Dick Porter

OMNIBUS PRESS
London / New York / Paris / Sydney / Copenhagen / Berlin / Madrid / Tokyo

First published 2015
This edition, copyright © 2025 Omnibus Press
(A Division of Wise Music Group
14–15 Berners Street, London, W1T 3LJ)

Cover design by Fresh Lemon
Picture research by Jacqui Black

ISBN: 9781915841728

Dick Porter hereby asserts his right to be identified as the author of this work in accordance with Sections 77 to 78 of the Copyright, Designs and Patents Act 1988.

All rights reserved. No part of this book may be reproduced in any form or by any electronic or mechanical means, including information storage or retrieval systems, without permission in writing from the publisher, except by a reviewer who may quote brief passages.

Every effort has been made to trace the copyright holders of the photographs in this book but one or two were unreachable. We would be grateful if the photographers concerned would contact us.

Printed in the Czech Republic.

A catalogue record for this book is available from the British Library.

www.omnibuspress.com

Contents

Chapter One – Seduction Of The Innocent	7
Chapter Two – Beautiful Monsters	27
Chapter Three – Rotten To The Core	47
Chapter Four – No Club Lone Wolf	65
Chapter Five – This Is Not Ordinary Music	86
Chapter Six – The Band From Ward T	105
Chapter Seven – How The Weird Can Get Started In Recording	124
Chapter Eight – The Bad Stuff	144
Chapter Nine – The Magic That You Do	164
Chapter Ten – Cramped	184
Chapter Eleven – Adult Kicks	203
Chapter Twelve – The Ones That Got Away	225
Chapter Thirteen – Buy The Ticket, Take The Ride	245
Acknowledgements & Sources	257
Discography	265

CHAPTER ONE

Seduction Of The Innocent

As long as there are girls and boys there's gonna be sex and it's gonna be in rock'n'roll – if it's good rock'n'roll. The people that keep sex out of rock'n'roll . . . it's not rock'n'roll any more.

Lux Interior

JUST over a year after Elvis Presley lit rock'n'roll's initial fast burning fuse by launching into Arthur Crudup's 'That's All Right' at the end of an otherwise unproductive July 1954 session at Sun Studios, Little Richard amplified that spark into a full blown conflagration by recording 'Tutti Frutti'. More than any other record, 'Tutti Frutti' established the template for rock'n'roll – to the extent that over 50 years later, the track was named as the number one selection in *Mojo* magazine's list of '100 Records that Changed the World'. The primal, onomatopoeic holler with which Richard opened the song was the sound of rock'n'roll being born, kicking and screaming, into a world that it would soon conquer.

Any examination of what made the Cramps such a vitally unique group has only to take 'Tutti Frutti' as its departure point. Like millions of others, Lux Interior and Poison Ivy Rorschach implicitly understood the significance of Little Richard Penniman's first major hit. Whereas Elvis Presley immediately embodied the kind of square-shocking rebellion that has always been a cornerstone of youth culture, Little Richard dramatically upped the ante by adding overt sexuality to the mix. Mindful of the necessity to court white audiences at venues such as Nashville's Grand Ole Opry, Elvis' pulsing sexuality was kept on a tight rein. Richard had no

Journey To The Centre Of The Cramps

such immediate concerns: He was an outsider – a black bisexual with a penchant for voyeurism and a talent for outrageous behaviour, on and off stage. At a time when the motions of Elvis' hips were subject to moral panics and seat-dampening enthusiasm in equal measure, Little Richard represented a loudly ticking timebomb. "It was really dangerous," observes Poison Ivy. "I've talked to people that remember the first time they heard Little Richard and they said it just scared 'em – older people that were young at the time, they said it was just terrifying."

Almost immediately, efforts were made to clean 'Tutti Frutti' up for mass consumption. The unmistakable intent of Richard's original lyric; 'Tutti Frutti, good booty / If it don't fit, don't force it / You can grease it, make it easy' was simply too lewd for an era where even milder innuendo was often considered shocking. While instantly aware of the track's potential, producer Robert 'Bumps' Blackwell also saw that it would be necessary to revise the song's 'minstrel modes and sexual humour' in order to get any kind of airplay. With the repeated substitution of the phrase 'Tutti Frutti, aw rooty' for the offending passages in place, Speciality Records had themselves a Top 30 hit on both sides of the Atlantic.

For some sections of the white establishment, Little Richard embodied the 'too black, too strong' notion that Malcolm X would refer to in his landmark 1963 'Message to the Grass Roots' speech. Many radio stations pulled the single as soon as they realised that Richard was black, and a new version of 'Tutti Frutti' was recorded by Pat Boone, a white, wholesome vocalist. Boone, who would later embark on a career as an evangelist, writing books such as *Pray To Win* and *A Miracle A Day Keeps The Devil Away*, as well as involving himself in politics by campaigning tirelessly for Ronald Reagan, scored a much bigger hit with the song, following it up several months later with a similarly sanitised version of Richard's 'Long Tall Sally'. "When 'Tutti Frutti' came out," explained Richard, "they needed a rock star to block me out of white homes because I was a hero to white kids. The white kids would have Pat Boone upon the dresser and me in the drawer 'because they liked my version better, but the families didn't want me because of the image that I was projecting." Richard's performances of 'Tutti Frutti' and 'Long Tall Sally' in the 1956 movie *Don't*

Seduction Of The Innocent

Knock The Rock are likewise sanitised, depicting him standing behind the piano lip-synching to the tracks before a seated white audience, all of them handclapping politely in an unthreatening fashion.

In many ways, the conflicting dynamics to which 'Tutti Frutti' were subjected established a template that would underpin the societal and generational conflicts that would serve to imbue youth culture with much of its vitality for the remainder of the century, with rebellion and sex constantly opposed by the forces of morality and commerce. In terms of rebellion, this template would usually involve the youth of the day taking things a little further than their predecessors and creating a media-led furore in the process. From Elvis Presley shaking his thing on the *Ed Sullivan Show* to Lady Gaga wrapping herself in the contents of the meat counter, successive generations appropriated and developed pre-existing aspects of popular or underground culture in ways that shocked and outraged their elders. This is a lineage that also included the Cramps. "It's important to remember that no less a figure than Frank Sinatra made headlines angrily dismissing Elvis and his contemporaries as 'cretinous goons'," observed Ken Burke in his book *Country Music Changed My Life: Tales Of Tough Times And Triumphs From Country's Legends*. "By contrast, the punk crowd – and the Cramps in specific – completely embraced the aspects of rockabilly that scared Sinatra. They nurtured no desire to assimilate into the so-called classier, more respectable end of show biz. In fact, they revelled in the garish garb and raucous rhythms their idols sought to escape."

While fifties rebellion opened up the generation gap, the manner in which rock'n'roll was sexualised created a more substantial schism by depositing youth culture firmly at the centre of America's moral battleground. At a time when any number of false syllogisms were being drawn by the likes of psychiatrist Fredric Wertham – who posited that juvenile delinquency was caused by reading comic books on the basis that a high proportion of juvenile delinquents answered in the affirmative when asked if they read comics, and perceived 'hidden' sexual messages in illustrations of shoulder blades – any overt reference to sex was a sure-fire way to create an uproar. "Rock'n'roll originally meant you know, sex – that's what it meant," observed Lux Interior. "It's the most powerful thing. Even to this day it causes people to be very uncomfortable; even at a party if someone mentions it, it causes people to squirm in their seats. I don't know why that is. Any type of intimacy upsets people."

For white audiences in the fifties, any overt references to, or displays of, sexuality within popular music were as novel as they were radical. Although America's vaudeville and Britain's music halls had historically featured risqué references to sex within humour and song, this seldom encroached into the mainstream. However, with post-war advances bringing a radio into every home and a television into many, the mass dissemination of this new kind of rebellious, sexually charged form of popular music was inevitable. While a conservative media scrambled to keep this thrusting, gyrating genie in its bottle by diluting rock'n'roll's potency for comfortable mass consumption, those who had been brought up with, or developed an understanding of, the blues wondered what all the fuss was about. "By being rock'n'roll, we're also a blues band in a way," Ivy observes. "A lot of people say that we're abnormally sex obsessed in our lyrics and with our band, like it's an unusual leaning, but I never hear anyone say that Muddy Waters was sex obsessed for singing 'Little Red Rooster', or whoever wrote it. Or Willie Dixon, or Howlin' Wolf – the things they sing about – they were never called abnormally obsessed with sex. That's all they sing about."

The chain reaction that was detonated by 'Tutti Frutti' set in motion a sequence of events that would not only lead to the formation of the Cramps, but also played a part in progressing wider societal issues such as desegregation, women's liberation and the advance of sexual freedoms. The links between rebellion, sex and rock'n'roll had been unbreakably forged. "A real rock'n'roll song is about sex most of the time," affirmed Lux. "So that leads you to 'I Wanna Be Your Dog'. That's one of the things that a lot of people would like to pretend, that human beings are above being like animals. We kind of enjoy that idea, that that's what we are: one more animal. Sex is pretty animalistic, I think. That was definitely part of the blues, kind of an attack on that idea that now we're cultured, civilised people and we're above that kind of thing. Seems like

Seduction Of The Innocent

the blues has always been about 'no, we're not above that kind of thing' . . . Without that it's like Iggy said, 'In this day and age if you want to be a success, you've got to make people come,' and I think it's the truth. I think that's what rock'n'roll is really all about – sex. There's a lot of other things in it, but that's the number one thing."

One of the initial waves of post-war 'bulge' babies, Lux Interior grew from a toddler to a teenager during the fifties, his awareness of the developments in music, movies and society in general growing as those changes gathered momentum. Lux entered the world on October 21, 1946 as Erick Lee Purkhiser, the second son of a conventional couple from the suburban town of Stow, Ohio. Situated around eight miles northwest of the county seat and economic hub of Akron, Stow was a growing residential community that had seen industry supersede agriculture as its main source of income during the first half of the 20th century. This shift was mainly due to the Goodyear Tire & Rubber company's main manufacturing facility being located in nearby Akron where similar firms, including Firestone and General Tire & Rubber, also subsequently built plants. Established as the largest rubber company in the world, Goodyear was the prime local employer, with Erick's father among the multitude of workers who passed through its gates each morning.

As Akron's industry sought to keep pace with the increasing demand for automotive spares and other vulcanised sundries, the city's population doubled, earning it the title of 'The Rubber Capital of the World'. As constant demand for rubber products increased the need for workers to man the plants, Akron briefly became America's fastest growing city. While Erick's hometown of Stow was pleasant enough, the city where his father worked as a foreman was dominated by industry, with giant smokestacks belching plumes of toxic smoke into the skies above, while the nearby Cuyahoga River regularly became clogged with black, heavy oil that captured debris within its visceral flow. In addition to such environmental concerns, those who laboured amid the clamour of Akron's industrial plants were subject to long hours of mundane and occasionally hazardous work carried out in difficult conditions, with the effects of the toxic air often exacerbated by humid, sweltering summers. "It's very

Journey To The Centre Of The Cramps

repressive," Lux explained. "Everybody works there 40 or 50 hours a week and when the weekend comes they just explode for a night or two, have a horrible headache on Sunday and get over it by Monday morning to get back in and punch that clock and go through another week's jail sentence. People really know how to go crazy in the Midwest."

Had Akron's population been primarily black, its immediate post-war social conditions would have made it a blues hub. As it was, it developed a reputation for being a place where real men did manly things – a notion underlined by the city's rocketing birth rate and an alcohol problem so severe that Alcoholics Anonymous was founded on Ardmore Avenue, situated a few minutes from the city centre. Aside from drinking and fucking, the other blue-collar staple – religion – played its part in keeping the citizenry on the straight and narrow. "I had a strict Catholic upbringing," remembered Lux. "I just had to go in – they made me go – and I'd just sit there and grit my teeth through it. I remember one time a girl: I broke up with this girl and got real religious for a couple of months. I mean *really* religious. But then I met this other girl . . ." Erick got an early taste of what was to become his one true faith courtesy of his older brother, Ron. "Rock'n'roll was something that was always there. I had an older brother that listened to it like crazy. And even before it was around, I remember my brother would play the piano and he'd play it really hard. I remember the first song I ever sang was 'Your Cheating Heart', the Hank Williams song. But it'd sound like rock'n'roll because he'd just bang it on the piano. I was really young, like six or five or something, and I'd just scream it."

Before girls and rock'n'roll began unsettling his equilibrium, the young, fair-haired, bespectacled Erick that looks out with a faint sense of mischief from his yearbook photo had sufficient time and space to develop the kind of questionable interests that would lead him along the path of the groovy outsider. Like most kids of any era, Erick was fascinated by the fantastic – anything weird, wacky, or way out would capture his fecund imagination. Access to such exotica was plentiful; television, movies, radio and comic books all provided a constant supply of cheap excitement. Although the moral panic led by Fredric Wertham had led to the cancellation of the more graphic comic books in 1954, EC Comics such as *The Vault Of*

Seduction Of The Innocent

Horror, *The Haunt Of Fear*, and *Tales From The Crypt* (which subsequently provided the basis of the Cramps' logo) had been printed in sufficient quantities to ensure that copies remained in common circulation throughout the decade. Additionally, while EC's competitors scrambled to formulate a self-regulatory code that would ensure they stayed in business while simultaneously neutering the output of their most successful rival, EC briefly branched out into science fiction – helping to fulfil the demand for little green men in flying saucers at a time when the USSR and America where frantically working to launch the first artificial satellites. "I think comics, especially the horror comics of the fifties, kind of spawned a kind of mindset in people you wouldn't expect, like Paul Simon, Carole King, these kind of people, they talk about having their minds bent by these kinds of comic books," observed Lux. "I think the horror comics of the fifties gave way to the pop art of the sixties and the hippies and LSD and all that shit that came later. It was really the first real deviant counterculture – that's where it began."

Television also played a prominent role in warping young Erick's mind in an agreeable and productive manner. As local stations began to multiply alongside the three major networks, old movies were seen as a useful means of filling expanding schedules. While science fiction tended to hold sway at cinemas and drive-ins, the Universal, MGM and RKO horror films of the thirties and forties were in steady rotation. "We all come from the Midwest and that's where there are 16 hours of horror movies a day on TV usually," Lux recalled. "We grew up with them." These included cult classics such as producer Val Lewton's *I Walked With A Zombie* [1943], a film that 15 years later – at a time when the very word 'zombie' was no longer permissible in comic books – exacted an irresistible allure on Erick and thousands of other young thrill seekers. Similarly, as Sputnik orbited overhead, the same kids gorged on a diet of B-movies produced to meet the heightened public interest in all things cosmic. These included many films that straddled the boundaries between science fiction and horror and set the whole mess down in a suburban context, such as the big screen adaptation of Richard Matheson's *The Incredible Shrinking Man* [1957] and the enjoyably daft *I Married A Monster From Outer Space* [1958]. "As a kid,

Journey To The Centre Of The Cramps

I'd take the bus to these theatres every weekend and see everything," Lux explained. "Until *The Brain Eaters* [1958]. My parents wouldn't let me go see *that*. I remember my dad saying, "*The Brain Eaters*? I'll be goddamned if I'm going to let him go see *The Brain Eaters*. He's fucked up enough already."

Erick's unquenchable thirst for the strange and macabre overcame all parental restrictions and, by early the next decade, he'd gravitated toward the real junk. "There are all these movies that were made by this guy named Herschell Gordon Lewis who owned a chain of drive-ins in the early sixties. He made them to show at his drive-ins," enthused Lux. "*Blood Feast* is about this weird guy who has an Egyptian temple in his basement where he sacrifices people, and *Two Thousand Maniacs*! It's real great. It's about a Southern town, and the first thing you see is a bunch of people putting up a detour sign at the crossroads. It turns out the whole town is full of people who came back from the grave after the Civil War. They were massacred by the Union soldiers and they came back from the grave after 100 years looking for revenge. They lure all these vacationers into the town and get them to join in all these quaint backwoods sports like rolling down a hill in a barrel; except the barrel's lined with knives. Eventually they just return to their graves for another hundred years."

In 1957, Cleveland's WHKK Radio brought a new disc jockey before its unsuspecting listeners. In addition to taking the art of radio broadcasting to new, wigged-out heights, Pete 'Mad Daddy' Myers firmly established himself as a key figure in Lux's pantheon of all-time heroes: "He was the person who set me on this road, which I've never been able to get off, which I hope I can set people on myself. He was a Cleveland radio DJ who named the term 'rock'n'roll'. People are so jealous of him for that, even today. They will not admit the fact that Alan Freed did not invent that term for the mid-fifties experience. He's just been wiped out of history, a guy that is pure genius for me." As radios throughout northeast Ohio quaked with his manic laughter, Myers oversaw four-hour shows packed with a high-octane mix of horror, rock'n'roll and R&B, and his unique machine gun patter, usually delivered in rhyme and introduced with such wonky wisdom as, 'Welcome, little stinkers, to the land of

Seduction Of The Innocent

winky blinkers! We've boiled up wavy gravy and it's ready to flow, so hang loose, Mother Goose, here comes the show.'

Pete Myers became an instant local sensation, quickly graduating to larger stations and making a well-publicised parachute jump into Lake Erie as a means of keeping his name in the press while contractual wrangles kept him off the air. The Mad Daddy's popularity reached a peak while he was at Cleveland's WHK Radio during 1958–59; he regularly hosted packed dances and boasted a large fan club of 'Mad Minions' that included Erick as a member and subsequently president. "I actually talked to him on the phone when he left Cleveland, the week that he left to go to New York to be snubbed," recounted Lux. "I called him on the phone and I told him that I was the head of his fan club in Stow, Ohio. He believed that and talked to me. I actually had a little three-inch reel to reel that I recorded with my friends and my parents threw it away, they were afraid that this was going to be a bad influence. They were very insightful. He talked to me on the phone for a couple of minutes in rhyme, just like on the radio show. Then later he said, 'I'm going to get the operator back, you can't afford this, I'm going to pay for this call.' And that actually happened, I thought we were going to have to explain that later, but it didn't show up on the bill." Although he was Cleveland's top disc-jockey at the end of the fifties, Myers was unable to transfer the popularity of his Mad Daddy persona to New York, where a lukewarm reception on the WNEW station led him to drop the character. After Myers briefly revived the *Mad Daddy Show* on New York's WINS station, he transferred back to WNEW in 1965, where he broadcasted as Pete Myers until taking his own life in October 1968.

While Mad Daddy Myers opened Erick's ears to the raw power of rockabilly and the rumble of rock'n'rollers like Link Wray, a second stream of bad influences was available to him through his older sibling, Ron. "My older brother was a real juvenile delinquent. He saw *The Wild One* with Marlon Brando; he had a motorcycle a week later. He had leather wristbands and motorcycle boots and he *was* Marlon Brando. He'd have all his hoodlum friends over and they'd play poker up in his bedroom, it'd be smoky in there, all of his walls would be covered in

Journey To The Centre Of The Cramps

albums. He was really cool." Erick's admiration for his older brother brought awareness that Ron was part of a scene. "There were two types of people – Brownies and Hoods. The hoods in the fifties wore all-black clothes, as tight as they could; there were no stretch pants then. They would wear pants tighter than mine; they would break the seams trying to get them on, they'd peg 'em that tight, but that's what got me interested in black clothes."

In addition to a developing sense of rock'n'roll style, Erick was also exposed to the possibilities that it offered. "I lived four houses down from Stow High School and the Town Hall was right across the street. Stow High School Bulldogs was the name of the [football] team and they had a thing called the Doghouse every Saturday Night – this was in the fifties when I was about 10 years old," he recalls. "I'd go look in the window and I'd see all these bands; the Ramblers, who had a hit with 'Lost Train' – That's when I decided I wanted to be in a rock'n'roll band. I watched them play, and then when they were coming out and loading their equipment . . . and the guy came out with a cigarette and the cop says, "Hey, no cigarettes" and the guy just went [Lux made a cool, snotty wise-guy face] and he just threw it right at his feet and walked right by – that's the moment I wanted to be in a rock'n'roll band. It took me forever afterward to do it though, what with distractions here and there."

While Pete Myers was languishing in New York, his local legacy became a lineage when a 39-year-old disc jockey and voiceover artist named Ernie Anderson was installed by his employer, Cleveland's WJW-TV, as the host of its late night *Shock Theater* series. As host Anderson's brief was to introduce the night's creaky horror movies and oddball sci-fi offerings in an appropriately spooky style. In order to achieve this, Anderson enlisted the help of his former comedy partner Tim Conway, with whom he had previously hosted the weekday morning movie feature, *Ernie's Place*. "Basically, Ernie would play the host, and I would come on as a different guest every show – because we couldn't get any real guests," recalled Conway. "One day, I was matador, a boxer, a Cleveland Indian. We had skits and I'd try to have lines, but Ernie didn't work like that. He couldn't remember lines. He was too freewheeling of a guy."

Seduction Of The Innocent

Taking inspiration from Pete Myers, Anderson created his Ghoulardi persona. The character was similar to the Mad Daddy in that he developed his own hip jive and regularly played tracks by rock'n'roll groups on his show. Peppering his announcements with phrases such as 'stay sick', 'purple knif' and 'turn blue' (all of which would find their way into the Cramps' lexicon), Ghoulardi's maniacal delivery matched his startling visual image, which included a lab coat festooned in badges, sunglasses with at least one lens missing, fake facial hair and a succession of implausible wigs. Instead of promoting *Shock Theater*'s weekly features, he'd regularly criticise them on-air. "He did whatever he wanted. He didn't just play movies like the other hosts of his day," explained studio engineer and frequent co-conspirator 'Big' Chuck Schodowski. "He thought the movies were awful, so he'd tell viewers 'Hey, group, these movies are so bad, don't waste your time. Turn off the channel and go to bed.'" Unsurprisingly, this failed to impress WJW-TV executives, already nervous about Ghoulardi's live antics that included letting off firecrackers, resulting in a minor studio fire. "No one in their right mind would go on the air and tell you to turn off the TV," added Schodowski. "The programme manager at the station couldn't stand him and openly worked against him so he wouldn't be successful."

Irrespective of in-house machinations against him, Ghoulardi struck the same chord with Cleveland's youth that Myers had and *Shock Theater*'s ratings tripled in three months, grabbing an unprecedented 70 percent share of the late-night audience in the process. "Every week. Everybody I knew, you had to be home in time to watch Ghoulardi," recalled Lux. "He was just way out of control, always causing trouble, always in trouble but he was so powerful that he could get away with it. Kind of like Elvis Presley shaking his hips on television, he was so powerful he could get away with it, everyone was upset about it but they couldn't do anything about it because it was bringing in too much money. When Ghoulardi was on TV in the sixties crime just plummeted because no one was out, they were all watching Ghoulardi. He was just a totally rebellious character. A good model for young people and one of the forerunners of what later became youth counterculture type thing."

Journey To The Centre Of The Cramps

At the height of his popularity, Ghoulardi represented a short-term marketing bonanza; badges featuring his trademark slogans, wighats (an acrylic multi-coloured wig), and blue milkshakes served in plastic cups adorned with his image became available. Erick was no slouch in grabbing himself some hip swag, investing in a pair of Ghoulardi-approved shoes called 'Batty Bucks'. "They were like brown Hush Puppies, but they had a big black bat right on the front of them and the laces went through the bat," he recalled. "That's when I first became a star at school with my Batty Bucks. I was constantly sick from the big Ghoulardi milkshakes – they were kind of fluorescent blue/green."

Ghoulardi's popularity led to his hosting WJW's Saturday afternoon *Masterpiece Theater* and even gave rise to a weekday children's show entitled *Laurel, Ghoulardi And Hardy*. By 1966, with a fair proportion of Cleveland's youth owning clothes that made them look like extras from a mad scientist's laboratory, Anderson abruptly quit WJW, abandoning his alter ego in the process. Partially motivated by Tim Conway's successful switch to CBS' hit *Carol Burnett Show*, Ernie moved to Los Angeles. "My dad was looking for a change in career and a change in life," explained Anderson's son, Paul. "He always wanted to be an actor, but it didn't work out, so he took a different path." That path led to Anderson becoming one of the most successful voiceover artists in US television history; the voice of ABC's *Monday Night Football* and narrator for scores of series and previews including *The Love Boat* and *Star Trek: The Next Generation*. Although Anderson died of cancer aged 73 in 1997, the impact of Ghoulardi continues to resonate. "He was this great influence on me," recalled maverick filmmaker Jim Jarmusch. "There was this anarchism and wildness about him, this outsider hipster, this anti-authoritarian, blowing things up with explosives that affected me as a little kid. He opened me up to all kinds of weird-ass music; his whole anti-hierarchical appreciation of culture definitely influenced me." For Lux, Ghoulardi's popularity in Cleveland and northeast Ohio was emblematic of a region where "you can learn to appreciate rebellion. There were all kinds of horror movie hosts from there. Personalities that came out of that region that messed up people's minds at some point in their life. It's always seemed to me the

Seduction Of The Innocent

most important thing in life – to start trouble and make people ask questions about what's going on."

Naturally enough, the Ohioan appetite for rebellion extended to rock'n'roll. Throughout the sixties the state gave rise to a bewildering succession of micro-scenes, populated by largely obscure bands and serviced by a wealth of small labels. As groups such as the Es-Shades and Bobby & the Bengals scored local hits on labels that include Cle Town and B-W Records, those discs comprised an important element of the local dancehall culture. "The dances that went on there and the clothes that people wore then, in the early sixties, were just the wildest, the absolute *wildest*," recalled Lux. "It was like a science fiction comic book, wild and bizarre and nothing to do with Pat Boone and all that stuff. Places away from the cultural centres, like northern California or the South or the Midwest, is where it was the most extreme. Those were the places where people weren't afraid of doing something that wasn't in vogue or the new trend or whatever. I think that'll always be the case."

Inspired by his fleeting glimpse of glamour as personified by the Ramblers, Erick found himself drawn to the noise and excitement of the local hops. "I had to stand out and look in the windows, but there were these girls, just the sexiest girls that you've ever seen in the tightest clothes and the one great dance was the Bug. I thought it was the greatest one ever, 'cos they'd just do all this stuff, they'd move around and touch themselves all over, searching themselves as if they had a bug on them, just like a cat or something, and they would just be grabbing it from every place they shouldn't have been, and then finally they'd grab it, and they'd throw it on the person next to them and then that girl would start doing her dance – oh, man. It was kind of a dance; it was more like a conniption fit, but wow, a very sexy dance."

With the link between sex and rock'n'roll now irreversibly established within Erick's young mind, he duly set about enhancing his credentials as a rebel by hooking up with some likeminded pals. "At that time I had a jacket that said 'Angel' and it had a little halo on it that I'd made out of glitter," he recalled. "I had a big shield on the back of my jacket, top hat, gloves and a cane. I actually got thrown out of school for a week because I

Journey To The Centre Of The Cramps

wouldn't stop wearing it, then they finally made us stop wearing the jackets – we told them it was just a club, but they said, 'No, it's a gang.'" Taking their cues from older brother Ron, Erick and his chums nailed their colours to the black-clad Hoods mast and set about indulging in the kind of minor criminality that afforded them some small change and, more importantly, something of a neighbourhood reputation. "We stole hubcaps," he recounted. "We just stole them to steal them – we didn't even know who to sell them to. I remember we stole the hubcaps off the local hearse. Just lots of hubcaps. Then we'd go around and we'd steal phones out of phone booths. We figured out how to get them out real quick. One friend, he knew how to do electronics and he made walkie-talkies so we could watch for the cops. We'd just bash 'em open – it'd take a day of bashing with a sledgehammer just to get them open and we'd get $55 or something – but it was fun."

Being somewhat older than Erick, Ron's petty crime inclinations tended to be a little more developed, and predictably enough these led to encounters with the local cops – particularly when Ron and his crew turned to piracy and stole a 17-foot boat. This was stored in a Stow back garden, where it was difficult not to notice it and the boys were duly arrested. "They were all cool enough to leave me out of it, 'cos I wasn't around when they got busted," Lux explains. "He scared me after a while so I quit hanging around with him. He got a job at Goodyear as a welder and it paid real well and it was Goodyear, so you could just work there forever and retire and you're set for life. So he did."

Like both his younger brothers, Ron possessed considerable musical aptitude. "He took organ lessons and then he got so good that they couldn't find teachers any more. Then he started teaching organ," explained Lux. "He's made quite a bit of money playing at roller rinks and all that." With his appetite for petty crime duly dampened, Erick focussed on developing his record collection and passing his passion onto his younger brother, Mike. "He always had a lot of records," recalled the youngest Purkhiser brother. "When I was a kid, I was always coming up in his room and I'm sure I was pestering him, so he would make me promise that if I could be quiet for 24 hours, he'd give me a record and I'd think, 'Man, that's a

Seduction Of The Innocent

really good deal, I don't have to say nothing and I'll get a record?' And it didn't dawn on me until years later when I thought, 'Damn him, he was just trying to get me to shut up for a day.' I did get a lot of records. I was his first fan, he was pretty much preaching the rock'n'roll gospel at a young age, like 'listen to this record' or 'listen to that record', and I just always looked up to him." Erick's influence paid dividends for Mike, who not only fronted notable Akron bands such as the Action and the Walking Clampetts, but also graduated from the local university with a degree in electronics, which led him to a successful career as a communications manager, amplifier repair specialist and studio producer/engineer.

As Erick entered his twenties, the swinging sixties began to take on a more sober demeanour. "All of a sudden, instead of rock'n'roll, there was rock music; you had the Vietnam War and revolution and everyone became real serious, and women's liberation became a big deal," he explained. "Suddenly, everyone had to be real natural looking and wear make-up to make themselves look as if they didn't have make-up on, all that kind of stuff." In 1964, America's deep involvement in the Vietnam conflict led to the initiation of the draft but, fortunately for Erick, having no full-time job ensured that he was difficult to track down. "I almost went to Canada, but that was too scary for me," he recalled. "I just laid low and didn't turn in my name and stuff the way you were supposed to." However, as America lost its grip on the conflict, the need for new recruits intensified and the possibility of conscription became increasingly likely. Despite a temporary amnesty for those who had evaded the draft so far, Erick decided that his best bet was to take the educational option and hope this would enable him to sit out the remainder of the conscription period, now an issue coming under increasing political fire. However, this would necessitate him leaving home, a move he made with some reluctance. "I have always loved Akron," he said. "I loved growing up there and there was always something fun or cool going on there. I remember back in '68 there was a nightclub on South Main Street called The Birth. I remember going to it one time and it was like the first psychedelic nightclub in Akron. It was strange because the kids who were going to it were all like the goth kids but they had no idea they were the goth kids, because there

Journey To The Centre Of The Cramps

was no such term, but I remember going there one night and I was there for like four hours and all night long they would play like 'Land Of 1,000 Dances' and no other record. They played that record all night long and the kids were dancing like crazy and they had a psychedelic light show and it was a really cool club."

After considering his educational options, Erick decided to go west, travelling more than 2,000 miles across the country to enrol at the California State University in Sacramento. It was an inspired decision. At Sacramento he found a sprawling educational campus where free-thinking students basked in the fading embers of the Summer of Love. He also found the woman who was destined to become his soulmate.

Poison Ivy Rorschach was born on February 20, 1953, as Kristy Marlana Wallace, the youngest of three children, entering the world in San Bernardino, some 430 miles southeast of Sacramento. As the youngest child, Ivy was treated as the baby of the family – to a sometimes exaggerated extent: "They had me in a high chair 'til I was five years old, that's an unusually long time and it really bugged me at the time, but I love being treated like a baby now."

While her father worked as an engineer in California's burgeoning aerospace industry, the family supplemented his paycheck with a series of astute real estate transactions, which also served to keep the Wallaces on the move. "Instead of maintaining one family residence, we moved from house to house. My mother, who was very artistic, would help remodel, and then we would have a parade of potential buyers come through until the house was sold," Ivy explains. "It was weird having total strangers gawk at us in our home, kinda like a human zoo. I moved nine times between kindergarten and the end of high school." Understandably, this had an unsettling effect on Kristy, who found it difficult to maintain lasting friendships due to constantly switching schools and moving home. Instead, she began to create her own world, one where she would apply her imagination to dressing up a long-suffering family cat in a series of dresses, blowing up Barbie dolls with firecrackers, or constructing paper villages that she would subsequently burn down.

Seduction Of The Innocent

Given that Kristy's maternal grandmother was a talented pianist, while her paternal grandfather was an accomplished violinist who once played in composer and conductor John Phillip Sousa's world famous band, it was hardly surprising that she developed an early interest in music. "When I was very little, I was especially fixated on a stompin' 45 record that my brother had, 'Martian Hop' by the Randells," she recalls. "He would play it when his friends came over because they got a big kick outta watching me jump and fly around the room and off the furniture every time I heard it. I also loved 'Witch Doctor' by David Seville and 'The Purple People Eater' by Sheb Wooley. My mom, who had a beautiful singing voice, would always sing along if an Elvis song came on the radio. My sister and I would sing together in the back seat of the car if a girl group song came on the radio . . . One of the first records I remember having – I think the first records I had, my brother gave me – was Johnny Horton's 'Battle Of New Orleans', which is about running off the British."

In addition to employing Kristy as a source of entertainment, her brother also introduced her to the instrument that she would subsequently master in her own, unique way. "I learned a little when I was young, but not a whole lot. My brother played some guitar and he taught me how to do 'Pipeline' riffs and some chords, but other than that I've never had any lessons. I just started picking out songs on my own."

At school, Kristy was the perennial outsider, often unable to penetrate the established cliques at educational facilities where she was a recent arrival. Uninterested in lessons she found pedestrian and repetitious and tired of being an easy target for bullies looking to take advantage of the skinny, red-haired new kid, she resolved to embrace her ostracised status and become a bad girl. She started smoking and adopted heavy make-up, which led her into conflicts with her teachers, resulting in two expulsions. "I was *avant-garde* but not a criminal. But the consensus was I was a bad influence – so scram," she recounts. "I feel like I've been sinister all my life. I also just love make-up, heavy eye make-up. I always wore slutty eye make-up and got hassled for it . . . As children we dug being obnoxious and scary and monstrous. I was a misfit, one of those loner ones. You either let it get the best of you or else you start digging it and wallowing in

Journey To The Centre Of The Cramps

it, and I think I learned to wallow in being that thing."

This created problems at home where, although she empathised with the difficulties Kristy was encountering, her mother attempted to instil some form of discipline. "She wasn't sympathetic to my way of acting out at all," explains Ivy. "I wish I could say I had some kind of bizarre religious background, but I haven't – I had just the opposite. Not enough magic as far as that when I was growing up and I think it made me just kind of explode the other way. Both my parents were total atheists. They don't believe in anything and I believe in everything."

In keeping with her new rebellious image, Kristy began developing a taste for outsider rock'n'roll that led her away from novelty records such as 'The Purple People Eater' and 'Martian Hop' and into the realm of the reverb-laden, seat-slashing instrumental. "My most identifiable influences would be Link Wray and Duane Eddy. I think those guys seemed neglected when our band started. I loved Chuck Berry, but it seemed like early rock'n'roll was centred around Chuck Berry. So just the simplicity of it, the starkness of the stark chords of Link Wray and the stark single-note thing of Duane Eddy," she explained.

Best known for his landmark 1958 single with the Ray Men, 'Rumble', Link Wray was of crucial significance in terms of the development of rock'n'roll. Utilising distortion, feedback and power chords in a totally new way, 'Rumble' set the perfect sonic template for rebellion – so much so that it became banned on the grounds that the title referred to gang fights and that the sheer sound of the instrumental cut encouraged juvenile delinquency. Along with 'Rumble', subsequent singles laced with a Western twang, including 'Rawhide', 'Comanche' and 'El Toro', influenced generations of guitarists, among them Jimmy Page and Pete Townshend in the UK. "Link Wray is my main hero, because I think he's really overlooked," adds Ivy. "He had the most apocalyptic, monumental sound I ever heard – real emotional and so simple and so violent. That stands for rock'n'roll, which is supposed to be violent and dangerous, and have this dangerous sound. He was initially my biggest influence, and he still is. No matter how long I've been doing this, I hear something new when I listen to him. Maybe because I'm not the same person, maybe I

Seduction Of The Innocent

know more from playing longer. It enables me to hear more now, so it seems like I'm always hearing something new and getting influenced by some new aspect of Link Wray. He's just so . . . it's like guitar at the end of the world. So austere. And so much drama. You know, he makes the most out of the least, for sure."

Gripped by Wray's scary coolness and sonic futurism, Ivy's palate of influences also extended to less vituperative, but equally evocative instrumentals. "I've had a lifelong obsession with Jack Nitzsche's 'Lonely Surfer' since it first hit the airwaves – I'm sure that's why I play guitar now," she observes. "I still think that's the most perfect recording ever made. When I listen to that, I literally can't talk. I just turn off; it's so perfect – like cathedral architecture. When I was little, I thought it was perfect. I didn't even know what Jack looked like back then, and then once in a while I'd see photos of this short-haired guy with glasses."

Kristy's early concert going brought her into contact with what she describes as "the music of my generation", which included the likes of the Yardbirds, Kinks, Rolling Stones, and Jimi Hendrix. However, it was a musical template established by the previous generations that provided Kristy with an identifiable role model. "I saw Bo Diddley with the Duchess at Memorial Auditorium in Sacramento, opening for Quicksilver Messenger Service. That did it," she remembered. Bo Diddley's band featured a second guitarist who was generally known as 'the Duchess'. Over the years the position was filled by a number of talented female guitarists including Peggy Jones, Norma-Jean Wofford, Gloria Jolivet, Cornelia 'Cookie' Redmond, and Debby Hastings. Aside from Jones, these guitarists generally played rhythm, and at a time when female musicians were massively underrepresented in rock'n'roll, the Duchess represented a new world of possibilities to Kristy: "They just did all of this synchronised box-step and stuff and she was in gold lamé. That just burned through my brain permanently. And so I had pants made. And the high heels. A lot of the time, if I'm not wearing boots, I wear high-heeled mules because she wore them."

Kristy was also preoccupied by chemical and spiritual possibilities, experimenting with psychedelics, often to remarkable effect. "Once I

Journey To The Centre Of The Cramps

starved myself for six days and then I ate some mushrooms and left my body instantly," Ivy recalled. "There really are other planes and other entities. They're always there but acid opens you up and makes you aware of them. They're not something you should go out of your way to see." Such lysergic adventurism combined with Kristy's natural capacity for slipping into altered states of consciousness to exacerbate her status as a loner. "It used to cause a lot of trouble in my life because I didn't understand what was going on and it was just taken as manic-depressive schizophrenia, whereas now I've learnt to develop it," she explained. Despite this, Kristy's natural intelligence enabled her to avoid flunking high school entirely, and a reasonable performance in her SATs meant that, like Erick, she was able to register at Sac State University.

CHAPTER TWO

Beautiful Monsters

When I met Ivy I'd been on mescaline for a month, without being off of it.

Lux Interior

I was a teenage hitchhiker and he gave me a ride. He's been giving me a ride ever since.

Poison Ivy

HAVING enrolled in Sacramento State University as a means of deferring the draft, Erick entered the halls of academe with little interest in doing any formal studying. "Saying it was a college is stretching it a bit," he recalled. "You'd get credit for going there and everything, but it was just a bunch of weirdoes. It was crazy. Half the teachers were just fucking the students and getting paid for it. It was really a great time, those days. Really a creative environment." The freewheeling campus environment suited Erick's developing tastes for the esoteric and bizarre as he set about becoming "a hell of a hippie" and took to sampling the delights of cheap wine and mind-bending drugs with commendable enthusiasm. "I lived on mescaline for a long time," he revealed. "I'd take it every day for about seven months – I guess that ain't acid but I saw a lot of things and I never felt like killing myself because I couldn't stand it. I lived in Northern California for a while so I've seen a lot of demons and shit anyway! There's a million different ways to get high, you do it by breathing or crossing your eyes and constantly staring at your forehead." His consciousness duly expanded, Erick resolved that he was now 'VipVop', a psychedelic guru. "How I got to be a

Journey To The Centre Of The Cramps

psychedelic guru was I just appointed myself one. Basically, all you have to do to become one was take enough drugs."

The adoption of this new persona continued a trend that had begun when he'd taken the name 'Angel' back when he was running with Akron's Hoods, continued through a brief post-glam phase as 'Raven Beauty' and subsequently find its ultimate form with 'Lux Interior' (which owed its origins to the 'deluxe interiors' of old car commercials). Rather than having any deep psychological root, Erick's penchant for reinventing himself was more indicative of a madcap imagination, sense of fun, and a faddish desire to reflect whatever was groovy at that point in time. It was a characteristic he shared with his future soulmate.

"I was 'Poison Ivy' in Sacramento," Ivy explains. "I still have a driver's licence that says that, and this was before any thought of a band. Lux was 'VipVop' on his driver's licence. When we went to Ohio, he was 'Raven Beauty' and eventually changed to 'Lux Interior'. I was already Poison Ivy before the Cramps. We were reinventing ourselves, but not because of the band. Only our shrink knows why."

Although the origins of Kristy's chosen name owe something to the villainess that featured in *Batman* comics from 1966 onward, it also derives some provenance from the Coasters' 1959 R&B hit (subsequently covered by Portland garage titans the Kingsmen and English beat combo the Paramounts, among a host of others, not least the Rolling Stones). In this respect, 'Poison Ivy' shares some common ground with 'VipVop', which was partially derived from a track entitled 'Vip Vop' recorded by fifties R&B duo Marvin & Johnny that featured the phrase repeated continuously throughout. Additionally, the pre-war blues pianist Jimmy Gordon, who accompanied the likes of Big Bill Broonzy, sometimes performed and recorded with 'His Vip Vop Band'. As a choice of name, 'VipVop' certainly got reactions, "It was a really cool name because no one could stand to say 'VipVop'. It sounded like they were singing or something. It wasn't like two names, just 'VipVop' – they were embarrassed to say it so they called him 'Vop', or 'Mr. Vop', or 'Vip'," Ivy recounted. "I had 'VipVop' on my driver's licence and every time I got stopped by the cops they would hassle me: 'VipVop – I oughta give you a ticket just for *that*,'"

Beautiful Monsters

added Lux. "The guy couldn't deal with it," Ivy recalls. "Like he was embarrassed to put it on his report."

Like Erick, Kristy had a *laissez-faire* approach to her studies. "I had no academic or career ambitions at all, and I don't know why. I like dancing, too, and when I went to college I mainly took the dance and art classes," she explained. "I wasn't taking any of the things that were required of any of the majors. I mean, I was running out of time to get caught up. There's like basic general things that everyone has to take, and I hadn't taken any of them yet. I was just goofing off." Within the loose parameters of post-hippie era progressive Californian higher education, Kristy found plenty of scope for avoiding anything resembling formal academic study. "It was a very strange art department in Sacramento at that time, too, because the whole student population was made up of hippies, and they were into witchcraft and metaphysics and everything else," she observed. "The textbook for that class was called *The Sacred Mushroom And The Cross*, and the subject of that book is how the real topic of The Bible is the *amanita muscaria* mushroom, and that Christ is a metaphor for this magic mushroom. The kind of instructors we'd have would say: 'I haven't seen you in class for a while, what grade d'you want?' And we'd say, 'Well, I guess an "A"' and they'd say, 'Okay'."

While Erick had been attending the University for some time, Kristy had only recently enrolled, and their initial meeting took place away from the Sac State campus. "First time I saw her she was walking down the street, hitchhiking, and she was wearing a halter top and short shorts with a big hole in the ass with red panties showing through," Lux recalled. "I was with this other guy, a friend of mine, and we both just went, 'Who-o-o-oh!' We pulled over and I think I had a hard-on about three seconds after I saw her." For her part, Kristy was similarly pleased to make her future paramour's acquaintance. "I'd seen him around the campus, and I thought he was extremely exotic. He would have these pants and each leg of the pants was a different colour. That kind of thing fascinated me," she explained. "I had seen him around town before and was already impressed, so I was really glad to meet him that way."

Although the perils of attractive, scantily clad women hitchhiking alone

Journey To The Centre Of The Cramps

would have been brought vividly to life by watching scores of exploitation and B-movies, Kristy not only felt entirely safe, but her gift for prescience led her to believe that meeting Erick had been pre-ordained. "Looking back, I figure it might not have been that bright. But at the time it was pretty common practice, it seemed like a natural thing to do," she reflected. "I think we would have met anyway. It was destiny."

However, destiny often requires a little extra assistance to work its magic, and having looked through the list of available courses during the brief journey back to Kristy's apartment, both parties opted to take a course in Art and Shamanism. The esoteric nature of the course was ideally suited to Kristy's interest in art and spirituality and also tailor-made for any halfway serious psychedelic guru (although Erick subsequently admitted that Kristy explained what shamanism was during the car ride). "That's where our real meeting began," affirmed Ivy. "I was sitting in class when I saw Lux walking in. It was a very large class, too, because everybody knew the teacher got high, and I was sending out psychic brainwaves of, like: 'Sit by me! Sit by me! Sit by me!' And he did. He came straight to me and sat next to me. We were making small talk and I said, 'It's my birthday', and he pulled a drawing out of his portfolio and gave it to me as a birthday gift right then. It was a female figure, but it was very abstract expressionist. It had a lot of physical energy that I can't describe in words. I don't know if it was past lives or what, but I felt like I'd known him all my life. It wasn't like we'd just met."

"I remember the first day of that class, the teacher had us all sit around in a circle on the floor and hold hands," Lux remembered. "It was some kind of weird exercise, some mumbo-jumbo crazy cult thing where there was supposed to be energy which would fly around clockwise, and then he made it go counter-clockwise. It was great, it really worked, but just holding hands with her I felt about a thousand times the energy that I was getting from him. She's incredibly beautiful, that was the first thing I noticed. And then when I talked to her she was incredibly smart, too. We just had a bond." With the powerful forces of mutual attraction far outstripping any shamanic vibes whipped up in the classroom, the two outsiders became a couple and set about creating a shared world of their

Beautiful Monsters

own that would endure for almost 40 years. "We met in a very free way, and we fell in love very quickly," Ivy revealed. "We were just together constantly, and we were pretty much out of our minds constantly, to be honest. We didn't come to the surface for quite a long time."

Within a fortnight Erick and Kristy had moved in together. "We just couldn't hardly stand to be away from each other. People would even tell us, 'That's not right, it's not healthy, you guys shouldn't be spending all your time together.' And they tell us that to this day," said Lux. "She was somebody really special when I met her, we immediately got along and we've never spent any time apart since. She's smart and interested in all the things that I was interested in."

Aside from relishing the varyingly intense experiences of falling in love and dropping liberal amounts of acid together, Kristy and Erick's shared interest in music led them to become immersed in the glam scene that was infecting California during 1972 and '73. "All we wanted to do was go to rock'n'roll shows," Lux recalled. "At that time, going to rock'n'roll shows in southern California was great cos everybody got dressed up like crazy and it almost didn't matter who the band was. The audience was more interesting than the bands." One exception to this rule came when the New York Dolls made a rare excursion from their hometown to play three nights at the Matrix Club in San Francisco. At the time, frontman David Johansen's androgynous pan-sexuality, guitarist Johnny Thunders' extreme evocation of rock'n'roll's bad-to-the-bone archetype and bassist Arthur Kane's penchant for bizarre outfits ensured that they were a visual, as well as a sonic, feast. "I remember when the Dolls released their first album, we saw them the day it came out. We hitchhiked down to San Francisco – we were living in Sacramento – and David Johansen wore a black and white T-shirt with Marilyn Monroe on it. He did the make-up; blue eye-shadow, red lipstick – then he came out and was doing the show and the make-up ran down the T-shirt as he sweated," recalls Lux. "The first time we saw them, Arthur wasn't playing – Peter Jordan was playing bass, but Arthur was there. And he was kinda banging out the rhythm and he was leaning on the amp and all," adds Ivy. "They were such a huge influence."

Journey To The Centre Of The Cramps

Almost immediately, the newly entwined couple developed a notion that would determine their direction for much of the next four decades. "I'd wanted to be in a band and she played guitar and we got this idea within days of meeting each other: that we should have a band." The idea quickly assumed the proportions of a quest. "I think we were just high off our own ideas of things," Ivy observed. "It seemed like it was feasible that we could do something ourselves, but it seemed to make total sense at the time. And that kind of thing where you think at a certain age, or because of a certain drug. You feel like you can take over the world or something. And not really taking over the world, but there were just things that we had to do – things that had to get expressed that way. I was really amazed that he wasn't in a band because music was all that he thought about . . . besides sex, or something. I was the same way."

Back in Ohio, Mike recalled receiving a letter from his brother expressing his desire to participate in the rock'n'roll world: "Basically he said, 'I want to do what you're doing, I want to play in a band and make music like you do.' And I thought that was pretty cool because I always knew him as an artist and as a music lover but not as a musician or performer."

In addition to the likes of Alice Cooper and T. Rex, the couple dug "anybody who was just sexy and wild and played rock'n'roll". While this would also include the likes of Iggy Pop (who was just beginning the process that would result in the Stooges' landmark *Raw Power* LP) and the then little-known New York Dolls, the pre-eminence of singer song-writers and whimsical or indulgent progressive rockers meant that exciting new releases tended to be few and far between. "We'd go to record stores looking for new records and there wasn't anything good," explained Lux. "So we started listening to this stuff you could buy really cheap in junk stores, and it was blowing our mind. It was just so wild and great. Anything with the word 'bop' in the title, we bought. It was really timeless music; there was nothing out-of-date or old-fashioned about it. It was fuelled by sex, and really exciting, thrilling music."

"We cleaned up at thrift stores," adds Ivy. "That great store opened, Ed's Rare Records on the K Street Mall – he kind of indoctrinated us. We'd say 'Why are these records so expensive, what are they?' And then

Beautiful Monsters

he'd play them and explain and that turned us on. We were kind of scouts for him, we'd go to the junk stores and bring things, and swap them for his records."

"Right after we found Ed's Rare Records, we met this guy named Robert at this other record store," Ivy explained. "He was this Mexican guy that lived in West Sacramento, he collected black vocal groups and he turned us onto that. That's what started us collecting records from junk stores, getting doo-wop records. One day, he gave us a box of about 50 records and it just got us started and it was all doo-wop. That's still our main fetish, the vocal groups, which clearly isn't part of what we do – we don't do harmony or anything, but that's what we're really into." For the young couple, it was doo-wop's otherworldly qualities that provided them with a vital fix of weird and they quickly developed a passion for the more esoteric end of the vocal group spectrum, and would later cite groups including the Four Plaid Throats, Jackie & the Starlites, the Medallions, the Versatones, and the Five Dollars as having recorded songs that made an impact upon them. "If you put on some of those Flamingos records, when they were on End Records – some of that stuff, it sounds like you're on drugs all of a sudden," Lux observed. "It's like you've just taken acid or something, they've got this big echo chamber and they all sound like they're from another dimension – all these weird warbling sounds in the background and everything. A lot of those early Bird groups from the forties and early fifties, that's what they were doing – it really was like a drug experience, it sounded like that. You got high from listening to those things."

Erick and Kristy would latch onto any records that looked cool, had a groovy title, or – most crucially – featured some form of sonic adventurism. Aside from the more exotic end of the doo-wop spectrum, this included acquiring garage rarities to fill gaps in Erick's collection, an exploration of early sixties instrumentals that developed out of Kristy's passion for Link Wray and Duane Eddy, or rockabilly. "We just ran into rockabilly by accident," explained Lux. "The B-sides, the balance of those rockabilly records, they're a lot like the doo-wop groups, there's these weird, strange things that usually sound like they're off centre – real crazy

Journey To The Centre Of The Cramps

stuff." To a large degree, it was the complete sense of detachment from the music industry evident within many of the more obscure rockabilly releases that particularly appealed to the couple. "When we first bought these records, we thought 'Gawd, they really thought this was gonna sell a million copies.' Because you can listen to them and you can hear they really thought that was gonna be a Top 10 hit. Singing about slopping out the hogs or something and they thought it was gonna be a number one, right up there behind Jerry Lee and Elvis," observed Lux. "I've just always liked obscure things, strange names – and once I found rockabilly I just couldn't listen to anything else."

While it was not exactly a musical epiphany, it's easy to understand why rockabilly would have such a significant impact on Erick and Kristy's future path. It is outsider music, owing its provenance to an unholy union between blues and country that extended from the hillbilly boogie and took root in the South's poorest rural areas. Given that many of its prime exponents were sons of the soil (both Carl Perkins and Billy Lee Riley came from families of sharecroppers) it is hardly surprising that the music often featured a rustic rawness that, as with the blues, juxtaposed recountments of poverty and anguish against unfettered musical abandon. "I think rockabilly was a quantum leap in culture," mused Ivy. "Something happened in the evolution of people's minds. Like that rockabilly vocal style that's so emotional – it's hyper-emotionalism, hyper-surrealism. It had to have been more than previous musical precedents leading up to it. Maybe it was the atom bomb; 'Let's do it now because we might get blown up.'"

Additionally, having assimilated the way in which doo-wop combined elements of the blues and swing and reinvented them for the street corner, rockabilly's fusion of musical forms from both sides of the fifties racial divide struck a positive chord with the future Cramps. "One of the things rockabilly started was white people listening to rock'n'roll, and one of the things rock'n'roll did was bring down segregation," reasoned Lux. "All kinds of white kids were buying Little Richard and Chuck Berry records and they thought that was fine. Rock'n'roll did that, and that's a good thing."

Beautiful Monsters

The simplicity and energy of early rockabilly recordings served to fuel Kristy and Erick's desire to make their own music. "It dawned on us because of some records we brought home; 'Geez, we could play this stuff'. There were all these bands, like the Rolling Stones and the New York Dolls, that took R&B and did something with it, but nobody had really done anything with rockabilly yet. We thought that would give us a real head start – that we'd have some resources to do something that came from the blues but hadn't been done yet." In addition to being relatively easy to play, a million miles removed from the complex, almost academic, progressive rock that was increasingly taking up airtime on the developing FM stations, Erick was gripped by the potential of rockabilly's direct, universal appeal. "There's something about R&B and rock'n'roll – the early stuff, now you say 'rock'n'roll' and that could mean anything – but real rock'n'roll, the stuff based on the blues when it first started, that music is so timeless it'll never get old. Five hundred years from now I think that people will be rolling around on their pod stems or whatever happens, and they'll be listening to these same records we're talking about. As you know, once you've been infected by this stuff, there's no cure. I don't think radiation would help – it might make it worse."

Now that the two students had a conceptual direction for their band, their exposure to the discipline of study led them to undertake further, rigorous research. "Because there were no reissues out then, like there are now, the only way you could get it was to find the originals and learn about it that way. And so we just learned about that music and fell in love with it," explains Ivy. This entailed a stepping up of their campaign to unearth whatever exotic vinyl bounty lay tucked away among Sacramento's thrift stores. "Ivy actually went out and got a job at a Goodwill so she could be there when the truck pulled in. Sometimes we would sit outside these stores in our car, half asleep, waiting for the truck, hoping there would be these golden records," remembered Lux. "The job stank – it was like a *real* job, so I quit," added Ivy.

A more productive seam of vintage discs came to light courtesy of a small article in *Rolling Stone* detailing the existence of a Sun Records warehouse in Memphis, Tennessee. Founded by Sam Phillips in 1952, Sun

Journey To The Centre Of The Cramps

represented the mother lode for anyone interested in compiling a comprehensive rock'n'roll collection. Most famous for releasing early singles by Elvis, Johnny Cash, Carl Perkins, Roy Orbison and Jerry Lee Lewis, the label's back catalogue was pitted with a rich selection of great material from lesser known rockers such as Charlie Feathers, Billy Lee Riley and Warren Smith. According to the article, these records were available for 20 cents each or five for a dollar and this proved the clincher. Even with Kristy and Erick's meagre means, it would be a pilgrimage to the cradle of rockabilly that was well worth making – the couple pointed their rusty '61 Chevy station wagon eastward and set about making the arduous 2,000 mile journey. "Fifty miles outside of Memphis our car fell apart, but we managed to get there and spend our last money on records," recalled Lux. "We went in and bought box loads of them, kept one of each, and used the rest to trade for other stuff."

Although some sharp collectors had got there before them and had their pick of the Select-o-Hits warehouse's blues stash, record collecting was still in its infancy and the couple were able to buy a good proportion of Sun's rockabilly releases. "There weren't nearly as many collectors as there are now," explained Ivy. "The records at Select-o-Hits were bought up mostly by foreigners. You had to already know about the old Sun records for sale. You had to say, 'I want to go back into the warehouse', because the front of the building was just a regular record store." After Erick had called his parents to borrow some money to make the purchases (under the premise of needing the cash to fix up their car), they returned home somewhat cautiously. "We were so loaded down with records that if we hit a little bump, the car went 'bang!' There was no spring left – It was just riding on the axle," recounted Lux. "It was the middle of winter, too," added Ivy. "The entire state of Texas was ice. I remember we went at 15 miles-an-hour across Texas . . . the car was skidding . . ."

In addition to vastly enhancing their rockabilly record stash, the Memphis trip also convinced Erick and Kristy of the need to leave Sacramento. "We were out of place completely there," Ivy explains. "We would get jeered at from the street. We went hitchhiking, later on we'd hitchhike together and Lux would be in drag. We went through different

Beautiful Monsters

phases, one where I'd try to look as much like Marc Bolan as I could and he'd look like this tall woman, we found we'd get a ride easier – guys would say, 'Girls, want to go to a party?' and I'd do the talking so that Lux wouldn't have to use his manly voice. We were total freaks, it was great. It's weird, because it was kind of a hippie capital, but very uptight unless you were like a farmer/hippie, just T-shirt and jeans, you were out of place there and people would just catcall us out of cars, we were in fear of our lives sometimes."

Aside from the cloying blue-jean orthodoxy of the local post-hippie crowd, Erick was drawing constant heat from certain members of the local police department, largely on account of his appearance and having 'VipVop' on his driving licence. "It was all about freedom. It was kind of like communism – you couldn't do anything different from anyone else, but you were free," asserted Lux. "There was a legal issue in California," added Ivy. "But I don't want to elaborate on that. We just had to get out of town."

The couple headed for Erick's old Akron stamping ground and set about reconstructing their private world in the Midwest. "They seemed very much like soulmates," observed Mike. "They just loved each other, they were always seen together and they might have had disputes between the two of them, but I never heard them say a bad word about each other the way some couples do." Having spent much of the previous year scouring Sacramento's record shops and thrift stores, Kristy and Erick were quick to take advantage of fresh hunting grounds. "It was especially amazing because we'd just find unbelievably rare things. All the southerners would come to Ohio to work in the Steel Mill and the rubber companies in the fifties and sixties, and they brought their records with them that never made it out of the south, and they ended up in the junk stores around Akron and Cleveland. We went in there and got that stuff," recounted Lux. "We found all these unbelievably obscure records . . . And they not only had Sun records, but they had stuff from a lot of other labels that were there, too. It was just amazing." To support their vinyl habit and pay the rent, the couple worked at a local circuit board factory that Ivy later described as being "really boring [with] a real fascist

Journey To The Centre Of The Cramps

boss. We weren't cut out for that kind of work; we're too delicate and sensitive."

Aside from regular record-hunting sorties, Kristy and Erick also took in gigs at the local Civic Theatre and other nearby venues. "We'd all take diet pills and go to all of the rock'n'roll shows," recalled Lux. "Everyone would get dressed up for every show and it'd be so much fun. I remember when we saw the New York Dolls in Kent, Ohio. They played at an abandoned amusement park called Myers Lake Park. It was all overrun by weeds, and they opened up this old dusty ballroom and had the show there. David Johansen was on top of the PA columns going wild." However, as glam entered its terminal mid-seventies decline, the couple found that they were increasingly delving into forgotten corners of the past in search of sonic kicks. "There wasn't much going on in the seventies that really thrilled us; the New York Dolls had broken up, T. Rex wasn't what it was before," reflects Ivy. "Through record collecting we were getting more and more passionate, being exposed to music that most people weren't."

Erick and Kristy became increasingly thorough, often visiting the most unlikely looking shops to ask the proprietor if there were any old records stashed away. Occasionally, they hit the jackpot, "There was a Salvation Army one right in the middle of Cleveland, very close to WJW TV. It was just amazing; it was like a department store of 45s. You could go there early in the morning and stay in there all day and not get through it," said Lux. Time and again, it was records culled from rock'n'roll's early years that delivered the most excitement and wonder. "They're just these real nervous records, absolutely full of energy. And there's a real tension in the idea of this backbeat with a guitar and the singer sounding like he's just about to have a nervous breakdown. That's an infectious sound and it really caught us," Lux explained.

For Erick, it was Charlie Feathers, never one of Sun's most celebrated names, who would provide him with his most enduring vocal influence. "He's my all-time idol – he's just really amazing," confirmed Lux, who would go onto appropriate elements of Feathers' fractured vocal style. "He's supposed to have invented the rockabilly hiccup, he's made a lot of

Beautiful Monsters

great recordings that are just astounding, contributed a lot to rock'n'roll but will probably never be inducted into the Rock And Roll Hall of Fame." While this remains true, Feathers' influence has been recognised by the Rockabilly Hall of Fame, while such notables as Bob Dylan and Quentin Tarantino have subsequently acknowledged his legacy. Although he worked at Sun Records as a session musician, he was not rated particularly highly by Sam Phillips and cut only one single for the label – the January 1956 release 'Defrost Your Heart'. The bulk of his best-loved recordings emerged on Syd Nathan's Cincinnati-based King Records. These included 'I Can't Hardly Stand It', which the Cramps would later cover as the B-side to their 1980 'Drug Train' seven-inch. After his King contract expired he issued a string of singles before taking a lengthy recording hiatus that would end when he re-emerged during the seventies with a slightly less frantic, but equally evocative approach that resulted in landmark singles such as 'That Certain Woman' and the rolling 'We're Getting Closer To Being Apart'. During the eighties, the support of groups such as the Cramps and Tav Falco's Panther Burns led to a new generation of rockers discovering Feathers' work and ensured that he was able to perform and record into his sixties. "He lives in his own world," Lux observed. "The weird world of Charlie Feathers. He lives in Memphis in a trailer, I think."

Perhaps surprisingly, Ricky Nelson was another major rockabilly influence that came to the fore of Erick's attention during this period. Nelson had become famous thanks to his role in the proto-reality situation comedy *The Adventures Of Ozzie And Harriet*, where the teenage Ricky appeared alongside his real life family in a long-running series of wholesome escapades. Having successfully made the transition from radio to television, the show not only ensured that Ricky grew up in public, but also provided him with an invaluable platform from which to launch his singing career. His April 1957 debut single (a cover of Fats Domino's 'I'm Walkin'') became an immediate Top 10 hit, initiating a popular bonanza that would see Nelson score chart success at a rate that was bettered only by Elvis Presley and Pat Boone. Although his biggest sellers tended to be ballads such as 'Poor Little Fool' and 'Teen Age Idol', Ricky had a

Journey To The Centre Of The Cramps

genuine passion for rock'n'roll, being a particularly big fan of Carl Perkins, and recording with Elvis' backing vocalists the Jordanaires. Another bonus was that the guitarist on many of Nelson's records was the ace session player James Burton, one of the best pickers ever in both country and rock. "He's when the sick world of rockabilly infiltrated the suburbs for the first time," explained Lux. "He made all these suburban kids pay attention to it and they may never have if it wasn't for him. Elvis was a little bit too greasy, dark and weird and black, to have touched some of the people that Ricky Nelson could touch. He was one of the very first people to record cover songs from Sun Records, which was the greatest label there ever was for rockabilly."

Such was Nelson's commitment to rock'n'roll that he took the gamble of dismissing seasoned session musicians early in his recording career, replacing them with a younger band that he then took on the road. "He was one of the first people to do rockabilly that wasn't some out of control, wild, Southern hillbilly, crazed on some kind of drug or alcohol. He was just a suburbanite, clean cut kid that was twisted by this music. He'd go on TV and do this every week and was twisting up the rest of suburbia," Lux observed. "You look at all these people like Elvis or Little Richard before him – they were all considered these wild animals from the South, or immoral nigger-lovers. But everybody knew and loved Ricky Nelson for years because of his television show. He was famous and successful and could do whatever he wanted, and yet his favourite star was not the huge pop stars of the period, it was Carl Perkins. He also made really great records and his band were just amazing."

Naturally enough, Erick and Kristy's increasingly detailed examination of rock'n'roll's roots led them into its pre-history, and their interest in the blues continued to intensify. At the time, the 'blues boom' of the previous decade was a distant phenomenon and the form from which all rock'n'roll owed its provenance subject to being forgotten or dismissed as a form of primitivism. "People will never understand the blues," asserted Lux. "They understand it less today than they did back then. Even black people today, a lot of them disown the blues. When people say 'trash', they're saying that they think the blues is trash, because that's all rock'n'roll is.

Beautiful Monsters

When people say 'trash' they mean you're not doing something like Pink Floyd. You know, 'good' music. It's probably worse here in America than it is over in Europe for people understanding what rock'n'roll is. It's not trash. It's a folk art. Which makes it more important than anything that comes out of a major studio."

During the mid-seventies, the record industry did not repeatedly strip mine its back catalogues in the way that is often customary today. Although some reissues were starting to become available, most labels were focused on new releases and while it was possible to get 'Best Of' sets from the most popular blues, rock'n'roll and doo-wop acts of the previous two decades, anyone seeking their rarer cuts – or obscurities in general – had to seek out the original wax. "Back then, there was only one way to get that stuff. You had to find it somewhere, in a junk store or something, you just had to discover it. Which was the more fun way of doing it, but I'm really thrilled that all these reissues are out now so people can hear it all," said Lux. "People had no idea of the great music that had happened, rockabilly in particular, just because none of it had been re-released. Outside of Jerry Lee Lewis and Elvis, you know, there wasn't much that anybody had even heard. It was pretty obscure stuff. Then when all these reissues started happening, people became aware of this amazing heritage of great American music that nobody knew about."

Pre-internet, the only other option was to send away to small ads that appeared in music magazines. "There were no reissues," confirms Ivy. "We even remember when we got a Sonics reissue that came out in the mid-seventies, we had to mail order that and the only other reissue things we had was two records we sent to Holland for – there was that collector label – and we had to wait for eight weeks for it to come from Holland, everything else had to be original. That's the only way that you could get exposed to any of that was through originals, through finding them in thrift stores – there was no other way. We didn't have cassettes even until '75, so there wasn't even trading cassettes going on."

For Erick and Kristy, finding space to house their rapidly expanding haul of vinyl treasure was not a huge issue. After a couple of short-term lets, they moved to Vesper Street, about a mile and a half north of the city

Journey To The Centre Of The Cramps

centre. "Akron was very inexpensive to live in. So we had this gigantic three-storey house for the two of us," recounted Ivy. Finding storage units however, was a different matter. "We had to argue with my parents – 'Let us borrow the pool table' and they thought 'Well, maybe he'll get good at pool, maybe he'll be good at something finally' and we just wanted something to hold our records," explained Lux. The spacious living/storage conditions also enabled the couple to begin their own musical experiments. "We used the attic for rehearsals," explained Ivy. "We must have talked about the band in Sacramento, though, because I actually bought Lux the fuzz pedal we use, which is a Univox Superfuzz, from a pawn shop. His brother sent him a Student Prince guitar and I taught him 'Baby Strange' by T.Rex."

Initially, the idea of starting a band was simply an extension of their relationship. "We decided that we had to have our own band. We were sort of wrapped up in our own little world, we didn't have people telling us that you can't do that, or that you're a fool, there's too many people doing that, so we just did it," said Ivy. "I think being together – not just as a couple, but as partners in crime – that you can get each other wound up in a way that a person alone can't. We convinced each other that it was a viable option to have our own band and that everybody would think it was really cool. It was kind of a delusion. Except that we succeeded with it."

Although Erick experimented with guitar, his previous experience had been occasional vocal stints with some of Mike's earlier bands. With Kristy already able to play a six-string, the roles that the couple were to assume within the Cramps fell into place organically. "Ivy always knew that she wanted to play guitar. Me and Ivy were the first ones to have the idea for the group, so she got to play guitar," remembered Lux. "I always wanted to throw myself around onstage and break mic stands. Originally I was going to play guitar, but I couldn't dance around much that way."

From the very outset, Erick's desire to dance around reflected the raw energy that the couple wanted their group to have. At a time when sitting around on beanbags absorbing extended flights of musical and

Beautiful Monsters

lyrical whimsy remained *de rigueur* for much of America, such uninhibited abandon would immediately place the new group in opposition to the mainstream current. "If there were going to be fun shows to go to, we would have to be playing, no one else was doing that," declared Lux.

To help evoke the spirit of excitement they wanted for their new group, Erick and Kristy would draw upon the knowledge of raw, primal rock'n'roll that they had been painstakingly accruing over the past three years. "We decided this music couldn't be forgotten forever," asserted Lux. "Rock'n'roll is a whole landscape, it takes you from here to there. And you can't look at that as great 'art'. It's not that socialised; it's an outlaw art. And you can't judge it unless you're living a rock'n'roll lifestyle, either."

Any doubts that Erick may have had about his vocal ability were dispelled by a trip to see a past-their-prime T. Rex, "I saw them in Cleveland where Bolan came on weighting 300 pounds, wearing this batwing costume and beating his guitar with a whip – 'Holy shit!' I thought, 'This guy is my idol!' Driving home I was singing better than he had onstage, so trying to form a group started to seem natural."

Further fuel to Erick and Kristy's plans to form a group and live the rock'n'roll life to its fullest extent came via a feature in *Rock Sound* magazine that outlined a new, exciting scene centred on an obscure New York bar named CBGB. The Bowery venue had opened a couple of years earlier and, after a spell as a hangout for Hell's Angels and marines, had been opened up for rock'n'roll on Sunday nights thanks to Television manager Terry Ork persuading owner Hilly Kristal that it would be a way of filling the bar on a customarily quiet night and getting his group to build a small stage. Within months, bands such as Television, the Patti Smith Group, Blondie, Talking Heads and the Ramones had all made their debuts there. While each of these acts evoked aspects of rock'n'roll's past to varying degrees, there was little else to connect them stylistically – Patti Smith spliced literary concepts, allied to a beat sensibility and elements of garage rock; Television were initially raw but soon veered toward a minimalist interpretation of progressive rock; Blondie projected the classic girl–group sound of the early sixties through a slightly shambolic, energetic lens; Talking Heads referenced a wide range of influences in a wired-yet-academic way; and the Ramones looked like a street gang and sounded like the Beach Boys on crystal meth. The personnel of these bands was drawn largely from remnants of the earlier Warhol and glam scenes, kids who'd learned to play from listening to Velvet Underground albums, some from the outer boroughs and others out-of-towners who'd arrived in New York with the same dreams as Erick and Kristy were currently nurturing.

Aside from a broadly common appreciation of girl groups such as the Shangri-Las and the Ronettes and a general recognition of the sort of basic garage rock that had been collected by Elektra Records founder Jac Holzman and Patti Smith Group guitarist Lenny Kaye for the 1972 *Nuggets* double album, what these groups did share (with each other and the future Cramps) was a complete lack of interest in following the prevailing musical orthodoxy of the era. Logically enough, Kristy and Erick resolved that this was something that they needed to experience themselves. "There was no place in Ohio where you could have an original band, and we knew that CBGB was starting to happen," recalled Ivy. The couple made two trips to CBGB during the second half on 1975 and were immediately impressed with what they saw. "Seeing Television back before they had their record deal, which took them a long time, was like seeing the Yardbirds or something," Lux enthused. "They would play 'Psychotic Reaction' and stuff like that, and they were just a real crappy rock'n'roll band, and all of a sudden they had a record deal and it was just like this fluid rock music thing. It's the same thing with the Talking Heads – they sounded more like disco when they had a record out, but they sounded more like the 1910 Fruitgum Company or something before they had a record deal. I love all those guys' records too, but that was the most fun about seeing all these bands before they had any record deals, cos they were really different bands."

These trips cemented the deal – if Erick and Kristy were to have a band, then it was an absolute necessity that they moved to where the action was. "We'd done the nine-hour drive from Akron twice and seen the

Beautiful Monsters

Ramones and Television, so we knew it was all there. Get a few days off, take speed, drive there, see the bands, drive back and there'd be nothing left of us when we got back to Ohio. But those two trips convinced us we had to move," recounted Ivy. "For years I'd gone to see bands and said, 'Wow, that's the only thing there is for me. I could do that so good.' Usually what it was, was I'd go to see bands and I'd be depressed and disappointed by someone I thought was going to be good. I'd say to myself, 'I could do better than that if I was up there.' It would always be like that. One day it just seemed that either I had to do this, or forget it."

The New York trips also provided the couple with another piece in their musical jigsaw thanks to a chance encounter at a Sixth Avenue restaurant called Chicken & Burger World. There, Erick and Kristy – who introduced themselves as Lux and Ivy – got talking to 19-year-old Kent State student Miriam Linna. Miriam recalled seeing the striking-looking Lux at a Kinks show. "A familiar-looking tall guy with long hair and a velvet jacket had sidled over to our table to say that he'd seen us at a show at the Piccadilly Inn in Cleveland a few weeks earlier, and then he told us that he and his girlfriend Ivy were in the middle of moving to New York to form a band, and that I should play drums with them," she remembered. "I was shocked. I told him I'd never played at all and that seemed to be a selling point." After returning to Ohio, Miriam received a letter from Lux saying that they'd visit her when they returned to pick up their stuff ahead of relocating to New York. When the couple duly dropped by Miriam recalled that, "We started going through stacks of magazines and records and talked about music and about the band they wanted to start." While nothing was firmly fixed, partly due to Miriam's reluctance to move to New York, it seemed that Lux and Ivy were enthusiastic about recruiting the novice teenager to play drums.

With little more than a rough outline of the kind of band they wanted to be, a uniquely striking look, a huge amount of faith in each other and a shared conviction in their chosen path, Lux and Ivy packed up some belongings, scraped together the meagre amount of cash they'd managed to accrue and, as the chill of autumn began to make its presence felt, set off for New York. "We had a *mission* to move to New York and become the

Journey To The Centre Of The Cramps

new New York Dolls. We were influenced by their glamour, two guitar assault and firm grasp of R&B, but we thought nobody – from the early Stones and Yardbirds to the Dolls and T. Rex, had included the most deadly ingredient of all – rockabilly," Lux insisted. And besides, as he later observed, "If I'd stayed I'd have a hole in my head. I don't care to live in the Midwest."

CHAPTER THREE

Rotten To The Core

You've just got to understand that 90 per cent of the people living in New York are completely crazy. I mean homicidally crazy.

Bryan Gregory

ON their arrival in New York in September 1975, Lux and Ivy's first priority was to find a base from which to launch their assault on the city's growing underground scene. "We had enough money for a hotel for two days, and couldn't find a place to live," said Ivy. "So we slept the third night in the car at a truck-stop in New Jersey and said, 'If we don't find somewhere tomorrow, we'll have to forget it and go back to Ohio.' That day we found our apartment. So we moved and proceeded to starve. But that was okay. We had to be there."

Cramps HQ was duly established at a fourth floor apartment on East 73rd Street, the Upper East Side being a swanky area so the couple's new home had location, if not size, in its favour. It was a half hour subway ride away from the Mecca of CBGB and, being the "size of a tomb", barely enabled Lux and Ivy to store their constantly expanding collection of records and bric-a-brac. "There was only one window in the apartment, facing into a back alley," recalled Miriam Linna. "There was a mess of records on shelves facing the jukebox, a walk-through bedroom with a massive old bed that took up the entire room, a tiny bathroom with a sink and shower, and a minuscule kitchenette, but it was homey."

Having joined the tired, poor and huddled masses that historically flock to the city, Lux and Ivy quickly found that their fun-filled excursions to

Journey To The Centre Of The Cramps

New York earlier in the year had left them with somewhat rose-tinted impressions. Economically, they could scarcely have arrived at a worse time; within weeks of the couple setting down their suitcases, President Gerald Ford was refusing to bail out Mayor Abraham Beame's debt-ridden administration. Hustlers, junkies and traumatised Vietnam veterans picked their way through the growing piles of uncollected rubbish on the sidewalks. Although Ford later relented, slashed services and a decaying infrastructure meant that anyone hoping to gain a toehold in one of the world's toughest cities would be facing even more of a struggle than was usually the case.

"New York was a very different place in those days," Miriam observed. "The city was nearly bankrupt, some unknown psychopath dubbed the Son of Sam was shooting disco people every couple of months, and there were no yuppies or rich kids anywhere in sight. Everybody was a scrapper." Additionally, the New York Dolls – who had epitomised the soiled glamour of the city's preceding underground scene, their allure playing no small part in enticing Lux and Ivy to make the move east – were in the process of disintegrating and had been dropped by their record company. "We came to New York thinking, because of this single picture, that everybody walked around looking like the New York Dolls. And of course nobody did – it was all jeans and boring," opined Lux. "We discovered that the Dolls were just weirdos, just like Elvis had been in the South," added Ivy." Instead of the heavy rock'n'roll subculture we expected, all we found was garbage all over the streets, and people who'd moved there to become dancers or actors. It hardly seemed like a great breeding ground for rock'n'roll."

As their subsequent careers would empirically demonstrate, Lux and Ivy were determined. Although their rent ate up the bulk of their meagre funds, the strength of their shared belief in their rock'n'roll mission and their unwavering faith in each other ensured there was absolutely no question of them abandoning their chosen path. "We never lost our faith," asserts Ivy. "We didn't doubt." Despite a bitter winter of barely getting by, the couple maintained their focus on forming a group. "We even bought a PA – we thought you needed to own your own PA in New York. I mean

Rotten To The Core

we didn't know anything about having a band," admitted Ivy. "We knew that rockabilly and the kind of music we were listening to was what everybody in the world wanted to hear! At the same time we were really moved and inspired by punk rock bands that were happening in New York at the time." For Lux and Ivy, the directness and pure rock'n'roll spirit of the bands making waves at CBGB bore evident similarities to the untrammelled sense of wild abandon personified by the rawness of rockabilly. "The Ramones were just like this blast of light onstage. The energy influenced us," Ivy recalls. "I love the music of rockabilly, but I think we're equally as influenced by what it was and what it meant. And it's exactly on target as to what rock'n'roll is. Not rock music or pop music, but what rock'n'roll – those words – should be. Which is stripped down, sexually fuelled, frantic, two-and-a-half minutes that get you excited, or make you come, or explode, or something like that," explained Lux. "Rockabilly was the punk rock of the fifties," concluded Ivy.

However, the themes that would underpin the Cramps represented far more than simply turbo-charging early rock'n'roll with the blistering velocity of the Ramones. Having wholly committed to realising their ambition, Lux and Ivy's group would need to encapsulate everything they admired, believed in, or valued. The band would be an externalisation of their personalities, interests and outlooks. While this would soon come to encompass a broad sweep of exotic popular culture including movies, television, comics and radio, part of their initial focus on rockabilly stemmed from an almost evangelical desire to bring this forgotten music to a new generation of rock fans. "There's something really intense that happened in the country at the beginning of white rock'n'roll, that went on for two or three years and was such an incredible thing, such a great thing in American history," Lux explained. "It's just as important as the hot dog, or McDonald's, or anything else. It was so big that it's disgusting that it was not known about. It's immoral that it's not known about. These people are still around, playing in swing bands or operating gas stations and stuff like that."

Aside from a PA and Ivy's guitar the group also had a name. "Ivy thought of the name a long time ago, in '74 or something – she wanted to

49

Journey To The Centre Of The Cramps

have a band called 'the Cramps'. It was mainly because we really dug the Kinks. We liked them a lot and felt like the Kinks stood for something that's wrong in society, something that people try to get rid of and straighten out. We were trying to think of a name like that, and what the American counterpart would be, and we came up with 'the Cramps' and made it a household word," recalled Lux. Having conceived the name as a modernised American equivalent to 'the Kinks', Ivy stuck with it, rejecting any alternatives. As she later recalled, these included "Bop Crazy Babies because of Vern Pullens, we found that record in a place just west of Cleveland and he had a song called 'Bop Crazy Baby'. At the time it was before punk rock names, but there were names like 'the Kinks' and 'the Pretty Things', where you're something like a gang. Everything was like 'Aerosmith' and 'Featherroot' or something. So that seemed kind of subversive, so like everybody can be a Cramp. By the time we got it going and up on stage there was the Ramones and the Dead Boys, so there must have been like a collective mentality. There wasn't when we were thinking of it though." Fittingly, the manner in which 'the Cramps' evoked menstrual pain hinted at the visceral, sexualised aspects that underpin all truly exciting rock'n'roll. "Everyone was into this sexual denial, hippy sensibility," recalled Lux.

With the ideas behind the group taking shape, Lux and Ivy continued to soak up developments at CBGB, with the likes of the Ramones, Blondie, the Heartbreakers, Talking Heads and Suicide all playing there or at Max's Kansas City on Park Avenue South, during the early months of 1976. "There was such an incredible scene at CBGB at that time, and it was like Mecca to us – everyone just kind of migrated there," says Ivy. "When we saw the Ramones that influenced us, Suicide influenced us. So by the time that we played ourselves, we'd been influenced by whatever happened up to that point and even what kept on happening." In particular, Suicide's confrontational approach to performing left a firm impression on the couple. Remarkable in any number of ways, the electro-terrorist duo had been around since the start of the decade, playing live for the first time in November 1970. Contemporaries of the New York Dolls, Suicide had been regulars at the Mercer Arts Center and gigged with many of the

Rotten To The Core

groups such as Joey Ramone's glitter rock combo, Sniper, which included personnel who would subsequently go on to populate the city's germinal punk scene. While keyboard magus Martin Rev would stand behind his ramshackle banks of home-built equipment, creating a sonic maelstrom that inspired everything from synthpop to industrial music, fearless frontman Alan Vega would interact with the audience on a very physical level – blocking the path of anyone trying to escape the relentless aural assault, or swinging a length of motorcycle chain above his head. "He showed us that antagonism could be fun," explains Ivy.

In order to make ends meet, Ivy took on a series of waitressing jobs. "I was a waitress at several places – Guru Berger, which is a chain, and some other bar. I was a cocktail waitress," she recalls. Lux scored himself a regular paycheck when he wandered into the Musical Maze record store on Lexington and 85th Street, hoping to buy a copy of Lou Reed's *Coney Island Baby* for Ivy's birthday. Lux fell into conversation with the store's owner, Perry, who was immediately impressed with his customer's detailed musical knowledge and duly hired him on the spot. Aside from providing the couple with some much needed income and an additional means of sourcing rare and obscure vinyl, Lux's new job brought him into contact with Greg Beckerleg, another recent arrival in the city who had taken work at the Maze while he attempted to establish himself as an album cover artist. The new co-workers quickly discovered that they harboured similar rock'n'roll ambitions and that Greg also shared a birthday with Ivy, so Lux invited him along to their celebratory dinner date that evening. Learning of Lux and Ivy's plans to put together a group, Greg immediately wanted in. "He knew he was a star and he wanted to collect somehow," observed Lux. "I described the kind of band I wanted and he said that was the kind of band he'd always wanted to be in."

A native of Detroit, Greg seemed to have all the attributes necessary to become a Cramp. Firstly, he was an outsider who, up until his 25th birthday, had drifted through life, harbouring dreams of becoming the next Brian Jones without having any practical notion of how that might be achieved. Musically, his sole experience involved tinkering with an organ. "I was living with this guy who had an organ. When he went away to

Journey To The Centre Of The Cramps

work, I'd sit on it for an hour, two hours, and just hold down all the bass pedals with my feet," recalled Greg. "It was like suicide music – it would be all this noise and I'd just sit there and vibrate myself to death." This complete lack of any formal music training or history of being in bands was exactly what Lux and Ivy were looking for, as it not only ensured that Greg was free of any received affectations, but also meant that he would fit into a group where any form of orthodoxy would represent a drawback. Given that the Cramps were conceived as a gang of outsiders, a misfit such as Greg would fit right in.

In addition to his avowed nonconformity, Beckerleg was a striking looking individual. His pockmarked skin had the quality of parchment torn from a book of forbidden lore, while his needlepoint pupils glinted from beneath a flick of long brown hair, arranged to cascade down one side of his face in the style of Veronica Lake. Possessed of a shifty quality that made people around him uncomfortable or wary, Greg was also somewhat effeminate – both in his slightly androgynous look and his soft, subtly lisping speech. "He had this kind of swirly way around," Ivy recalls. "He was more girl than me – that was great too."

Interviewing the Cramps in 1979, *NME* journalist Nick Kent was transfixed by Beckerleg's appearance, observing that, "Equally unsettling is Gregory's complete serenity of manner, his voice always remaining at one speciously gentle pitch strictly at odds with a pair of eyes so venomous-looking that, replete with the gamut of tattoos covering his arms, Gregory looks like he walked out of the human snake-pit of a Todd Browning film." He also shared Ivy's interest in unconventional spirituality, maintaining that he had been told by a psychic that he would meet someone on his birthday that would profoundly change his life. Furthermore, he projected a studied air of cool mystery that would enable mythologies about his past to be constructed, with Lux subsequently asserting that, "He once worked on a car assembly line, and the story goes that he accidentally fell into a half-completed body and couldn't be found until the finished product rolled off the ramp" – or, less plausibly, that, "He worked in a nuclear weapons plant in California, but they fired him cos he was eating too much of the product."

Rotten To The Core

After the meal, Lux and Ivy reasoned that Greg might well make an ideal bassist for the new group. "We were shocked the next day when he had already gone out and bought a Giannini guitar at a pawnshop and stencilled 'The Cramps' on its case," remembered Ivy. Not wanting to puncture Greg's enthusiasm by telling him that they'd mentally pencilled him in to play bass, Lux and Ivy went with the flow – the Cramps would have two guitarists. "I took one look at it and said, 'Let's do it!' The three of us made a pact that if we didn't make it, we'd join hands and jump off the Empire State Building," Lux recounted. "That was the seriousness of it. The purpose was to have fun. In the beginning we'd be totally happy if we had 20 totally insane fans who came to see us every time we played, and we could have fun doing it." In addition to the new guitar, Greg had decided that he wanted to be known as Bryan Gregory, "because it sounded like a movie star". From the newly rechristened Bryan's point of view, the key thing was that the group looked exciting and different. "I'd always wanted to be in a band, but I never thought I'd meet anyone as cool as me 'til I met these people," he revealed. "Bryan's creative forte was more visual than sonic," observed Ivy. "When we met him, he had just moved to New York to pursue a graphic-arts career. He loved art, jewellery making, decorating – I think it was the visual aspects of the Cramps that appealed to him most."

In order to further enhance his already impressive image, Ivy later presented Bryan with a Flying V guitar. "When we gave the guitar to him, he immediately decorated it with polka-dot price stickers and painted our name in fancy script on the case, and you know what? It looked hot," she recalled. Equally striking was the unusual new six-string that Ivy subsequently selected to replace her Plexiglas Dan Armstrong model. "I had this kind of rare Canadian guitar called a 'Lewis'," she explained. "Actually, I had two of them. I bought the first on 48th Street in New York City in 1976, then the second in Vancouver in 1983. They're both solid-bodies with Bigsby-like vibrato bars and they both weigh a ton. One unusual characteristic about both of them is that the necks are flat and wide, like a classical guitar. I wish I could find out more about them. When I bought the first one, the salesman told me it was a Canadian make." As it turned

Journey To The Centre Of The Cramps

out, the wide-necked guitar would prove ideal for Ivy's meticulously picked leads. "Now all we needed was a drummer," she added.

Although Lux and Ivy had approached Miriam Linna to play drums the previous year, she had yet to commit to the move from Ohio to New York, so when Bryan suggested that he should call his sister Pam, she was accepted sight unseen, despite having even less musical experience than her brother. "We didn't let these details stop us from forging ahead with our mission," explained Ivy. While Pam was relocating from Detroit, Lux and Ivy set about introducing Bryan to the CBGB scene. "I just remember taking Bryan, who hadn't seen the Ramones yet, to a show," Ivy recalled. "He'd had less than half a glass of wine and a hit off somebody's joint, but when the Ramones came out, this energy was so overwhelming, he threw up in the gutter outside. He just got so overwhelmed by them, it was too much. He couldn't deal with it. They were like white light and white heat, like a nuclear blast or an explosion. When the Ramones came out onstage, it was like a magnesium flare – you didn't see anything else."

Despite the shock of close exposure to the Ramones' ferocious assault, Gregory assimilated the notion of what could be achieved with savage blasts of serrated distortion, the impression the Queens quartet made on him playing a part in the foundation of his own, uniquely untutored guitar technique. As Lux and Ivy got to know Bryan, the trio began to develop the 'us-against-them' mentality that was concomitant with the idea of the band being akin to a gang. "We were almost the same size and could fit into each other's pants and shoes." Ivy explained. "We understood each other because we weren't the boy/girl next door, and we'd both already been through a lot and knew how to hustle tooth and nail to survive. We could be our scary selves without horrifying each other."

Once Pam had arrived in the Big Apple in June and taken on the suitably rhythmic sounding surname of 'Balam', the quorum was complete. They set about rehearsing songs (and in Bryan and Pam's case learning their instruments) in the basement of the Music Maze, where Perry had allowed them to come in and practise. Having purchased an inexpensive drum kit for Pam, they set up after the store had closed and began by

Rotten To The Core

attempting a cover of 'Quick Joey Small (Run Joey Run)', originally a minor transatlantic hit for the Kasenetz-Katz Singing Orchestral Circus in 1968. A Farfisa-infused shard of bubblegum-garage attitude, the track proved an excellent choice for the Cramps, who "were impressed that we could play a song with a beginning, middle, and an end". A subsequently recorded demo provides evidence that Lux's Iggy-range, assertive vocal delivery was there from the very start (albeit delivered via standard guitar amplifier), while Ivy's precisely savage guitar slashes enliven a stomping version of the song. Store owner Perry was equally impressed with the group and attempted to get them to sign a hastily scrawled management contract.

Additional cover versions were selected from Lux and Ivy's vast stash of classic rock'n'roll, including the Phantom's frantic 1960 cut 'Love Me' and Roy Orbison's 1957 Sun Records recording 'A Cat Named Domino'. While an early rehearsal recording of the Cramps' version of the latter provides further evidence that Lux's vocal hysteria came into this world fully formed, Ivy's note perfect lead indicates her determination to master her instrument from the very start. The summer 1976 demo version of 'Love Me' similarly gives indications of what would become trademarks of the Cramps' sound: the controlled use of feedback, deployment of echo and Bryan's banks of distortion. The group also imbue the track with a sense of crepuscular menace absent from the original, while still retaining its lyrical psychosis and stop/start humour. "That record by the Phantom, that's like the craziest record ever recorded," Lux declared. "That guy recorded that insane crazy thing and said, 'I know where Pat Boone goes to church – raaaargh' and he ran out of there and grabbed Pat Boone coming out of church and said, 'You've gotta listen to my record, it's crazy, it's rockabilly, it's from Hell, it's out of control – you'll love it, Pat!'"

Both 'Love Me' and 'Quick Joey Small' show the importance Lux and Ivy attached to material that had been widely dismissed as 'novelty records' at the time of their release. "I think there's a great danger with children, if they don't have novelty records, they can grow up, get a job, go to school, and then die and they never become crazy or anything. You've got to be very careful," announced Lux. Other covers the group attempted during these early sessions included 'Hurricane Fighter Plane', originally recorded by Texan outsiders the Red Crayola, the Ramones' 'Beat On The Brat', 13th Floor Elevators' founder Roky Erickson's 'Two Headed Dog' and Peanuts Wilson's 1957 rocker 'Cast Iron Arm'.

As the group thrashed away, rats fled the dingy cellar and John – a Down's syndrome sufferer who acted as the shop's security and sometimes worked on the oldies section with Lux – would take similar flight, escaping into the street with his fingers jammed into his ears. "[John] once said the Cramps sounded like a song called 'Dead Man's Scroll', which we'd never heard of," remembered Lux. "We later found out it's a fabulous and rare record, also issued as 'Midnight Stroll', by the Revels." Lux and Ivy had already composed a number of original songs, and the novice group applied themselves to developing those alongside the cover versions. "When we first got together we would try all kinds of things," explained Lux. "We would try to copy records and all kinds of weird things, a lot of them never made it to the stage, when we were searching for what we were going to sound like. We really couldn't play any instruments at all for a while."

Despite this, Ivy declared herself delighted with the progress that Bryan and Pam were making. "They'd both never played before and I was amazed what they picked up," she enthuses. "Some people that have never played; they still have something maybe they'd never thought of. She's really good . . . I don't know if she got tips from other drummers – I don't think she did." Similarly, Ivy had come to an understanding with Bryan about the way in which the twin guitar dynamic would function. "He mainly functioned as bass player. He played bass lines on guitar, he'd tune it down real low," she explained. "The two guitar thing – the Dolls were an influence on that – the way they had two guitars, we'd seen a lot of bands but no one had done that before. It was always just lead and rhythm, none of this weaving in and out . . . they were just like 3-D guitars."

The quartet settled into their roles within the group: Lux – the unhinged vocal ringmaster; Ivy – responsible for lead and melody; Bryan –

Rotten To The Core

alternating between providing bottom end and twisted layers of fuzz; and Pam – laying down a stomping, thunderous jungle beat. "When we first went into the basement of the Musical Maze record store with Bryan Gregory and his sister Pam to jam, we didn't know how we'd sound. So we just did it. We didn't have enough going on to discuss it," Ivy explained. "It was a natural, organic thing . . . it's really more self-expression of our personal tastes." Lux agreed, "When we started it wasn't like a lot of bands do, starting out with a concept and they plan this whole certain thing around a concept. It's more like some kind of art presentation than a rock'n'roll band. From the beginning we wanted to be a rock'n'roll band and play the kind of stuff we dug listening to for years."

The Cramps' earliest originals included 'Sunglasses After Dark', which owed its title to Dwight Pullen's 1958 B-side to 'Teenage Bug', but took its musical cues from Link Wray & the Raymen's 'Ace Of Spades'. "Because my favourite guitarist is Link Wray, and I guess the thing I like in what he does is what I wanna do, too," Ivy observed. "I just like hearing a lot of strings splashing all at once. And just the austerity and the starkness of how he plays, you know? The drama that's created by not overplaying." Even in demo form, it was evident that the Cramps were putting their own spin on songs such as these. Whereas Wray's lead motif is maintained, the group slow the pace somewhat, evoking the air of menace with which Wray had infused 'Rumble'. The addition of haunting echo and muted fuzz increased the feeling of unreal peril, which juxtaposed against Lux's demented warning about the perils of wearing shades. "We set out to become a patchwork hybrid with a life of its own – a rock'n'roll Brides of Frankenstein," explained Lux.

Pam Balam, whose "fierce rockin' drum sound" was later credited by Ivy as providing the basis for the group's subsequent rhythmic template, led the way for the demo version of 'TV Set'. Adding horror and cult television to the Cramps' lyrical formula, the song was destined to become one of their most popular numbers. By taking straightforward rockabilly syncopation and transferring it to the toms, Pam constructed a tribal rhythm that enabled Ivy and Bryan to take the track further out by adding raw rhythmic garage guitar and bursts of precisely placed noise. Such

Journey To The Centre Of The Cramps

subversion and adaptation of the early rock'n'roll that inspired them demonstrated that, right from the start, there was little question of the Cramps being mere revivalists. Instead, they consciously avoided anything that might resemble orthodoxy, and in doing so the group can be said to have successfully assimilated the experimental spirit of early punk. "When we got to New York we made a pact not to play Chuck Berry," says Ivy. "We love Chuck Berry, but the reason was because everybody did it."

The Cramps also recorded an early version of 'Under The Wires' during their initial practices. Originally titled 'Subwire Desire', the track would remain unreleased for almost five years, finally surfacing in 1981 on the group's second album, *Psychedelic Jungle*. A hilarious and groovy evocation of the sex-pest phone caller, its germinal version is a churning bump'n'grind bonanza that features Ivy's precision picking, underpinned by Bryan's savage sonic slashes. More than any other track on the summer 1976 tapes, it shows how close the Cramps were to their subsequent recognisable form at this early stage of their development.

While the group was coming together nicely, Ivy was becoming increasingly sick of her job as a cocktail waitress, so much so that she jumped at the chance to leave when Maze owner Perry's girlfriend offered her the opportunity to work at the Victorian, a midtown establishment offering bondage and domination for its clientele. "The people who came in were very powerful, and for an hour or so they'd want to give up their power. To this day, whenever I see that as someone's fetish, I can't imagine somebody doing that without getting paid. But occasionally when I get pissed off I'll get going," she revealed. "When someone's on TV or something I'm wondering about things like that, if it's a powerful person, I'm wondering what they do to balance it out. That's a facet with some people, like they need to get walked on or something, but as soon as they're done, that's it."

A photograph of Ivy from the period shows her resplendent in sunglasses, cupless bra, suspender belt and stockings, evincing the kind of dangerous sexuality she would subsequently bring to the Cramps' stage shows. More immediately, it paid far better than her previous jobs. "It was a very interesting time. I was making way more money than anyone else in the band. And the work suited me. We didn't struggle in the way we would have if I'd just stayed waiting tables. It enabled us to be independent . . . I was cut out for the work," she explained. "Having worked as a dominatrix, I think that way about people. What they're really about. And I didn't know what an English Massage was before I worked there – it's a beating. I think that you can probably learn more about someone in that line of work than a psychiatrist can."

Aside from the slightly unsettling way in which a premium was placed on employees at the Victorian who looked close to the legal age of consent (as Ivy explained, "It was worth a lot to be of legal age but not look your age"), she feels that her continued employment there may have served to alienate Pam, who quit the group during that summer. Although Lux subsequently explained that she left because "she was young and wild and had other things on her mind, like boys", he was also quoted as saying that "she didn't really like" being in the group. Pam's departure occurred at around the same time that the Cramps wore out their welcome at the Music Maze. However, by August, both problems had been resolved: they found a proper rehearsal space at West 39th Street, in Manhattan's Garment District. "We'd get off at Times Square Station and briskly walk past all the hookers and junkies with our guitars," Ivy recalled.

As Pam's replacement, the group recruited Miriam, who'd returned to New York in time for the bicentennial celebrations. "We all ganged up and went to see the New York Dolls, I swear, in a shopping centre on Long Island, or New Jersey, whatever – a total teenage weekend bash, Cleveland/Detroit versus the world," she recounted. "I'd met up with Lux and Ivy and had stayed over at their place, a small, low-ceiling walk-up on East 73rd Street. A cool old jukebox took up a good chunk of the living room – Lux said he paid a guy five bucks to carry it up the stairs, strapped to his back!" There, Miriam met Bryan for the first time, before heading downtown to catch the July 4 fireworks. "The streets were packed with surging crowds, the noise level was insane, the big ships were in. It was simply as exciting as life could get for a kid from the boonies. I was in a band and I had yet to find a pair of drum sticks, let alone a job and a place to live."

Journey To The Centre Of The Cramps

The dust had scarcely settled from America's biggest ever public party when Miriam was thrown in at the deep end. "So here I was now, not knowing what I was getting into, and not knowing which end was up on a drumstick, in with this snap-happy trio with a name, and a selection of photos, and zero experience, or musical ability for that matter," she recalled. "Lux handed me a brand new pair of sticks and pronounced me the world's greatest drummer. Let's go. Just like that. No audition, no test run, no lessons, no suggestions of what to play or how fast."

Two tracks recorded at a session at their new rehearsal loft that October surfaced on the Cramps' 2004 rarities collection, *How To Make A Monster*, and indicate that Miriam slotted neatly into the group dynamic, adopting the pre-existing tom-tom-orientated, primal-beat-keeping pattern. This process was undoubtedly made easier by the way in which Ivy and Bryan had developed over the four months since the group began playing together. While Lux's vocal on the rehearsal tape is sung in a slightly higher register than usual, their rendition of 'I Was A Teenage Werewolf' is close to the version that would subsequently appear on their 1980 debut album, *Songs The Lord Taught Us*. With the group noticeably tighter than they had been on their earlier rehearsal tapes, this version of that song is notable for the way that the Cramps were beginning to use space as a means of evoking a sense of menace, while Ivy and Bryan's developing guitar interplay gave the song's threatening ambience a physical form. The song shares its title with the 1957 creature feature that starred Michael Landon in the title role. "That's also a film that's very hard to see in the States right now because Michael Landon won't allow it to be shown. He tries to suppress it. It's a great picture where they did all these bizarre camera things, like all the way while when he was walking across the gym he was upside down. They did all kinds of disorientating things like that," explained Lux. "In America now he's a real well-known TV star in *Little House On The Prairie*, he's got this real clean image now, he's in *Bonanza*," Ivy added. Although both song and movie imply similarities between lycanthropy and puberty, Lux maintained there was little connection between the two. "'I Was A Teenage Werewolf' has nothing to do with the film of the same name. That song is absolutely true. I wrote a song called 'Man With The X-Ray Eyes' once after seeing *The Man With The X-Ray Eyes* [1963] on mushrooms, but we never did it."

Also included on the October 1976 tape is an early version of the group's cover of Charlie Feathers' 1956 cut 'I Can't Hardly Stand It'. This rendition begins very slowly, building to a hypnotic, plodding rhythm adorned by Lux's yelps and his amped-up interpretation of Feathers' unique vocal style, which gives the song an organic slapback feel. "I hear it in Lux's voice, Lux doesn't sound like Charlie Feathers but I hear the influences. I don't know if Lux is aware of it or not though," observed Ivy. This gave the already otherworldly source material an extra coating of weird and was, in turn, enhanced by Miriam's understated use of her drum rims. "Since nobody really knew how to play, it was pointless trying to faithfully cover any songs that anybody would know," observed Miriam. "The idea was doing original versions of gnarly, attitudinal old obscuros, things that Ivy could deliver a dangerous guitar line, that Bryan could fuzz blast away to, that I could pound around, that Lux could verbalise over with his well oiled vocal chords and seasoned imagination, stoked by hours of late night creature features on TV."

Ivy kept things similarly simple, maintaining the twangy motif and allowing the track's unhinged, lovelorn vocal to carry it home. "I think some guitarists get led into an ego thing where they want to perform in some technical way, which even if you can it's not always the best thing to choose to do," she explained. "I still like the idea of playing for the pure euphoria. My favourite thing to play, still, is rhythm. It's just so euphoric that I really get high playing. Certain things I play don't even feel like it's me playing it, and that's my favourite kind of playing. Guitarists can get caught up in trying to be recognised for something technical or intricate that they're doing, but they lose the whole world of getting high just from playing when they do that." Although 'I Can't Hardly Stand It' would miss out on inclusion on *Songs The Lord Taught Us*, it would surface later the same year as the B-side of the UK release of 'Drug Train'.

Miriam turned 21 that same month and was given a pair of hand-painted Japanese slippers and a vintage Oriental jewellery box by Ivy, while Lux – whom she'd taken to visiting old record stores with – presented the

Journey To The Centre Of The Cramps

drummer with a pair of albums by Washington garage titans the Sonics. In addition to getting along well with her new bandmates and finding her place within the group's structure, Miriam had overcome her initial homesickness and was digging life in the Big Apple. "I remember waiting for the downtown Lexington Avenue train with Lux. I guess I was missing home, and told him I'd been writing to my friends back home and that maybe I should go back," she recalled. "He took me by the shoulders, looked me straight in the eyes, and told me, 'You're a Cramp now! You can't go back.' There was a phone call home, bawling to mom, and another with my brother threatening to come and get me and bring me back. It never happened, though, and my proclamation to [my friend] Nikki that I could never live in New York would fade." Miriam's period of adjustment was helped by Lux and Ivy's fierce commitment to the cause, which saw them organising photo sessions and printing business cards almost from the band's inception.

This single-mindedness finally bore its first tangible fruit when they finally persuaded Hilly Kristal to give the Cramps their first shot at playing CBGB. He booked the group to play the Monday night audition slot on a bill topped by the Dead Boys, who also had roots in Cleveland and had begun carving out a reputation as the latest authentic punk rock sensation. Guitarist Cheetah Chrome and drummer Johnny Blitz had previously served time alongside future Pere Ubu mainstay David Thomas in Cleveland's proto-punk garage combo, Rocket From The Tombs. "One thing people assume is that we knew those people," said Ivy. "We didn't. We weren't aware of them playing, except that we saw Rocket From The Tombs supporting Television in a hotel in Cleveland. We didn't meet any of them until we moved to New York. We didn't know anything in Ohio except our stupid jobs and mainstream gigs. We didn't know there was an underground. So we had to get out of there."

This need to break out of Ohio had been shared by the Dead Boys, who had taken inspiration and encouragement from the Ramones, making a splash with their 1977 debut single, 'Sonic Reducer', and following it up with the landmark *Young Loud And Snotty Album* that October. Live, the Dead Boys tended to make the Ramones look like a symphony of

Rotten To The Core

subtleties – punking it up almost to the point of parody with borderline misogynistic material such as 'I Need Lunch' and 'Caught With The Meat In Your Mouth'. Described by Ivy as "notably off the wall" and as having "the filthiest sense of humour we'd ever encountered", Dead Boys' frontman Stiv Bators was a one-man circus, slashing himself with microphone stands, indulging in onstage fellatio and gaining a reputation for parading around with his pants down and his penis tucked between his legs. Stiv and Miriam knew each other from the old neighbourhood, and shortly before the Cramps' debut at CBGB, he wrote to her of his desire to run his 'hot throbbing tongue up your curvaceous thighs' and enthused about the prospect of the Dead Boys' forthcoming gig with the Cramps. The Dead Boys' lewd, snotty demeanour either initiated or conformed to any number of punk stereotypes, which gave them a kind of novelty transgressive appeal. Despite this, their initial set of songs contained more hooks than a fisherman's hamper and by November 1976 there was a considerable buzz around the band, who were also beginning to attract interest from major record labels – including Sire, home to the Ramones, with whom they would soon sign a deal. Hilly Kristal was particularly keen on the Dead Boys and they quickly became regulars at CBGB, where Stiv's notoriety was enhanced by rumours about him coming in the venue's uniquely awful chilli.

While Hilly was less enamoured of the Cramps, it was the Dead Boys who opened CBGB's doors for the new group. "That's why we feel so grateful and so fortunate with the scene that was there at the time," explained Ivy. "Monday night was audition night at CBGB, but not everybody could get on. We did straight away because we'd made friends with the Dead Boys, who were really hot at the time. So the Dead Boys headlined this audition night, and we played our first show to a packed house. New York was just a magnetic Mecca for people and there was just this swell of energy. We were hanging out at CBGB and Max's every night of the week, and so was everybody else." On November 1, 1976, with the intimate venue unusually busy for a Monday night, the Cramps took the stage for the first time having taken some well-intentioned, but ultimately naive, preparatory steps. "We didn't want to break strings so we

63

Journey To The Centre Of The Cramps

put brand new ones on our guitars right before we stepped onstage," Ivy recalled. "We were too naïve to know they would go out of tune instantly! So they were totally out of tune and we thought, we can't stop now, we're out there so we'd better keep playing. We got encores, so I think everybody just couldn't believe we had the guts to stay up there. And some people thought we were doing some *avant garde* atonal thing."

Although Hilly later told the group that they "sounded like a total joke", the Cramps' relatively short de-tuned set made an impression, as songs such as 'Sunglasses After Dark', 'I Was A Teenage Werewolf' and 'TV Set' received their first public airings. "Back then I really don't think we thought, 'How long are we going to do this?' The first time we played CBGB, the first time we auditioned, I think we were thinking that we'd go out and nobody would like us that much and we'd only play once," recounted Lux. "Before stepping onstage we would have been happy to just play that one gig and say, 'Woo, we did it.' But upon stepping off that stage . . ."

Having successfully negotiated the hurdle of their debut live performance, the first stage of Lux and Ivy's rock'n'roll mission was complete. In little over a year, the couple had relocated to New York, found work, and assembled their group and a set of material. "I think we thought we were successful after that first gig at CBGB – that was a success for us," observed Ivy. The Cramps were now a going concern that referenced Lux and Ivy's influences in the way that they had planned. "One of the things about rock'n'roll that makes it great, is that it's the person – y'know, it's the singer not the song; it's that person," Lux explained. "If somebody's a true original, like Elvis or Jerry Lee, they're always going to be great because nobody's going to turn them into some kind of a goofy thing. It's part of their rockabilly philosophy. They believed they were kings, and they became kings, that's that."

Anyone fortunate enough to catch that epoch-making first show could scarcely deny that the Cramps were also true originals. It was a show that would be followed by well over a thousand more. The Cramps were now also on the road to becoming kings of their own highly individual realm.

Ivy, Miriam, Bryan and Lux squeeze into CBGBs tiny, graffiti-encrusted toilet, 1977.
STEPHANIE CHERNIKOWSKI/MICHAEL OCHS ARCHIVES/GETTY IMAGES.

Portrait Of A Young Fiend: Lux plays it straight for a Stow High School Yearbook mugshot, c1963.

"We took a lot of acid together", Lux and Ivy surf the tail end of the hippie wave, Sacremento, 1972.

Pam, Bryan, Lux and Ivy rehearsing in the Music Maze basement, 1976. QUITA BODLEY

The notorious Napa State Hospital concert, June 16, 1978. RUBY RAY

Ivy: "All there was was CBGBs and Max's – In the world." The Cramps at Max's Kansas City, May 1977. BOB GRUEN/WWW.BOBGRUEN.COM

On the edge – Ivy, Lux, Bryan and Nick at Peter Ball's 1978 Independence Day Party, Bratenhal, Cleveland.

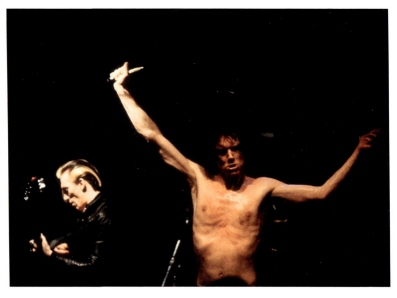

Ivy: "We've been pretty lucky that way as far as Lux hasn't gone to jail for getting naked". Letting it all hang out, 1978. DALLE/PHOTOSHOT

Handbill for the Cramps gig at Memphis State University, Nick Knox's live debut.

Ivy: "Bryan's creative forte was more visual than sonic." Gregory lords it in Santa Monica, 1979. DONNA SANTISI

(Post) Teenage Werewolf: Lux lets rip at Santa Monica, 1979. DONNA SANTISI

The Cramps bring the sickness to England, Kings College, London, 1979. DAVID CORIO

"We're karmically entwined" – The *folie à deux* at the black, pulsing heart of the Cramps, London, 1980. PAUL SLATTERY

The Cramps strike a pose for the press, backstage at the Electric Ballroom, London, 1980. PAUL SLATTERY/RETNA PICTURES

Julien Hechtlinger (aka Julien Grindsnatch) temporarily steps into Bryan Gregory's python skin shoes, August 1980. EDDIE MALLUK

"He's just got this urge to hit" – Nick Knox lays down the primal rhythms, Santa Monica, 1980.
EDDIE MALLUK

The strangeness in them – "We have always been flamboyant dressers and stuff…"
MICHAEL LAVINE

CHAPTER FOUR

No Club Lone Wolf

Let's wipe out Jethro Tull.
Lux Interior

This is it – dig it or walk.
Poison Ivy

ALTHOUGH CBGB would play its part in raising the Cramps' profile, owner Hilly Kristal's initial ambivalence toward the group had scarcely been dented by their debut show at his bar, "So you wanna gig at CBGB," he teased. "Well, I ain't gonna give you a gig at CBGB." Instead, the quartet would get the opportunity to develop their live chops at Max's Kansas City. Situated about a mile north of Hilly's bar, Max's was CBGB's older counterpart in New York's underground binary system. The venue was originally opened by Mickey Ruskin in December 1965 and quickly became a hip hangout, largely thanks to the patronage of the city's literary and artistic elite, with the likes of William Burroughs, Roy Lichtenstein, Allen Ginsberg and Robert Rauschenberg regularly showing up at the club. Most significantly, Max's back room became the sanctum of choice for Andy Warhol and his coterie of 'superstars', friends, and hangers-on.

Warhol's association with the Velvet Underground led to the band performing regularly there and by the early seventies the bar had become the glittering epicentre of New York's small glam scene. While the likes of Reed, Bowie and Pop held court, Deborah Harry was one of the steady

Journey To The Centre Of The Cramps

stream of young hopefuls drawn by Max's hip allure and the necessity to earn cash by taking work there. "The first incarnation of Max's was heavy duty. That's not a phrase I like to use, but it clearly defines what was going on," recalled the future Blondie siren. "All Hollywood came. The photographers, sculptors and artists were all at the bar, in the front, while the back room was full of the Andy Warhol crowd, the late night people and musicians. Who did I serve? You name 'em. Who's the actor who was *Our Man Flint*? James Coburn! He was so gorgeous. Stevie Winwood, Jefferson Airplane, Jimi Hendrix. Then there was Andy with all of his nutty superstars . . . Max's was a perfect place to work. You were a fly on the wall. You could be as visible, or as invisible, as you wanted to be. I could meet people and talk to them – or not. I was just the waitress."

For Debbie, and others such as fashion designer Carlos Falchi, who worked at Max's as a busboy, waiting on tables and hustling for attention or tips provided them with early exposure to the bitchiness and perversity that tends to be a feature of creative elites. "I used to cry a lot then generally. It wasn't just them, they just triggered it off. They were very frustrating people to wait on," she explained. "I met all the stars and served them their steaks. Most of them were so stoned they couldn't eat and still gave me five dollar tips. I'd wrap up the steaks and take them home." As the glam era faded, so did Max's cachet and toward the end of 1974 financial difficulties led to Mickey Ruskin closing the club.

While Ruskin went on to open a string of less successful bars and clubs, Max's Kansas City was re-opened the following year by Tommy and Laura Dean, who initially planned to catch the rising disco tide, but subsequently hired disc jockey and club manager Peter Crowley to book live acts for the re-booted nightspot. Crowley had arrived in New York in 1959 following a season working at the Cole Bros. Travelling Circus. After taking a series of corporate jobs, he discovered the folk rock scene that was developing amid New York's coffee houses and set about carving out a career in the entertainment business. By 1975, Peter had spent more than a decade immersed in the city's subculture and this, allied with some well-developed, adventurous instincts, led him to book a succession of New York's brightest new bands that included Blondie, the Ramones, the

No Club Lone Wolf

Talking Heads and Television. "I booked the bands I found worthy," he explained. Crowley's definition of worthiness was more often than not accurate, and Max's quickly became re-established as a hip hangout, vying with CBGB as the main place to see New York's young punks. "Nearly every band on the scene played both venues – and any other dive that would have them," he recalled. "Some people tried to create animosity between the two clubs, but Hilly and I refused to cooperate with them. We got along fine."

Although it was now under new ownership, Max's continued to play host to the kind of hard-to-please crowd that necessitated the booking of robust, road-hardened groups such as Suicide, and Johnny Thunders' and Jerry Nolan's post New York Dolls group, the Heartbreakers. A recording of an early Cramps show at Max's from January 1977 is partly notable for the barrage of wiseass heckles that included such barbs as 'This place is *The Gong Show*' and 'That drummer is dynamite – if only she knew how to play' alongside entreaties for the group to 'get a job' and 'take a break'. Having caught the Cramps' exciting-but-shambolic live debut, Crowley figured that the group would have the stones to cope with being thrown in at the deep end as a support act at Max's. "A lot of people saw us, as chaotic as we were, including Peter Crowley who booked Max's Kansas City. He loved us and immediately booked us. Hilly Kristal thought we sucked, which we probably did, but Peter loved us," recalled Ivy. "He said, 'I want to book you every Saturday night from now on,'" added Lux.

The Cramps' first Saturday night at Max's came on November 21, where they supported Suicide alongside openers Fuse. Having played Max's during its earlier incarnation, Suicide's Alan Vega and Marty Rev were more than used to giving significantly better than they got in respect of tough crowds. "Marty was great at what he did, but Alan – if someone got up to go to the bathroom, he'd leap up and take the mic stand and block their path with it. He'd do stuff like that all the time, intimidating the audience. It could get quite scary sometimes," remembered Lux. In addition to their street-hardened, confrontational aspects, Suicide's ethereal keyboards and otherworldly artificial rhythms keyed directly into Ivy's penchant for the exotic and unusual. "It might be a 15-minute set or a

Journey To The Centre Of The Cramps

45-minute set, he'd wear a huge silver wig and a leather jacket. Marty's loops remind me of ice cream trucks that I used to hear when I was a kid," she recalls. "You'd hear [Beethoven's] *Für Elise* from far away, which is the theme for so many of the Universal horror movies from the thirties and forties."

Crowley saw the Cramps and Suicide as two differing facets of outsider rock'n'roll, "It was the perfect matchup," he asserted. "You have the hillbilly version and the New York City, Times Square version." Suicide's Marty Rev also felt a connection: "The Cramps were kind of simpatico with us, but we spoke little the first night." The two groups also shared doo-wop as a common influence, with Marty having fallen in love with its harmonies while growing up in the Bronx. This influence was evident in tracks such as the crystalline 'Cherie' and the haunting 'Keep Your Dreams', which contrasted starkly with the duo's habit of playing at club-clearing volume. Despite this, Suicide were held in sufficient regard by Crowley and Tommy Dean to merit inclusion on that year's inaugural *Max's Kansas City* compilation album, where they submitted an insidiously effective version of 'Rocket USA' to a set that also featured tracks from Wayne County & the Backstreet Boys, former Rocket From The Tombs mainman David Thomas' experimental Pere Ubu and former *Pork* actress and Bowie publicist, Cherry Vanilla.

Opening for Suicide helped establish the Cramps as a regular support band at Max's, where they subsequently provided backup for the likes of Blondie and Mink DeVille as well as lesser known groups including the Kieran Liscoe Rhythm Band. "At this time we were always the opening band and the people that showed up were coming to see someone else," Ivy explained. "They had no idea what they were in for. Fights broke out between our few fans and our detractors. Our early shows were like the confrontational Dada 'events' of 60 years earlier. The audience was a big part of it – we always evoked a hostile reaction." Wayne (now Jayne) County was Max's resident DJ during this period and recalls these gigs with great affection: "I was totally impressed, being born in the Deep South; I was raised around that twangy guitar sound. My neighbours could play the guitar just like that. Like Duane Eddy, Chet Atkins and the

No Club Lone Wolf

Ventures. It was used in a lot of the very primitive country music of that time. Some of the Pentecostal Churches used bands and had that twang sound, as well as the screaming and moaning in ecstasy over the Blood of Jesus. So when I heard the Cramps I smiled and then laughed out loud, in pleasure! It was like being back in Georgia in the fifties."

As punk rock's breakthrough year kicked off in the UK with the Sex Pistols' dismissal by EMI and the official gala opening of the Roxy club in Covent Garden, the Cramps saw in 1977 with a run of eight gigs at Max's. In addition to their earliest tracks such as 'TV Set' and 'Sunglasses After Dark', their set had expanded to include several new songs. The recording of their show supporting Mink DeVille and Suicide on January 14 features a slightly tentative rendition of 'Don't Eat Stuff Off The Sidewalk'. Although it is structurally close to the version that would be released on 1981's *Psychedelic Jungle* album, the track began life with a thinner sound, driven on by Ivy's Link Wray flourishes and Miriam's perpetually pounding tom-toms. While Lux's vocal has yet to assume its full authoritative resonance, Bryan's use of distortion to create drones and squealing sonic undercurrents is particularly effective. Although the version of 'Jungle Hop' contains a few bum notes and peters out rather than ending, and Miriam's technical limitations are particularly noticeable during the guitar/drum interplay on 'I'm Cramped', much of the nine-song set bears close resemblance to their subsequent recorded versions.

The key to this was that Ivy's playing had very quickly reached impressive levels of accuracy and confidence – her picking is note perfect and the way in which she alternates between single notes and chords during 'Sunglasses' is particularly sure-footed. Although Ivy would somewhat belatedly become recognised as an outstanding guitarist and sonic pioneer, her talent is not only glaringly evident even at this early stage, but also served to provide the solid core that held the group's sound together. Whereas Miriam's drumming was little more than beat keeping, she occasionally lost her grip on the tempo (as is evident on the recording of 'TV Set' from this gig), Ivy remained resolutely on course, only becoming uncertain during a messy guitar break during the Cramps' new cover of the Sonics' 1965 garage classic, 'Strychnine'. Additionally, her guitar interplay

Journey To The Centre Of The Cramps

with Bryan was developing effectively, particularly across 'Sunglasses After Dark' and during 'Domino's instrumental break, where the trio of musicians mesh together spectacularly. 'I Was A Teenage Werewolf' had also developed from its earlier demo incarnation, as the group become increasingly assured in their use of space and Bryan's one-note buzz provides a neon-tube counterpoint to Ivy's precise lead.

Similarly, Lux was growing in confidence and effectiveness, reaching an unhinged peak during 'Love Me' and demonstrating that he could handle the heckles from Max's more vituperative regulars. So far as the Cramps' towering frontman was concerned, he was following his true calling. "I don't want to do anything but be a singer in a rock'n'roll band," he declared. "All I did before this group was collect records and listen to records and make tapes of records to play in my car. It wasn't that I couldn't do anything else. At one time I did paintings: I won't say I was an artist because I hate the word, but I painted and stuff, and a lot of people thought I was real good. I've always had the feeling that I could do whatever I wanted to do. It's just that I never wanted to do anything like I want to do this."

The support slots at Max's snagged the Cramps a small number of early fans, while a write-up of their CBGB debut in the *Village Voice* and the group's own fly-posting activities helped further spread the good word. "We got a following just from that. We put these flyers up all over town and that's where the 'psychobilly' tag came from – we thought it up just to get people interested in us," explained Ivy. While the phrase 'psychobilly' would subsequently come back to haunt the Cramps, the dozen or so shows they played at Max's during the winter of 1976 and 1977 were of critical importance to the group's development. Right from the outset, the group demonstrated assured belief in the material that they were playing. This in turn stemmed from Lux and Ivy's unwavering commitment to the band and their mission, and was increasingly evident with each passing gig at the Park Avenue club.

"It was how much we meant it," confirmed Lux. "We're more interested in our personalities and our energies coming out onstage than how well we play. How much we can drive the kids nuts and how much they

No Club Lone Wolf

can drive us nuts – that's what's important." While Ivy conceded that "at first it was so rough that it was hard to really dance to it", this can be viewed as being indicative of a degree of perfectionism on the guitarist's part – for a band that had played just a handful of gigs, they already stood out thanks to a strong set of material that was already coming close to its fully realised form and a developing visual image built around Lux's imposing presence, Ivy's smouldering sexuality and Bryan's all-round strangeness. "Bryan was capable of creating the most insane snarls and shrieks out of that crazy deal," recalled Miriam "He also had a gift for moving his cigarette around his mouth with his lips and shooting it out at some poor kid in the audience. It was bizarre and terrifying but you couldn't help but be riveted. He seemed to be constructed entirely of sinew, not an ounce of excess on his frame. That tough look from all concerned was real. Believe me, at the time, it wasn't all nice audiences and fun-loving appreciative types who 'got it'. There was a lot of crap to deal with." Despite this intermittent hostility, the band had already validated Peter Crowley's faith in them. "Of the bands who made it, only the Cramps acknowledged my contribution to their success," he later observed.

By March, Hilly Kristal had sufficiently overcome his misgivings about the Cramps to allow them back through CBGB's battered doors for a second shot at supporting the Dead Boys. This led to the band being approached by New York filmmaker Amos Poe, who had previously made *The Blank Generation*, a hand-shot documentary of the local music scene that featured the Ramones, the Patti Smith Group, Blondie and a host of others. Poe had also directed *Unmade Beds*, an adaptation of Jean Luc Godard's *Breathless* that featured Deborah Harry and Tuff Darts' vocalist Robert Gordon among its cast of little-known actors. For his latest film, *The Foreigner* – a *nouvelle vague* espionage drama that got an art-house release in 1978 – Poe again featured Debbie Harry, while also offering Ivy, Lux, Bryan and Miriam the opportunity to make their acting debuts. "The band got something of a rep for being hardasses," recalled Miriam. "Which was why Amos Poe cast the Cramps as thugs in his film."

The partially improvised scenes featuring the Cramps were filmed at CBGB and depict Bryan and Miriam beating up drunken punk Max

Journey To The Centre Of The Cramps

Menace (played by actor and director Eric Mitchell) while local group the Erasers thrashed away in the largely empty club. A second scene has the entire group, led by a flicknife-wielding Lux, battering the same unfortunate victim to the floor of CBGB's graffiti-daubed toilets, before carving him up a little. "Now that's method acting," Miriam declared. "I remember the first hint of theatrical get-ups for the group. Photographer/dancer Anya Phillips wanted to take some studio snaps of the Cramps. She set up lights and umbrellas and then ran off, returning with some sort of rubber shirt with bones on it, dangling from a wire hanger. 'Put this on,' she said to me. 'Uh, no,' I said. She tried to encourage me to squeeze into the goofy get-up, but nothing in the world could get me to cooperate."

After an end-of-the-week two-nighter supporting Suicide at Max's, the Cramps got a major break when they were hired to support the Ramones at CBGB for the first time on April 1, 1977. "They gave us our start really," Ivy recalled. "Before we played with them we weren't known much at all, we even had difficulty getting booked into CBGB. Then the Ramones came to our shows – all the bands would go and see each others' shows. They invited us to open for them and their fans liked us, and they'd said that it was like throwing Christians to the lions if you opened for the Ramones. It was great – that was the biggest break we've had in our entire lives, because then we could play and get booked on our own and things started from there."

At this time, the Ramones had released two albums on Sire records and were very much at the top of the CBGB totem pole. Although Blondie and Talking Heads would later eclipse them commercially, the way in which they had kick-started the punk rock scenes on both sides of the Atlantic ensured that they would be by far the most culturally significant act to emerge from New York's underground during this period. "I think the Ramones are the only punks in New York. I think they define what punk is supposed to be in the seventies. I don't think anyone else can live up to it. They don't consider themselves a punk band, but they consider themselves punks," observed Miriam. "My admiration for them would never fade. The one drum lesson I ever got was from Tommy Ramone, who showed me how to hold the sticks."

No Club Lone Wolf

These shows initiated a relationship between the two bands that would continue for over a quarter of a century, with Joey and Johnny Ramone becoming close friends with Lux and Ivy. Impressed with the Cramps' version of 'Surfin' Bird', da brudders asked if they could take their own crack at the song and returned the favour with assistance and advice. Having established their reputation with simple, stripped down material delivered at escape velocity and garnished with Socratic irony, the Ramones' best friend and longtime artistic director Arturo Vega felt that the Cramps had a little too much going on. "He said, 'You guys are never going to make it because you're too good. You have to be lousy to make it.' I think that's just about it – there's too much substance to the Cramps. There's too much to be frightened of,'" recalled Lux. "He said that there were too many facets and that would just confuse people. If there was just one simple thing then they'd go, 'Okay, I know what that is' and you can name it, categorise it and put a package around it, but you couldn't do that with us."

The Ramones also installed the Cramps as their openers for a pair of gigs at My Father's Place in Roslyn – the first time that the Cramps had ever played off Manhattan Island. Opened in 1971 by Michael 'Eppy' Epstein, the club was Long Island's equivalent of Max's, hosting the likes of Bruce Springsteen, Bob Marley, Ian Hunter and Billy Joel. "That was the hot place," Joel recalled. "When acts were just heating up, outside of Manhattan, where would they all go? My Father's Place." This provided the Cramps with exposure to the Ramones' out of town crowd and they also doubled up on both nights with their first headlining shows at CBGB where they were supported by the quirky, geekish Come On and arty no-wavers the Contortions. A third CBGB gig the following night saw the Cramps backed by confrontational street punks, the Steel Tips. A further concert five days later supporting the Ramones resulted in the Cramps receiving some mixed early reviews.

Whereas *Creem* correspondent Wayne Robbins paid the group a back-handed compliment by writing that they presented 'the kind of music my cockroaches play at 4 a.m., when they hold jam sessions banging pots and pans in my apartment', a *New York Rocker* review of the same gig reported

Journey To The Centre Of The Cramps

that Ramones fans were 'bitching around the bar about how they couldn't play', while a later write-up inexplicably criticised the band for being 'sterile' and 'calculating'. In addition to being unrepresentative of the way in which many Ramones fans subsequently came to dig the Cramps, this kind of sniffy assertion was indicative of the manner in which certain sections of the local media were dismissive of, or even hostile to, the band. "Everything in New York is very cliquey," explained Lux. "If you want to join that clique they'll do anything for you, but then you're part of that thing. There are several cliques – the Max's Kansas City clique, the *New York Rocker* clique, all these little 'clubs'. I never had any friends all my life. I don't know why I should have friends now just because I'm in a rock'n'roll band." From Ivy's viewpoint, the *New York Rocker* barb was simply representative of the way that the paper operated at the time: "It was that kind of power position, with people in England reading it like it is some kind of bible of New York rock'n'roll, but it is someone writing about their boyfriend's band as if it is the best band. Like their list of top unrecorded bands, the first two had members of *New York Rocker* in them."

Even within a scene that represented itself as being removed from the mainstream, it often seemed as if the Cramps were cast as perennial outsiders. While the New York punk circuit was notoriously bitchy – and continues to be so today, with regular disputes opening up across social media networks involving ageing participants looking to settle old scores – this kind of cliquey cattiness is emblematic of many such scenes. It is essentially part of a dynamic whereby those peripheral to the action seek to impose their own notional hierarchies as a means of positioning themselves closer to the centre of events. In the main, this tends to stem from journalists, fanzine compilers and assorted hangers-on, rather than the bands themselves. For the Cramps, this initially took the form of them being consistently ignored. "When we first started playing New York, the Dead Boys and the Ramones would have us open for them and right away we got a huge following and started headlining. We'd play CBGB and Max's once a month at weekends and draw huge crowds, but the press would never mention us," Lux recounted. "We were never mentioned in

No Club Lone Wolf

Punk magazine. We played a benefit for them and even after the benefit they never mentioned us. I don't think they knew what to make of us, because we weren't exactly punk – we didn't have the safety pins."

Although very few of the bands that initially appeared at CBGB and Max's during punk rock's initial flowering actually bore much resemblance to the subsequent media-led interpretation of the genre, Arturo Vega's observations about the Cramps' complex palette of assimilated influences proved to be prescient – the band were referencing ideas and material so removed from the experience of many of those orbiting that particular milieu that they had difficulty understanding exactly what they were confronted with. "We were misunderstood; some people thought we were trying to be arty or something," Ivy explains. "One thing that really bugged me in the early days was that a lot of people thought we were just making fun of something, a parody of something," added Lux. "They thought we weren't serious about what we were doing. I think that was a misunderstanding, or just a lack of knowledge of what rockabilly was all about. Not that what we're doing has all that much to do with rockabilly, but it does have something to do with it and I think those rockabilly tendencies caused us a few misinterpretations. It isn't camp at all."

Part of this lack of comprehension stemmed from the fact that the Cramps weren't trying to *be* anything other than the people they'd been all their lives. "We never felt like we were part of that scene either, even though we played there, sold out shows once a month," said Lux. "I think they looked at us like we were a bunch of hicks – and they're right, we weren't a bunch of art students like most of them." Like the Ramones, the Cramps as an entity coalesced naturally, without any conceptual contrivances. "We've loved rock'n'roll all our lives, and this band is the end of it. We're not using the band to get into galleries or become mime dancers or anything. We want to be a rock'n'roll band, and I'll do it till past when I'm dead," asserted Lux. "It's funny cos the Damned, the Ramones, us – all that whole scene was like art students and stuff, all three of us were kind of like considered not art students or something, I dunno what it was."

As 1977 wore on, the nature of the bands playing at CBGB in particular began to change, drifting toward the subsequent 'No Wave' movement,

Journey To The Centre Of The Cramps

which spliced elements of *avant garde* music, jazz and experimentalism to a punk rock attitude and approach. Centred around groups including Teenage Jesus & the Jerks, Mars, and the Contortions, No Wave was conceptually rich, a product of the aesthetic sensibilities of a fashionable elite that tended to move on to the next fad as soon as others latched onto their scene. Although it had energy and immediacy in common with primal rock'n'roll, No Wave's innate nihilism served to make it the antithesis of much of what the Cramps were all about. "There was a lot of talk about minimalism and these art school words were going around about composition, and everybody was describing the music compositionally and all that crap," Lux recalled. "We're minimalistic because we love the punk rock records of the sixties and the rockabilly records of the fifties. We love great, simple rock'n'roll that you dance to. That's where our concept, if you will, comes from. Whereas a lot of bands don't have that awareness of the fifties and sixties and they base their minimal concept on nothing but nothingness. It doesn't work. It's very hard to take very few elements and make something intense out of it. It's much harder than making a musical statement with lots of instruments and arrangements – anyone can do that." Customarily, the profoundly hip tend to be more concerned with looking cool than letting it all hang out, an attitude that flew in the face of the Cramps' determination to put on a show and have a good time. "Some of these audiences in America, they just sit there like they're at the opera watching a piece of art," Lux opined. "A lot of the bands in New York, these art bands are contributing to the problem. I have nothing to do with these bands that call themselves 'new wave' when all they are is a bunch of snotty-nosed little art students that don't know or care anything about rock'n'roll."

Additionally, the Cramps were also criticised on account of a perceived lack of technical prowess, which – given the prevailing do-it-yourself ethos of the era – seemed reactionary. Although Miriam's drumming was rudimentary, there was no question about Ivy's mastery of her chosen instrument, and anyone looking for the *avant garde* could find it within Bryan's experimental approach to playing. "I hate all the people on the New York rock scene who are treating us like shit. They know who they

No Club Lone Wolf

are," declared Lux. "Some people in New York hate us because they feel that we haven't paid our dues, but we've paid a hell of a lot of dues. We haven't played guitars before, but we've paid a lot of dues. I think they hate us because of our intensity. There is about 10% that hate us and 90% that love us. So many people say that we are bad musicians and that is not true." In a wider respect, this early exposure to the hyper-critical nature of some sections of the media served to instil a them-against-us mentality within the Cramps, who would subsequently view some journalists with a degree of suspicion from this point on. "I do find that in the press somebody will say one thing and all of a sudden I'll see 10 reviews of us someplace else that will use the same phrases. It's like they read other reviews rather than actually trying to find things out," Lux retorted.

Despite their beefs with sections of the local media and a few mendacious hipsters, the Cramps' participation in the CBGB scene proved to be a largely positive experience. "It was a real lifestyle," recalled Lux. "No newspapers wanted to know anything about it, it was a completely secret thing for a long time, before the Sex Pistols hit – that was when the news really started paying attention that something weird was happening. But before that it was just a completely secret thing that nobody knew about except the bands. The same bands would go see the bands that were playing – a band that was playing on Wednesday night, the next night would then go and see the band that came to watch them the night before. It was really fun. Back in those days New York was kind of a scarier, more dangerous place than it is now, it's a real swell kind of place and all yuppified and that sort of thing. It was great fun and I'm real thrilled that that's where we started." The band particularly enjoyed hanging out and playing with the Ramones, Blondie and the Talking Heads, and it seemed that even CBGB's previously unimpressed owner was warming to them. "At one point, Hilly Kristal was messing with the idea of having local bands cover Rolling Stones songs and everybody was making dibs on tunes," recounted Miriam. "I remember blowing through 'Off The Hook' a few times, anticipating recording it, but the whole project fell through. Around the same time, we were messing with the Troggs' 'Night Of The Long Grass'."

Journey To The Centre Of The Cramps

While the Ramones were working toward their third album on Sire records, label boss Seymour Stein had also signed Talking Heads, the Patti Smith Group were on RCA subsidiary Arista, Television had a deal with Elektra, and even Blondie – who had unfairly been considered the runts of the CBGB litter – had records out on the small Private Stock label and were being courted by the Warners' distributed Chrysalis imprint. Such industry frenzy demonstrated the manner in which Hilly's Bowery bar had achieved a reputation on both sides of the Atlantic, and although CBGB and Max's were becoming a one-stop shop for A&R men and label executives, they seemed uncertain of precisely what to make of the Cramps. "I kind of like it that we were the one band where they couldn't see anything worthwhile," Ivy observed. "Because with Talking Heads, Ramones, Television, Patti Smith – who were all very different from each other – all these labels could see something that they could use, but with us it was just, 'There's nothing there,' they couldn't see anything useful in what we did. They would all say that, 'We just don't see anywhere where this could fit in.'"

To a degree, this hesitancy on the part of record label personnel derived from the gulf between the manner in which the Cramps evoked the unconstrained spirit of early rock'n'roll and the more tangential way that punk rock had assimilated it. Whereas the Ramones evoked the leather-jacketed menace of Gene Vincent and played with the kind of uninhibited abandon that could be found on a Little Richard record, the Cramps actually sounded like a supercharged adaptation of these influences. The Cramps referenced the fifties in a far more direct way than any other band around at the time, but were not a nostalgia act in the style of Sha Na Na or Darts. Throughout the seventies there had been a seemingly endless succession of attempts to repackage the fifties and market it for contemporary consumption. Like many exercises in packaging, this resulted in a sanitised product – films such as *American Graffiti* or *Grease* and television shows including *Happy Days* presenting saccharine, finger-poppin', soda-jerking re-enactments as all manner of revivalist groups served up some truly anaemic rock'n'roll. For any A&R man looking to plug into the punk power surge, any direct references to the fifties would have been

No Club Lone Wolf

tainted by these contemporary representations and viewed as deeply unhip. Few of them knew who Link Wray was and fewer had a clue about Charlie Feathers. This being so, they either dismissed the Cramps out of hand or did not know what to make of them. "We had a really strong idea of exactly what we wanted to do before we started and the way it came out probably sounded so weird to record companies that none of them wanted anything to do with us," Lux explained. "They couldn't have a clue how you could make that sound like something good, so I think it was lucky in a way that we weren't even approached by record companies. I think even if we were, we would have told them, 'Get lost – we can't do anything but what we do.'"

The clarity of Lux's and Ivy's vision was such that any artistic interference on any level, from any outside agency, was completely out of the question. Although they'd yet to have any outside experience of the way in which record labels sought to remould their investments for the marketplace, the Cramps had seen this in operation often enough to realise that they wanted no part of it. "What amazed us at the time, was that a lot of bands who got signed by the labels – Blondie, and Talking Heads, and Television – what the public ended up hearing was nothing like what any of those bands were like live," recounts Ivy. "They were all rock'n'roll bands and they all had this punky, edgy, tough kind of quality to them and it might be hard to imagine, but they all seemed to have something in common. By the time they had their record deal and went in the studio with their producer and it came out to the public, and that's their first record, it was nothing like what we would see, because we would go and see Blondie and Talking Heads and it all went together to us – it was all rock'n'roll. So that changed, it wasn't just that bands aren't around now, but just immediately, as soon as the labels got them, the whole machinery kicked in."

The fact that the image that the Cramps presented onstage was little more than an amped-up version of the people they actually were led several label executives to conclude that little could be done to market them as – regardless of their resistance – there was no changing them. Occasionally, they missed the point quite spectacularly. "I remember one

Journey To The Centre Of The Cramps

record company that said, 'Well, they play really good music and everything, but they have no overt sexuality in the band, so we couldn't think of what to do with them,'" marvelled Lux.

After returning to Max's for a headline show supported by Lollipop on April 24, the Cramps' next gig took them to Mickey Ruskin's latest venture, the Lower Manhattan Ocean Club on Chambers Street. Opened in 1976, the restaurant and bar was again aimed at attracting the art crowd, and featured interior decor created by a number of artists, including sculptor Forrest Myers, who were paid in a combination of cash and free food. Musically, the venue emphasised the groovy, showcasing the likes of loft-jazz saxophonist David Murray and underground dance experimentalist Arthur Russell, as well as New York's breaking wave of new groups. Having established Max's reputation via the patronage of upcoming artists, Ruskin saw no need to change a proven formula. "They're the most intelligent humans and the only ones I can deal with," he explained. The club duly attracted a variant of the hip elite that could be found haunting CBGB. "The young women were mostly in Danskins and stovepipe slacks and Capezio jazz shoes, and the guys in second-hand sweaters and worn Levi's and scuffed, canvas Sperrys like the ones the Ramones wore," recalled *New York Times* journalist Gerald Marzorati. "Everybody below Houston Street, it seemed, was making some form of art, or trying to, or looking as if he or she did." By now, the Cramps' regular slots at CBGB and Max's had enabled them to develop a following that ensured that the Ocean Club's cool clientele would find their hangout invaded by a significant number of people who had come specifically to see the group. Additionally, the rise of punk-orientated fanzines in the US helped spread the word on the Cramps, with do-it-yourself publications such as *Slash*, *Fanzeen* and *New Order* among those that featured the band during 1977.

On a national level, the June issue of *Rock Scene* magazine included a photo feature on the Cramps, shot by heavyweight photographer Bob Gruen during the band's mid-May show at Max's where they were supported by local power-poppers the Fast. Gruen's images depict the black-clad quartet in glowering action, accompanied by a strap line stating that 'Rumour has it that we will soon have a record of their intense

No Club Lone Wolf

music.' Most likely, the source of this rumour was none other than *Rock Scene* co-founder Richard Robinson, who had taken the Cramps into Bell Sound Studio on West 54th Street with the notion of capturing some tacks for subsequent release.

In addition to launching *Rock Scene* in 1973, Robinson acted as the magazine's managing editor alongside his wife, Lisa – who had also mentioned the Cramps in her *New York Post* column – Lenny Kaye, associate editor and Patti Smith Group guitarist, and Wayne County, who contributed a problem page. Billed as 'the alternative to the alternative', the magazine was graphics led, featuring spreads from many of the hottest photographers of the day including Gruen, Leee Black Childers and Roberta Bayley as well as contributions from those active on the scene such as Blondie mainstay Chris Stein and Ramones manager Danny Field. Gossipy in tone, the publication would customarily feature several pages of after-show photographs that mixed visiting stars such as the Stones and Bo Diddley with regular updates on what the Ramones, Patti Smith, the Heartbreakers, Kiss and other New York acts had been up to. *Rock Scene* had also included an early shot of the Cramps in its May edition, describing the group as 'recent arrivals on the NY rock scene' and would go on to feature them in a two page 'Cramps Standing In The Shadows' piece the following month. The six posed shots were snapped by Robinson, who had also worked in production – having overseen Lou Reed's 1972 solo debut and the Flamin' Groovies' 1971 album *Teenage Head*. "This was stunning to me," enthused Miriam. "Not in my wildest dreams could I believe that the guy who recorded my favourite band wanted to record us. I honestly felt that I was on *Candid Camera*, that this was all a dream, or a hilarious hoax that was being played on me."

However, Miriam's excitement soon evaporated as the Cramps' debut studio session proved to be an unsuccessful and frustrating experience. "We weren't quite ready," observes Ivy. "The engineer kept making us do multiple takes – we wondered what it was he wanted." The band laid down eight tracks – seven from their established live set and one newer number, 'What's Behind The Mask' – a reworking of Dale Hawkins' rockin' 1957 single that replaced the original amorous lyric with Lux's

Journey To The Centre Of The Cramps

longing to see the face of a mysterious *femme fatale*. The song splices Lux and Ivy's fascination with mystery and horror to the group's churning rockabilly backing in a witty and entertaining manner, continuing the pattern established with songs such as 'TV Set' and 'I Was A Teenage Werewolf'. Ultimately, Robinson's efforts to capture the Cramps for a record release fell short, sounding significantly less like the subsequently issued articles than their earlier demos had. As the session dragged on, disappointment grew with the engineer's insistence on continually re-recording the same track, leading Lux to exclaim, "If you're waiting for us to get good, then it's gonna be a long wait."

The failure of the Bell Sound session represented the Cramps' first genuine setback. In addition to giving Ivy pause to wonder whether the group would ever record anything that would emerge on vinyl, it also served to set her and Lux wondering if the group chemistry was exactly right. While they were pondering this, the band had the consolation of a three-night slot at CBGB supporting the Ramones, whose popularity was now such that they could easily fill far bigger venues, resulting in a trio of sweaty, sold-out shows. The two groups represented an irresistible double-header, channelling their shared garage influences in varying ways and enabling the Cramps to pick up further followers from among the Ramones' growing contingent of fans. The manner in which both groups were a *gestalt* of their collective personalities, playing with enthusiasm, a healthy degree of humour and without any pretension or contrivance, ensured that they were an excellent match. Among those that 'got' the Cramps during this period was Lux's brother, Mike. "It was so Ghoulardi, so Mad Daddy, it was that whole kind of schtick and I knew that was what Rick was all about and Ivy, too," he explained. "The music surprised me because it was so raw, and I was the Beatles fan and he was the Stones fan, he liked the raw stuff. But later I realised what it was all about – it was about the feeling and the emotion just like those early records were. They weren't really doing anything too different than the early rockabilly or blues records; they just put their own twist on it." Although the Cramps were yet to release any of their material, their June 10 set subsequently emerged on the Trademark Of Quality label, one of innumerable live

No Club Lone Wolf

bootlegs that became available during the eighties as their popularity increased.

With the Cramps having demonstrated that they could draw a decent crowd of their own to CBGB, Hilly made a not uncharacteristic leap of logic and decided that they would be ideal for headlining a three-day weekender showcasing a collection of Canadian bands including the Viletones, Diodes and Teenage Head. Toronto combo the Viletones had developed a reputation for extreme performances in their hometown, and a contingent of around 60 Canadians made the trip south to catch their local heroes in action at punk's epicentre. Among those was Linda Lee, a drummer who played with groups such as the Curse and True Confessions under the name of Patsy Poison. Having arrived at the club she took the opportunity to sample the delights of CBGB's charming unisex washroom, where she experienced an encounter with the unearthly. "It felt like you'd walked into a subway that somebody had been violently ill in, and that was used to piss in for the last 20 years," she recalled. "I felt a presence come in and it was Bryan Gregory, who was the guitar player in the Cramps. There's a rumour going around that he actually was so evil that he was decapitated; he was that bad of a human being. He walked in and he was about my height; really, really, really thin, and he had the most incredible pockmarked skin – like jagged looking. He had blond hair and one bit of it was behind his ear and it was long and greasy, and the other strand hung right down across his face. He was incredibly ghastly looking. He just stood there and took out his comb and admired himself for two minutes, and I was just standing there looking at him."

The mixture of Canadians and Cramps diehards served to counteract the growing groups of hipsters who hung around the venue looking cool and demanding to be impressed, and the gigs proved to be raucous affairs, with Viletones' frontman Steven Leckie (also known as 'Nazi Dog') drawing attention from legendary critic Lester Bangs for his on (and off) stage gymnastics. "This guy Natzee Dog hung from the rafters, crawled all over the stage, and hurled himself on the first row until his body was one huge sore," he wrote. "Somebody asked me what I thought and I said, 'Fine with me – in 1972 every band in the world was Grand Funk, now

Journey To The Centre Of The Cramps

every band in the world is the Stooges.' I didn't tell Natzee Dog that, though."

The visiting bands hit it off with the Cramps and personnel from the Viletones, Diodes and Teenage Head joined Lux, Ivy, Bryan and assorted friends for an impromptu house-warming party at Miriam's new pad on 5th Street. She'd moved there from "an abandoned, and certifiably haunted old basement shop with no hot water" on Warren Street in Lower Manhattan that she'd shared with Teenage Jesus mainstays Lydia Lunch and Bradley Field, and that also served as the Cramps' rehearsal space. "The Canadians, especially the band Teenage Head, were nuts about the Groovies and were insanely impressed that we had recorded with grand, exalted poobah Richard Robinson," she recalled.

The early hours celebration was to be Miriam's last hurrah as a Cramp, as she quit the band shortly afterwards. Miriam had different influences and a different circle of friends than Lux and Ivy and did not entirely share their vision for the group and the timeworn cliché of 'musical differences' played a part in the separation. Miriam was also feeling exhausted from the non-stop New York lifestyle that she'd submitted herself to since arriving from Ohio 12 months earlier. "My first year in New York was a necessary hazing, too, a full-time, full-on occupation that just happened to be filled with loud music and sweaty people, day in and day out – at least the earplugs were optional. Not entirely a bad thing, not by any means. And for someone who shot out of the hopper at full-tilt, I had a relatively soft landing, thanks to fellow Groovies fans Trixie A. Balm and Shawn Brighton, who showed up at my door the proverbial morning after with a hell of a pep talk and plans for, what else, a band."

That band proved to be Nervus Rex, where Miriam enjoyed a brief tenure before joining the Zantees, a revivalist combo that included her future husband Billy Miller, with whom she would found the Norton Records label in 1986. In addition to running the label (which specialises in 'wild rock' by the likes of Hasil Adkins, the Flamin' Groovies and Link Wray) Miriam published a number of magazines such as *Kicks*, *Smut Peddler* and *Bad Seed*. She is also an acknowledged expert on pulp fiction and in 2004 co-edited *Sin-A-Rama: Sleaze Sex Paperbacks Of The Sixties*.

No Club Lone Wolf

"I'm also thankful for the days to Lux and Ivy and Bryan. That first year shot me into an overdrive that I've yet to come down from," she observed.

"Some time before the Cramps left New York, Lux and Bryan came to see the Zantees at Hurrah's, and to say goodbye. I was so happy to see them there, and remember standing on the stairs, halfway up, halfway down. It was only Lux and Bryan, and the three of us kind of just stared at each other. I felt real bad. I had that hollow break-up feeling in my throat. It was the last time I would see Bryan, and I know he heard me choke on hard tears when I hugged him goodbye and shook his ring-covered hand."

CHAPTER FIVE

This Is Not Ordinary Music

We were into making posters saying things like 'rockabilly voodoo' – All these weird things that would make people think, 'What's going on?'

Lux Interior

I believe that the Cramps are the new kings and queen of rock'n'roll.

Bryan Gregory

WHILE the Cramps were temporarily out of action in the wake of Miriam Linna's departure, the man who represented the source of much of the band's influences and ethos suddenly died. The death of Elvis Presley on August 16, 1977 from introducing a bumper cocktail of around 10 prescribed drugs into his already sickly system brought notions about the cultural importance of rock'n'roll into sharp focus. Such was Elvis' status that even four decades later, his death remains the most significant of any that have taken place within popular music. While media retrospectives of Elvis' life and reportage of his demise reached saturation point and crowds gathered outside Gracelands to mourn him, the incoming wave of rockers reacted with hostility: though Johnny Rotten observed that "Elvis was dead before he died and his gut was so big it cast a shadow over rock'n'roll in the last few years," *NME* journalist Danny Baker and *Zigzag* editor Kris Needs reminded those who'd cheered DJ Jerry Floyd's announcement of Presley's death during an Adverts gig at the Vortex in London that without the King, they would have little in the way of punk to rock to. "A lot of people look for the negative in everything these days," asserted Lux. "People laughed at Elvis because he got fat or

This Is Not Ordinary Music

something and forgot that he completely changed the world with some weird thing he did, but it was his own original idea and was very powerful, equally as powerful as the Sex Pistols or the Beatles or anybody else."

The varying nature of reactions to Presley's death was not only indicative of the partisan dynamics that had existed within rock'n'roll at least since the first pitched battles between mods and rockers, but also underlined the basis of Cramps' dislocation from the scene that they were operating within. The first wave of punk embraced a form of 'Year Zero' nihilism, ostensibly rejecting rock'n'roll's past, which was at odds with the Cramps' deep regard for earlier sub-cultural forms. Although this served to distance them from anyone taking that aspect of the punk ethos at face value, it was largely superficial – while Johnny Rotten grooved to Peter Hammill, Hawkwind and Can, the Clash disowned the past and decried the USA while simultaneously immersing themselves in America's rock'n'roll legacy. "I don't understand it. I hope that somehow people will forget about this 'No Elvis, Beatles, or Rolling Stones' and get back into the history of rock'n'roll, and get back into the simplicity of it and the stripped down rock'n'roll, nuclear warfare, over-the-topness of what it was when it first started," observed Lux. "He was a freak, he was from outer space, he was a pioneer in his day," Ivy declared. "It's a shame that he's not recognised as that, that he's been trivialised so much. I think it's misplaced frustration to blame him for something like that. I can understand the frustration, but I think they're misdirecting their wrath. I just wish people understood the origins of rock'n'roll more than they do."

From Lux's and Ivy's perspective, glib comments about Elvis' weight, or assertions that he had simply appropriated black culture and had little in the way of anything original to offer were short-sighted and ill-informed. It's unfortunately naive and it's an example of Americans not understanding their own culture. "I've heard that criticism about Elvis Presley in particular, which is really a shame. He didn't rip off anybody. He actually was incredibly original. He synthesised many styles of music in a very innocent way, and no one was doing what he was doing," insisted Ivy. "What he did was phenomenal; no one else had done it. There wasn't

Journey To The Centre Of The Cramps

anyone, black, white or purple, who was doing what he was doing . . . People focused on his health problems or his mortal failings to begin with as a way of putting him down. And now this is just one more new way. I think he was too intense for anyone to realise how significant he was. It'll probably take a hundred years for people to look back and realise."

While the Cramps would subsequently present some of their ideas about Elvis' uniquely intense life within the concepts surrounding the titling of their 1986 *A Date With Elvis* album, at the time of his death the group had to contend with continuing incomprehension regarding their rockabilly influences from audiences that were either ignorant or dismissive of any notion that punk rock was part of a wider, ongoing lineage. This would often compel Lux to make the point that punk itself was scarcely a new phenomenon. "The Shadows of Knight are my favourite punk group. I also like the Sonics a lot. If there is such a thing as punk rock today, then we're it. I wouldn't call us that – anything that is simple rock'n'roll now gets called punk rock. We're punk in the sense that we never played instruments before this," he explained. "I feel that we're a garage band," added Ivy. "We're definitely a rock'n'roll band – that's exactly what we are." So far as Lux and Ivy were concerned, such sub-generic definitions were so subjective as to be useless, and as they all broadly fell within the sprawling realm of rock'n'roll, that was essentially the only terminology that held any genuine value. "I always hated that word 'punk' – William Burroughs said that he always thought that punks were guys who took it up the ass. I always thought that what we were doing was the only good thing and all these other bands on the radio were just pop shit," Lux declared. "If I had my druthers, I just wish that it was called 'rock'n'roll' because that's something that there's very little of around today. Just pure rock'n'roll, that's what we are. Don't nickname it, you might as well claim it."

Being keenly aware of the manner in which rock'n'roll was compartmentalised by the music industry and its associated media as a means of marketing it to target demographics, almost as soon as the group had formed, Lux and Ivy sought to coin amusing and evocative ways in which to describe the Cramps as a means of helping them stand out. This creative

This Is Not Ordinary Music

thinking backfired somewhat as the phase 'psychobilly' was initially perceived as being an actual sub-generic descriptor by journalists and fans, before subsequently taking on a life of its own. "We used to make little posters, they were just Xeroxes with pictures of our band and then we would hand write with a pen various catchphrases to bring people to our shows – things that we thought sounded dramatic and carnival-like," recalls Ivy. "'Psychobilly' was one of them. 'Rockabilly Voodoo' was one of them, but these were like carnival come-ons. Since that time there's been bands, [and] psychobilly kind of became known as a style. Although it's a style, I think that all rockabilly was psychobilly anyway. There's nothing new about combining horror with rockabilly, it was an element that existed from the first rockabilly."

Although the Cramps' conflation of the words 'rockabilly' and 'psycho' originated in an offhand way, the manner in which it came to encompass a group of bands directly influenced by how Lux and Ivy adapted their own influences also serves to highlight that in the late seventies, the Cramps were travelling an entirely singular path. "To us, it was a mixture of garage punk from the sixties and rockabilly and all that, and all the things we do," Lux subsequently explained. "There is a thing called 'psychobilly', which is real fast, 90-mile an hour rockabilly-flavoured punk rock, and I don't think we're that. I think the same thing happened to punk rock. It's become something different from what it was originally, and so what people think of as punk rock now is not the same thing as what I thought of as punk rock for years."

This preoccupation with genres and labels was an aspect of the balkanisation of youth culture during the latter years of the seventies and was particularly prevalent in the UK, where the music press reported on, and at times conceived, a succession of terms to describe the next big thing after punk rock. "There are labels that aren't even accurate labels, but they're good words," Ivy observed. "I like those words and I don't object because it still sounds cool. We're just a rock'n'roll band. If people were more familiar with rock'n'roll these days they'd realise and just call us that." The period's general lack of interest in the wild, unrestrained nature of early rock'n'roll served to undermine understanding of the spirit in

Journey To The Centre Of The Cramps

which Lux and Ivy had conceived the word. "The really good, lesser known and obscure rockabilly from the fifties was very psychotic in its day and really stands up as being psychotic by today's standards – so all good rockabilly was psychobilly originally," confirmed Ivy. "That's one of the prime ingredients of rockabilly, is that it's got to be psychotic to begin with. So that's kind of redundant," added Lux. "We never meant it as a style, different from rockabilly, it was just like a dramatic word," concluded Ivy, who surmised that any issue concerning the term was essentially down to people taking matters rather too literally; "'Rockabilly voodoo' is a phrase that we invented too. All it means is the magic of playing rockabilly. It doesn't mean that we were into voodoo. Voodoo's a religion, we don't practise religion."

Although Lux and Ivy would endure questions about the precise meaning of 'psychobilly' for the next 30 years, the more immediate problem of finding a replacement for Miriam was resolved with the arrival of another Ohioan expatriate. In common with Lux, Ivy and Miriam, Nick Knox had made repeated trips to New York, lured by the promise of a rock scene that offered far greater potential than the one back home. Born Nicholas George Stephanoff, Knox grew up around the small adjoining towns of Parma and Independence, around nine miles south of Cleveland and developed a teenage fascination with rock'n'roll that would lead to him becoming a regular at local gigs. "I had seen him at various rock shows we had gone to, but we didn't know each other until we met in New York," Lux recounted. "The first time we saw him he was wearing purple hot pants in Canton, Ohio, at an amusement park with the greatest rollercoaster you've ever been on and the best New York Dolls concert you've ever seen. The first thing I said to Ivy was, 'Wow! Look at that guy!'" Unlike Pam and Miriam, Nick was not wholly without any previous drumming experience, having briefly been a member of the legendary Cleveland proto-punk group the Electric Eels. That said, there was little within the Eels' manic experimentalism that would have furnished him with anything remotely resembling formal training. The group had been formed by a trio of pupils from the Lakewood High School, whose leftfield sources of influence included the likes of Captain

This Is Not Ordinary Music

Beefheart and progressive jazz artists such as Albert Ayler and Ornette Coleman. Comprising novice dual guitarists John Morton and Brian McMahon and vocalist/clarinettist Dave 'E' McManus, the group struck out in a determinedly unorthodox direction. Taking their cues from *musique concrète* and foreshadowing the industrial concepts later embodied by groups such as Test Department and Einstürzende Neubauten, the Electric Eels regularly utilised sheets of metal struck with hammers to provide their rhythmic base.

After Brian McMahon left the Electric Eels toward the end of 1973, the band took on slightly more orthodox form. His replacement, Paul Marotta, could play keyboards and guitar to a reasonable standard, and the Eels further embraced a form of conventional structure via the recruitment of a drummer named Danny Foland. Despite this, the Eels' debut gig supporting Jamie Lyons (who had previously fronted garage titans the Music Explosion, scoring a Top 10 hit in 1967 with 'Little Bit O'Soul') led to Morton and McManus being arrested on the grounds of being drunk and disorderly. A beating from the local police meant that Morton played the Eels' second gig with his hand in plaster and a slide taped to the cast. This show also ended badly as McManus' use of sheet metal and sledge-hammer to provide additional percussion sat uneasily with the bar's proprietor, who pulled the plug 25 minutes into their set. Such adventurism failed to impress the local bar owners, who by and large gave the band a wide berth, preferring to book soft-rockers and covers groups rather than exposing their clientele to the Eels' unholy din, frontman McManus' confrontational approach to delivering the band's material and John Morton's penchant for indulging in fisticuffs with anyone who cared to take him on.

Having achieved a certain degree of local notoriety, partly due to being arrested during their debut gig, their use of Nazi imagery and satires of the far right, the group's finest hour came in December 1974, when they appeared at Cleveland's Viking Salon headlining over Rocket From The Tombs and the Mirrors. This 'Special Experimentation Night' served to cement the Electric Eels' place among a tiny pre-punk Cleveland underground scene that subsequently spawned groups such as Pere Ubu and the Dead Boys. An attempt to repeat this experimental event a few weeks later

Journey To The Centre Of The Cramps

resulted in the Eels being barred from the Viking Salon after they incorporated a lawnmower into their stage show. Mirrors drummer Michael Weldon later recalled that Dave McManus, "started a power mower during a song and when John was preoccupied fighting with an audience heckler, entertained by singing television commercials and theme songs from programmes like *The Patty Duke Show*. People in the audience were amazed by the show, but the owner locked up the Eels' equipment to pay for damages and banned them from his club." This led to Marotta temporarily leaving the group in frustration with being excluded from the last bar in town that would give them a gig, while McMahon returned. Shortly after, Nick Knox joined the band for the final few months of its existence. Although Nick got to play only one concert with the Eels, his place in the band was preserved for posterity when Rough Trade released a posthumous single featuring two tracks, 'Agitated' and 'Cyclotron', that were recorded at rehearsals during the first half of 1975. Other tracks from these sessions later emerged across four subsequent retrospective album releases.

After the Eels disbanded in the wake of their final, violent concert at Case-Western Reserve University, Nick began making trips to New York with groups of like-minded friends, which on one occasion included Miriam Linna – who dubbed him "Nick, who looks like a Kink". This party also included future Teenage Jesus & the Jerks drummer Bradley Field, who having relocated to New York and shared accommodation with Miriam had also got to know the Cramps. Field recommended Nick to Lux and Ivy. "He told us that Nick would be the perfect drummer for us and convinced him to come to New York to try out for our band," she explained.

"[Nick] came from Cleveland with eight or nine guys," recalled Lux. "They all came around me and Ivy's place one night and he was the only one who talked to Ivy." However, Nick's taciturn nature failed to make him a hit with Bryan Gregory, who took an immediate dislike to his future bandmate. "We went to a coffee shop with him. He ordered and ate two gigantic banana splits, scowled a lot and barely said a word," recounted Ivy. "Bryan instantly hated him." Opting not to risk alienating their sensitive guitarist for the sake of recruiting an untested drummer, Lux and Ivy

This Is Not Ordinary Music

initially decided to look elsewhere for Miriam's successor. "Lux explained to him that we didn't think things would work out," revealed Ivy. However, having made the trip from Cleveland Nick was not about to return home without achieving his objective of trying out for the Cramps. Aware that Lux and Ivy regularly hung out at CBGB, he tracked the couple down at the club. "He walked up to me and demanded an audition," Lux remembered. "I said, 'OK, why not,'" and it's a good thing I did because Nick told me if the answer had been 'No', he would have punched me on the nose, right then and there."

At the audition, Nick's experience with the Electric Eels and natural talent ensured that even Bryan was convinced of his worth. His prodigious strength enabled him to hit the toms with sufficient force that it filled in the band's bottom end, mitigating against their lack of a bassist. "He was the coolest guy back then, a talented drummer who surely had to be severely dumbed down to bash moronically," Miriam later observed. The quintessential strong-but-silent outsider, the customarily black-clad drummer quickly proved to be the perfect match with the rest of the group and subsequently bonded with Bryan to establish a decidedly oddball double friendship. "Nick was such a misfit that he fit in with us perfectly, and it didn't hurt that he had the same crooked smile as one of our heroes, Ray Davies," Lux proclaimed. "He's crazy as a loon, but he's completely loyal to our band and we like that. We like a little craziness. He's from Cleveland – you've got to forgive him for that." Ivy was equally taken with her new drummer. "I think having drums to hit keeps him out of trouble. He's kind of got a short fuse," she observed. "He said that he figured that when he grew up he'd be either a baseball player or a drummer, which I think is kind of funny as even a baseball player hits with a stick. He's just got this urge to hit."

Shortly before their enforced break from gigging, the Cramps had made their debut at the Village Gate, a well-known nightspot that had built a reputation through hosting performances by such luminaries as Miles Davis, John Coltrane, Aretha Franklin and Jimi Hendrix. As its name indicated, the Gate was situated in Greenwich Village on the corner of

Journey To The Centre Of The Cramps

Bleecker and Thompson Streets. Like the nearby CBGB, the club had previously been a flophouse and the Cramps were booked to play alongside CBGB regulars Tuff Darts, another New York band that would subsequently be signed by Sire Records. The group was fronted by Robert Gordon, who had appeared alongside Deborah Harry in Amos Poe's *Unmade Beds* and shared Lux and Ivy's passion for rockabilly. Also on the bill was Alex Chilton, a former teenage sensation with the Box Tops, a soul-infused pop quintet from Memphis that topped the singles chart with their 1967 debut cut 'The Letter', which also made the Top 10 in the UK, Canada and Australia. Chilton, who was 16 when the Box Tops broke globally, recalled, "At the time I was failing the tenth grade and I was going to have to repeat my sophomore year in high school, but I got lucky and had a number one hit that summer. So my mom and dad were like, 'Why don't you go ahead and give this rock thing a try?'"

After a series of smaller hits, the Box Tops disbanded in 1970 and Chilton began working on his own material at Memphis' Ardent Studios and developing his guitar technique before relocating to New York where he remained for several months before returning to his home town where he formed a new group, Big Star, having turned down the opportunity to front rock fusion heavyweights Blood Sweat & Tears on the grounds that they were too commercial. Initially, Chilton had planned on teaming up with another Memphis prodigy, Chris Bell, as a duo, but when Bell seemed less than keen in going down the Simon & Garfunkel route, Big Star was conceived as a quartet that also included bassist Andy Hummel and drummer Jody Stephens, who had been playing with Bell as a trio named Icewater. "Chris' band was already in place when I joined," recalled Alex. "They weren't very big on R&B, or black music, at all. So I just sort of did what the original concept of their band was. I tried to present things that were compatible with the concept of this group that was already in place. When I say 'they', I guess I'm really referring to Chris. I just tried to get with Chris' stylistic approach as well as I could." Modelling their songwriting partnership upon Lennon and McCartney, Chilton and Bell set about composing a set of material that would result in Big Star's optimistically titled debut album, *#1 Record*, which emerged on

This Is Not Ordinary Music

Ardent Studio boss John Fry's own label in 1972. Although the album received widespread critical acclaim, with *Billboard* noting that "every cut could be a single", poor distribution through Stax ensured that it was often hard to find, and *#1 Record* shifted less than 10,000 copies. This served to fuel considerable tension within the band, and after Bell and Hummel had come to blows and trashed one another's instruments, the former quit Big Star and the band briefly disbanded before reuniting to begin work on a second album in 1973.

Again recorded with John Fry at Ardent, the resultant *Radio City* LP served to further enhance Big Star's reputation. *Village Voice* music editor Robert Christgau observed that "The harmonies sound like the lead sheets are upside down and backwards, the guitar solos sound like screwball readymade pastiches, and the lyrics sound like love is strange – can an album be catchy and twisted at the same time?" Released in February 1974, *Radio City* had a rougher sound than its predecessor, which subsequently led it to be cited as a formative power pop milestone. "When Chris Bell was still in the band, he took more interest than anybody in the production and technology end of things. He had a good production mind," explained John Fry. "The reason why the second album is rougher, with fewer harmonies, is due to the absence of Chris' influence in the studio."

Despite his physical absence, Bell made a contribution to two of the album's 12 tracks, funky opener 'O My Soul' and 'Back Of A Car', which subsequently became one of the group's best-loved cuts. Despite this, Chris had agreed to take no writing credit for his input. "When Chris left the band, we made an arbitrary decision – Chris and us – which was that we took those songs, and didn't cut him in on them, and he might have taken some things that we had helped him on, for which he didn't cut us in on either," said Alex. "I know Chris didn't want to be cut in on any of the songs on the second album, as far as credit or money goes."

Like *#1 Record*, *Radio City* was again blighted by poor distribution, Stax once again unable to support the now struggling Ardent label sufficiently to ensure the disc was widely available. Ultimately, *Radio City* would sell around 20,000 copies, ensuring that Big Star would join the list of bands

Journey To The Centre Of The Cramps

like the Velvet Underground and the New York Dolls whose initial record sales were subsequently far outstripped by their enduring influence. Shortly before the album's release, Hummel left the band to concentrate on his college studies and was briefly replaced by John Lightman, before the group once again went their separate ways.

Described in one review as 'the sound of everything falling apart', *Radio City* marked the point at which Alex Chilton embarked on something of a sex, booze and drugs odyssey. "I got into it in 1974. I really started going wild about then," admitted Alex when asked about his drinking. "I was taking a lot of drugs, too. I think that Chris' influence was bad about that. Chris was always doing Valium . . . I can remember a time in '73 or '74 when I had the key to Ardent recordings so I could go in and record things late at night and just do anything I wanted. I can remember one time bringing a girl in there with me who was quite drunk and had a glass of gin and tonic in her hand, and she got really pissed off at me and threw it at me, only I stepped aside and there was the recording console. There was gin and tonic in all the faders."

This access to Ardent's facilities resulted in Chilton and Stephens reuniting in September 1974 to record what would ultimately emerge as Big Star's final album, *Third*. Featuring a large cast of guest musicians that included former Booker T & the MG's guitarist and Otis Redding sideman Steve Cropper, the sessions were produced by Jim Dickinson, who'd played piano and sung lead on the Jesters' 1966 Sun Records classic, 'Cadillac Man', and would later oversee Chilton's 1979 *Like Flies On Sherbert* long player. The material recorded was in the main vastly different from *#1 Record*'s harmonies or the nascent power pop of *Radio City*, an intimate, sprawling mixture of experimental and more conventional material, incorporating string and woodwind instruments and adorned by Chilton's then-girlfriend Lesa Aldridge's haunting vocals. Often starkly realised, the 14 tracks that comprised the original album were indicative of Alex's deteriorating mental state at the time. "I was getting very destructive in a lot of ways then, and I was trying to capture that on recordings," he admitted.

After the sessions had dragged on for several months, Ardent owner Jim

This Is Not Ordinary Music

Fry called a halt to proceedings and a test pressing of the LP was mastered in February 1975. Despite travelling to New York and California in an attempt to get the album issued on a label with decent distribution, neither Fry nor Dickinson could generate much in the way of industry interest. "We'd go in and play it and these guys would look at us like we were crazy," Fry recounted. By this time, Big Star were no longer a functioning entity, and it is questionable whether *Third* (which was ultimately released on the independent PVC records imprint in 1978) represented the work of the group whose name it carried. "Jody and I were hanging together as a unit still but we didn't see it as a Big Star record," asserted Alex. "We never saw it as a Big Star record. That was a marketing decision when the record was sold in whatever year that was sold. And they didn't ask me anything about it and they never have asked me anything about it."

While the album took on a later life of its own, again garnering significant critical praise and being re-issued in several different forms, often containing additional tracks and using the alternate title *Sister Lovers*, this was of little benefit to Chilton who declared himself unhappy with the finished product. "I was just throwing ideas at the wall. The idea was to choose, at the end, what to use. But then, in the end, I was pushed out of the process," he asserted. "Jim Dickinson took over the entire thing, and then he chose. That project was taken out of my hands at the critical moment where all decisions about what to use and what not to use were being made. I mean, I was just writing things, and doing things. The plan was to cooperatively decide what got used, but I got pushed out."

After recording the shambolic *Bach's Bottom* solo album in 1975, Alex subsequently dropped off the cultural radar for about a year. "I was just hangin' and messin' around," he explained, "drinking worse than ever, still taking drugs", before joining the rock'n'roll exodus to New York in 1977. There he formed a loose group named Alex Chilton & the Cossacks, which included Television guitarist Richard Lloyd sitting in for one session, and Chris Stamey, who later became known as part of power pop combo the dB's. The Cossacks began gigging around the city's bars, playing and hanging out at clubs such as CBGB and the Village Gate, where they'd appeared on the same bill as the Cramps on June 15. Having

Journey To The Centre Of The Cramps

caught Lux and Ivy's band live at both venues, Alex sensed that they might be kindred outsiders and introductions were duly made.

"We met him through a photographer, Stephanie Chernowski, who lived in a cool apartment near CBGB," recalled Ivy. "She let us rehearse in the building's basement and Alex hung out at her place. He'd been to our shows and dug us." With Jim Fry's door at Ardent still open to him, Chilton offered the band studio time in Memphis. Having missed out on an entire summer of gigs due to Miriam's departure, Lux and Ivy jumped at the opportunity, "He said, 'I can take you to Memphis', and we were like 'Memphis, wow'," recounts Ivy. "We crammed the whole band, our then manager and Alex into a drive away car and went non-stop to Ardent Studios in Memphis."

With session time arranged by Chilton at Ardent, the band arrived in Memphis in October 1977 where they booked into the Alamo Motel. "The first time when we went down to record there with Alex Chilton, that's where we stopped. It looks nice on the postcard," remembered Lux. "It has an Alamo motif, it looks interesting but it's got that weird indoor/outdoor carpeting and it's permanently damp and mouldy. Really gross," added Ivy. "We resorted to sleeping on floors at friends' houses instead – that was an upgrade." Having had about a fortnight to get up to speed with the Cramps' set, new drummer Nick found he was pitched straight in at the deep end, as in-between laying down tracks at Ardent he made his live debut with the band when they appeared before a large crowd at Memphis State University. "We played at this outdoor amphitheatre somewhere," recounted Lux. "There were all these guys standing around, hitting their fists together, like 'Kill you, faggot' when we first started playing. By the end of the set they were going crazy and everything."

The concert pulled in over a thousand people, by far the largest crowd that the Cramps had played for to date. Much of this was due to Alex Chilton's status as a local antihero, although such was his reputation that a proportion of the crowd may have comprised vengeful boyfriends and husbands. "He's probably fucked every chick in the state – literally. And those chicks' boyfriends are out to get him," asserted Lux. "There were

This Is Not Ordinary Music

guys with guns, man, all sorts of crazy things. He's done the most reckless suicidal things and gotten clean away. Talk about a cat having nine lives. Alex must have ninety."

For Ivy, the concert was something of a triumph, especially given that it was the first time they'd appeared with their new drummer. "Nick Knox barely knew us, he'd never played live with us. His first live show was in Memphis. He'd never seen us live," she recalls. "Something just shifted as soon as we got Nick; we felt like a gang, it hadn't before. We really became the Cramps when we got together with Nick. It was cool with Bryan's sister, but it still wasn't what it became with Nick. He was somethin' else." Similarly, Nick's greater power and technical prowess made a huge different to the way that the Cramps sounded on tape. "We couldn't believe it was us," Ivy enthused. "Hearing ourselves with him drumming, it was so rockin' and that was all we'd ever wanted. He was so loyal for 13 years. To me it was a technicality that there was Cramps before that and there'd been other members."

Equally positive was the band's experience of Alex's unorthodox working practices. "It was really great with him, because he was basically fucked up and getting loaded, falling asleep on the console. It was so different from our other experience, where a man behind the glass would command, 'Go! Be creative now!'" recalled Lux. "It was the opposite of our New York experience," confirmed Ivy. "Alex would say, 'Y'all are in the groove, just keep playing.' We thought, 'Really?'" Aside from being uniquely charismatic, Alex Chilton was steeped in rock'n'roll in a natural, unaffected way that appealed to Lux and Ivy's affinity with Memphis' cultural heritage. "He's the greatest liar I've ever met too," declared Lux. "He'd drive out to where he claimed 'the real blues was born' or something and it'd be some old shack! And you knew he was jiving you but you'd go along with it cos he was so damn funny. He's a real Southern boy is Alex. He believes in the Lord and the Lord sure as hell takes care of him. I mean, one night he was so fucked up on booze and drugs he pissed on his electric cable – like there was 1,000 volts of electricity open and he just urinated on all these open wires. Anyone else would've been burnt to a crisp, but not Alex."

Journey To The Centre Of The Cramps

A further benefit of the Cramps' liaison with Chilton came when he introduced them to Jim Dickinson who was looking to find a group that could back him for some time he had booked at Sam Phillips' studio. Again, Lux and Ivy leapt at the chance to get inside the legendary facility where much of the key early rock'n'roll that they adored had been recorded. "It's very hard to get in there," Ivy explained. "The studio just sits there rotting most of the time. You can't just give him your money and get in. You've got to talk him into doing it. All the time you know you're just lucky to be in there."

With the Cramps duly providing backing Dickinson laid down a version of 'Red Headed Woman', a song that rockabilly pioneer Sonny Burgess had initially recorded as the flip side of his landmark 1956 Sun seven-inch, 'We Wanna Boogie'. "By that time we had almost collected every Sun label single," remarked Lux. "So we were really in awe of that building and Sam Phillips. And then we met him. We had to stay over-night in the studio because we got locked in and we met him. It was like a dream or something. Could this be happening? We were told he never comes to the studio, but he showed up with a chainsaw to cut down the vines that had grown up over his name plaque – it was a magical experience."

The encounter with the man who had founded Sun Records and given Elvis, Johnny Cash, Carl Perkins and a host of others their start provided the highlight of the Cramps' successful visit to Tennessee. Still an imposing figure in his mid-fifties, Phillips stopped for a brief chat with Lux and Ivy. "We didn't talk to him too much. But we told him that we had every Sun single, and he says, 'Well, you know something?' And we said, 'What?' And he just says, 'You're lucky.' He had these huge glasses on that magnified his eyes until he looked like a monster from outer space. He's a real character, he had a crazy look in his eyes, you can just take one look in his eyes and say, 'Yeah, this is the guy,'" Lux recalled. "He's like a vampire," Ivy added. "You see photos of him from years ago and he looks younger now and we thought he must be Sam Phillips' son when we met him. He knows everything."

In addition to meeting Sam Phillips and recording with Jim Dickinson,

This Is Not Ordinary Music

the Cramps' visit to Sun also brought them into contact with Phillips' son Knox and his close friend Don 'Rooster' Ezell, a local taxi driver whose association with Sam Phillips ensured that he was often around the studio during its fifties golden age. Like Alex Chilton, these Memphis natives had the spirit of rock'n'roll coursing through their veins, and at a time when Elvis' death was a raw memory, they regaled their attentive visitors with tales of Presley's early years. "We were told that Elvis wasn't discovered as such at all. He was just some freaky looking kid always making a nuisance of himself around Sun Studios and nobody wanted to know him. Like, here's this guy who dyed his eyebrows and dressed in black pimp clothes – and this was the fifties in the South, you've got to remember – and Sam Phillips and all the session guys thought he was some disgusting little faggot!" exclaimed Lux. "What Don Ezell said Elvis was – I believe he used the term 'nigger queer' – it meant to a Southerner that Elvis hung around on Beale Street, he dressed flashy," explained Ivy. "Most of these guys on Sun were farmers, sharecroppers, redneck types. What does a redneck think of a teenager in a pink suit who wears mascara and hangs out on Beale Street? What would they have in common?"

Aside from rock'n'roll, this common ground turned out to be an enthusiasm for amphetamines, which Presley had access to on account of his mother being prescribed Benzedrine to combat her weight problem. "All those Sun guys just lived on speed, man. So, when Phillips found out that Elvis could get bottles of these things, he let him hang around. So here was Elvis every week bringing huge bottles of these pills to the guys at Sun until, as he was the studio's main source of supply for speed, Phillips was more or less obliged to let him cut a record," Lux recounted. "I don't think Elvis was a hustler," reasoned Ivy. "He was just a sweet kid whose love and passion was for gospel and the blues. That's all he cared about."

The sessions at Ardent proved fruitful, with the band laying down early versions of the bulk of their established live set as well as newer songs such as cover versions of Ricky Nelson's 1958 Top 10 hit 'Lonesome Town', rockabilly blond bomber Ronnie Dawson's 1959 single 'Rockin' Bones', and a reworking of rockin' trio Bill Allen and the Backbeats' 1958 cut 'Please Give Me Something', which the band re-titled as 'Twist And

Journey To The Centre Of The Cramps

Shout'. The Cramps also recorded a couple of new original songs, 'The Mad Daddy', Lux's tribute to Pete Myers, and 'Human Fly'. "I think 'Human Fly' is an anthem – an anthem about being a human monster," observed Lux. Despite this fecundity of recorded material, getting any of it mixed in Memphis proved impossible. "It's real laid-back. Someone that records an album down there that lives in Memphis, they'll take months, they'll go in and record one night and think about it for a month and that's the way they're used to doing it down there," explained Lux.

Instead, the Cramps made their way back to New York, fitting in a two-nighter at the Rat in Boston supporting local favourites Reddy Teddy on October 27 and 28. Lewis King, who subsequently went on to occupy the drum stool in rockabilly band Levi & the Rockats, recalled the indelible impression the group made with their first Massachusetts concerts: "The Cramps came out onstage looking like something out of a monster movie. Lux was a dime-store Frankenstein and Ivy was his equally second-hand bride. Bryan looked like an axe murderer with one-sided hair that had a shock of grey-white in it. And Nick – he looked like he drove a hearse for a living. But unlike bands like Kiss, they didn't look like they dressed up for the show. You believed they really looked this way all the time."

After returning home, the Cramps made their first appearance at CBGB since the Canadian showcase in July. The two shows on November 3–4 saw them supported by trash/glam ensemble the Sic Fucks, which included sisters Tish and Snooky Bellomo, who had previously sung backup to Debbie Harry in a germinal incarnation of Blondie. Largely comprising personnel that had been around the New York scene for some time, the Sic Fucks evoked the period before it had turned into a global phenomenon, peppering songs such as 'Fags On Acid' and 'Take Drugs' with in-jokes and barbs aimed at the likes of Lou Reed. The group had a highly theatrical aspect, which often saw the Bellomo Sisters dressed as sexy nuns and their connection to the core of the city's hip elite generally ensured that they drew a decent crowd, even if their name was sufficient to deflect rumoured interest from the more adventurous labels such as Chiswick.

This Is Not Ordinary Music

By the autumn of 1977, the nature of the groups playing at CBGB had noticeably altered. With many of the original axis of bands that had played a part in punk's genesis having outgrown the tight confines of Hilly's bar, a new generation of groups such as the Feelies, the Fleshtones and the Mumps alternated with visiting attractions from the UK including the Jam, Eddie & the Hot Rods and Dr. Feelgood. While Ramones gigs at the venue tended to sell out quickly, and Patti Smith or the Talking Heads would appear for special occasions, only the Dead Boys and Suicide continued to play the club with the same kind of regularity that they had when the year began. In a brave attempt to fill the increasing void, Hilly had even started booking reggae nights. "It went down the tube," asserts Lux. "Good rock'n'roll only seems to last a couple of years and then it fades away and a few years later it rears its ugly head again and everybody gets concerned and worried – with good reason. You've got your big business types trying to make this happen all over the place, but that's not the way it ever happens. You get some nasty little 15-year-old kids who make music in their garage, and that's the way it happens – they get tired of waiting for somebody to do something for them and they do it themselves."

With Blondie on the cusp of UK chart success with 'Denis' and the Ramones rounding out the year with a landmark concert at the Rainbow that was recorded for posterity as their *It's Alive* double album, many of the newer bands seemed to be looking to the scene from which those groups had sprung for inspiration, or reacting to the way in which punk rock was developing in Britain. "All those bands got so much better because they were influencing each other and knew each other and were passionate about music," observed Lux. "These things don't last forever," says Ivy. "They're really intense, everybody's united in some way that they don't fully understand and it enables them all to write – that is why you get a lot of bands and artists out of one era and place."

Having started out a couple of years after the likes of the Ramones, Blondie and Television, the Cramps had initially been treated as outsiders, but now found themselves being increasingly perceived as one of the key groups playing regularly at CBGB. Given that they were some distance

Journey To The Centre Of The Cramps

away from releasing anything on vinyl, and that they had taken a four month hiatus from playing in New York at a time when trends appeared to be shifting on a weekly basis, this says much for the way in which the Cramps stood out from those around them. Now all that they had to do was get a record out.

CHAPTER SIX

The Band From Ward T

We don't study music, we just shake our butts to it.

Poison Ivy

This band, the Cramps, that I've produced, they are the greatest rock'n'roll band in the world.

Alex Chilton

THE cultural fallout resulting from punk rock's initial transatlantic detonation some 18 months earlier led to significant changes within the record industry. By the end of 1977, there was something of a corporate scramble, with major labels that had been caught flatfooted by the cultural shift rushing to make up for lost time by offering deals to new bands far more readily than would have been the case in previous years, in the hope of slipping into punk's slipstream and picking up the next Ramones or Sex Pistols. In the UK, the do-it-yourself ethos spread as groups such as the Buzzcocks issued their own records that sold in decent quantities, thanks in part to a growing network of independent record shops such as Rough Trade and Small Wonder. Additionally, a wealth of smaller, hipper labels sprung up to challenge the old order by generating hits and publicity in equal measure. The following year would see an explosion of diversity displayed on the racks and walls of Britain's record stores, as labels such as Stiff, Chiswick and Beggars Banquet released a deluge of cleverly packaged singles from an increasingly wide range of artists.

Despite this, there were always those groups that seemed – initially, at

Journey To The Centre Of The Cramps

least – to fall through the cracks. While 1978 would result in what was subsequently, and somewhat cynically, dubbed the 'punk landfill' as a succession of identikit outfits issued derivative material, some of those being imitated (including Siouxsie & the Banshees and the Slits) began the year without a record deal. Although America's far larger geographical area made the development of any national independent music network less viable than was the case in the UK, on local levels a similar set of dynamics were already beginning to operate. Whereas the Ramones and Talking Heads had signed straight to Sire Records (which had hooked up a distribution deal with the giant Warner corporation in 1977), Blondie and Television had both issued their first singles on minor labels. In the latter case, this happened as far back as 1975 when Television manager Terry Ork took matters into his own hands and released their debut single on his own, newly instigated, label.

While the Ork label had essentially been a mechanism to get Television onto wax, and the group were subsequently snapped up by Elektra, Ork Records branched out during 1977. Having previously only issued singles by Television, their former bassist and vocalist Richard Hell (1976's landmark *Another World* EP) and power poppers the Marbles, Ork made the acquaintance of Alex Chilton. This not only resulted in the label releasing Chilton's five-track, 33 rpm, *The Singer Not The Song* EP, but also singles from the Cossacks' Chris Stamey and Prix – a Memphis-based studio ensemble that featured contributions from Chris Bell and Jon Tiven, who had produced Chilton's *Bach's Bottom* album and played guitar on his Ork EP. With Chilton also involved in production at a Connecticut studio where Terry Ork had connections, it seemed logical that the most straightforward means of getting some of the songs the Cramps had recorded with Chilton in Memphis onto vinyl would be through Ork's label. However, while this resulted in Lux and Ivy accompanying Alex on a lightning visit to London to mix the tracks at Advision Studios, where the Heartbreakers had laboured over their *LAMF* LP some three months before, none of Ork's recent singles had made any money and the label was facing financial difficulties that would put it out of action until 1979.

Although the trip provided Lux and Ivy with a set of decent mixes that

The Band From Ward T

they could retain for later use, this sudden dead end seemed typical of the kind of thing that tended to happen around Chilton. "He came into our apartment one time when we were trying to play him a tape that we made somewhere and everything in the apartment broke, something like four tape recorders we had there – everything from Panasonic to reel-to-reel just broke. My amplifier wouldn't work; wires fell out of the back of the speakers. We all use a jinx-removing spray that we bought at the voodoo store in Memphis when Alex comes around," explained Lux. "He believes in magic and we all do too, that's important to us. We believe that accidents can happen and that can be much better than what you've planned," Ivy added.

Still, there was little doubt that as 1977 approached its end, the Cramps were ready to take their place on the increasingly bulging record racks – they had developed into a tight unit, gained a reasonable following and were recognisable enough that CBGB ran an advertisement for a three night engagement in December that consisted simply of an uncaptioned photograph of the group. Their performances were also scaling new heights, with Lux increasingly developing the kind of kinetic stage act that would become his trademark. While their gig at the Ocean Club in May saw him chow down on a glass, miraculously escaping injury in the process, he'd been less fortunate at CBGB where an ill-advised swan-dive from the venue's low stage had led to a broken nose. An out of town excursion to Philadelphia's Hot Club in November had likewise resulted in him tearing a cartilage. Such injuries were viewed as an occupational hazard by Lux, who scarcely seemed bothered by his bashed beak and swollen knee. "The adrenalin gets going," he explained. "It's like whirling dervishes," added Ivy. "We get in this state where we've done things that should have hurt us – there's no physical way that couldn't have injured us, but didn't . . . I really do feel like we're immune."

In addition to honing his stagecraft, Lux had also now fully developed his commanding vocal style, which mixed his natural Iggy-like baritone with a dash of wry humour, while his mastery of Charlie Feathers' rockin' hiccup had reached the point where it sometimes sounded as if he was providing his own backing. From Lux's point of view, the lack of label

Journey To The Centre Of The Cramps

interest in the Cramps stemmed from the same kind of incomprehension that had seen rockabilly become an almost forgotten, marginalised form. "They don't know what category to put us into," he declared. "It seemed to me what we're doing, is the same thing everybody was doing in 1962, but for some reason they don't seem to know what we're doing. I guess we don't sing about some of the same things that people sang about in 1962 and the music is not the same, exactly, but it's in that spirit."

While the sector of the mainstream music industry not preoccupied with cashing in on disco's rise was looking for ways to market punk's energy as part of the contrived new wave phenomenon, the Cramps' style and content again marked them as outsiders – they didn't sound like anybody else and so labels arrived at the flawed conclusion that there was no interest in, or market for, the band. "It's part of the history of rock'n'roll, it's always been that way with big, major record companies," asserted Lux. "They want to get something because they want to get it before anyone else and they want to say 'Look what we discovered.' They're all on ego trips – 'Nobody knows about it and we got it. It's ours, we discovered it.' Meanwhile it just stinks, and it sounds like something that's on the radio now, which also stinks, and it's always been that way."

Between making their uncertain debut at CBGB in November 1976 and their first 1978 appearance at the bar just over a year later, the Cramps had established a unique identity and sound. "By this time, the audience knew what they were getting. We were regularly headlining three-night weekends at CBGB," recounted Ivy. This latest triple-header saw the band supported by a variety of acts including Teenage Jesus & the Jerks, between January 12 and 14. A recording of the band's Friday night set (which was given away to those attending the venue's 20th anniversary show in 1993, and subsequently surfaced on the *How To Make A Monster* retrospective) demonstrates the considerable improvement that Nick Knox made to the band's sound, and provided further evidence of the impressive way in which the Cramps were gelling. "We had come a long way from our audition at CBGB a year earlier," Ivy observed.

Right from the start of set opener, 'The Way I Walk', Nick's pounding regularity imbues the group with additional bottom end, supporting the

The Band From Ward T

song's instrumental sections as Ivy and Bryan cut loose with force and confidence. The band's growing female following is made evident by the shrill shrieks that accompany Lux's customary introduction to a thunderous rendition of 'Love Me', which he later identified as his favourite song from the set. "Girls were throwing their well-worn panties at us, which made very nice hats for Lux," explained Ivy. "I like to hear the girls scream," grinned Lux. Throughout the 13-song set, the Cramps lock together tightly, the only exception being during new number 'Uranium Rock'. Originally recorded in 1958 for Sun Records by Warren Smith, who was best known for scoring a minor hit with the Roy Orbison-penned 'So Long, I'm Gone' a year earlier, the Cramps mutate the original's rolling rockabilly into a rampant, if slightly shambolic, foldin' money hoedown that features an unusually straight vocal from Lux and would subsequently appear on IRS Records' 1984 compilation *Bad Music For Bad People*, where it provided completist interest among a selection of already-issued Cramps songs.

Just as Ivy's increasing mastery of the guitar provided the Cramps with melody and structure, Bryan had become adept at controlling the sheets of misdirected noise that he coaxed from his Flying-V. The rendition of 'Human Fly' captured at CBGB coruscates with unnatural energy, and the moment Ivy's opening descending scale gives way to Nick's jackhammer beat and Bryan's monstrous wall of distortion provides a rock'n'roll experience that can be felt as well as heard. Similarly, Gregory's merciless buzzsaw adorns Cleveland creature feature 'I Was A Teenage Werewolf' with textures that cause it to flicker like an electrified flytrap, while Ivy provides a mesmeric lead to 'Sunglasses After Dark' and makes effective, subtle use of single notes during 'What's Behind The Mask'. The influence of Duane Eddy is evident in her twang-heavy lead to 'Baby Blue Rock', a newish track that had evolved out of 'Twist And Shout' before mutating into 'Drug Train'. The Cramps' growing confidence is evident in their stagecraft, several songs segue neatly into the next, and 'I'm Cramped' is embellished with an extended discordant opening, before thundering in at breakneck speed to be further adorned by Nick's precision solo bursts. The triumphant closing 'TV Set' is a shuddering summary

Journey To The Centre Of The Cramps

of the Cramps' strengths – hypnotic and unsettling guitar interplay, unstoppable rockin' rhythms and commanding vocals.

In addition to being recorded for posterity, the Cramps' performance was also filmed by a CBS television crew for inclusion in a two-part report on the 'Punk Rock Phenomenon', which was fronted by long-time anchorman John Tesh, who later went on to a prolific and successful career as a pianist and also interviewed the band. The Cramps were also featured – playing up to any number of received notions about punk rockers – in Channel 2's press advertisements for the show that promised to spill the beans on 'hate power instead of love power' and the 'far-out, black leather world of the punk movement'. These ads ran in the *New York Times*, *New York Daily News* and *Daily Post*, and although the image used bore little relevance to anything the Cramps were doing it was part of increasingly impressive levels of media exposure for what was, after all, an unsigned group with little in the way of conventional management behind them. Apart from being plastered all over New York's daily press and featured on a major news channel, they were picking up coverage from the city's music press with *New York Rocker* running a feature in its November 1977 edition, while mentions in the growing fanzine sector were becoming increasingly regular. The power of the Cramps, the enthusiastic receptions that their set was receiving at gigs, and the widening scope of the media attention they were receiving, made it crystal clear that if nobody else was going to release these unholy sonic monsters, then the band would have to do so themselves.

From the six songs recorded in Memphis with Alex Chilton and mixed in London several weeks later, the Cramps selected two non-originals for their debut single – 'Surfin' Bird' and 'The Way I Walk'. However, writing the original songs was about the only thing the group didn't do. "We did everything on the record; the artwork, the photographs – no professionals. Everything we've done with this band, we've been told, 'You can't do it this way', but we want to prove you can," Lux recalled. Given that the Ramones had beaten the Cramps to the punch by over six months in getting a high-octane version of 'Surfin' Bird' onto vinyl with its inclusion on their *Rocket To Russia* album, it seemed a curious selection –

110

The Band From Ward T

'TV Set' had been widely mentioned as a possibility that would have mitigated against those unaware of the song's recent provenance, thinking that the Cramps were copying the Ramones. Determined to do their own thing, Lux and Ivy believed that the song represented something special, not only to them but within the wider context of popular culture. "Our first song was 'Surfin' Bird' and a lot of times we ended our set with that. I think that really stands for something in the history of rock'n'roll – not just our version, but that song in particular," asserted Lux. "The great thing about songs like 'Surfin' Bird' is that they're beyond art – beyond good or bad. Rock'n'roll is bigger than just records, it's a way of life – you don't even need music to have rock'n'roll."

Furthermore, for a band that was coming to represent a new strain of mutated rockabilly, selecting a surf rock song also appeared to be an odd thing to do. To an extent, this is indicative of the way in which Lux and Ivy prefer to perceive a wide spread of sub-genres as being what they essentially are – rock'n'roll. Musically, 'Surfin' Bird' shared common ground with instrumentals such as the Surfaris' 1963 classic 'Wipe Out', one of a series of such cuts from the early sixties that held an enduring appeal for the couple. "Psychologically, I kind of think of the fifties as lasting through the early sixties," asserted Ivy. "There was still a really cool instrumental thing going on until '63 or '64. What's weird is that people say that nothing happened between rockabilly and the British Invasion, but, man, that's when the instrumentals just flourished. It was really wild stuff. I wish I knew what name to put on that kind of music, because it was not rockabilly, but it was just really stomping dance music instrumentals. I guess electric guitars were still new and people were impressed by something as simple as reverb and tremolo, so they just pushed it as far as they could. Everyone thought it was the sound of the future, so you had that kind of futuristic innovation applied to it."

The Cramps' version of 'Surfin' Bird' was certainly in this spirit. Running more than twice the length of the Trashmen's and Ramones' cuts, it unfurls from a relatively conventional beginning into a juddering, twitching phantasmagoria of demented vocals, churning, distorted guitar and pounding drums, takes a detour into the realms of sonic psychosis,

Journey To The Centre Of The Cramps

before Ivy's Link Wray slashes bring it all back together ahead of its lunatic home stretch. This was not the 'Surfin' Bird' we were familiar with – it was, depending on your subjective standpoint, either a work of mad genius or evidence of what happens when you let crazy people into a recording studio. It might have been a cover, but it was in no sense derivative. "Our whole life has been collecting records – and now we can make 'em. That's our biggest kick. We make a record and we get done and we can really say 'Wow – it really sounds good'. Just like I guess Vincent Van Gogh can paint a painting and he'd say, 'Yeah, I can dig that, I won't kill myself. I won't cut off my other ear,'" enthused Lux, who subsequently cited the original rendition as being alongside Sandy Nelson's 1961 twang-infused instrumental stomper 'Let There Be Drums' as the songs that have influenced him the most. In any event, the origins of 'Surfin' Bird' remained every bit as tangled as its more recent history, the Trashmen's cut being based on a version of the Rivingtons' 'The Bird Is The Word' that the garage group had picked up on when they heard another band covering it, then adding elements drawn from the Rivingtons' first hit, 'Papa-Oom-Mow-Mow' and its subsequent follow-up 'Mama-Oom-Mow-Mow'. "There would be a single that I'd want on a desert island," declared Ivy. "'Mama-Oom-Mow-Mow' by the Rivingtons – 'He finally found himself a woman who could understand', that's the main lyric of it."

'The Way I Walk' featured similar retro-futuristic properties, taking Jack Scott's original and taking it into science-fiction realms with a series of unearthly shrieks and a hypnotic churning beat that gave it a crepuscular, B-movie quality far removed from its initial version. As with 'Surfin' Bird', the Cramps' singular adaptations of their cover material seemed to inspire others. "We were kind of pissed off when we turned on the *Midnight Special* and there was Robert [Gordon] singing 'The Way I Walk'," recalled Lux. "At the time of that first record, we were getting ripped off by a lot of people and getting a lot of flak and not much help because we were a rock'n'roll band in New York. We were a pure, crude rock'n'roll band in New York, which is a hard thing to be. A lot of people were stealing things from us right and left – our stage moves, our ideas. All

The Band From Ward T

of a sudden, a lot of song titles came out that were a lot like ours." A far more orthodox presentation of the song than the Cramps' adaptation, Gordon's version of 'The Way I Walk' was issued as a single on Private Stock during 1978. Produced by Blondie sound man Richard Gottehrer, it also featured trademark guitar embellishments from Link Wray, with whom Gordon had recorded an album the previous year.

Issued on the Cramps' newly formed Vengeance label and given the appropriately horrific catalogue number of 666, the single provided a fitting introduction to the group, their unique sound and their knowledgeable palette of influences. "In a way, putting that single out was like our big flying 'fuck you'. 'The Way I Walk' is representative of our sound but 'Surfin' Bird' – the attitude is, but the music isn't," said Ivy. These influences were further evident on the cover, which in addition to a neatly mysterious photograph of the band taken by Steven Blauner, presented the Cramps' logo, which drew upon typography used to ghoulish effect on the title header for EC Comics' ground-breaking *Crypt Of Terror* series. "We have most the ones from the forties and fifties to all the golden age stuff," explained Lux. "Those small companies were the ones that made way-out comics, beyond the limits of what really allowed – they managed to get stuff out. That stuff is really kind of evil stuff for kids to be reading. That collection is really important to us."

Lacking the funds to promote their debut single to any great extent, the Cramps resumed playing short runs of gigs or one-off shows. The band's first assault on Washington took place over two nights at the Atlantis Club on April 6 and 7, a week later they were back at CBGB for a three-nighter, before returning to the Rat for a pair of gigs supporting local new wavers the Atlantics. By late spring 1978, the likes of Blondie, the Ramones and Talking Heads were completely absent from CBGB listings. While the successes of those groups ensured that many of the component elements of the scene of which they were part were now spread far and wide, the bar continued to be successful and Hilly briefly explored the possibility of opening a second, larger music venue on Second Avenue. CBGB now had what contemporary marketing executives would term 'brand identity', its reputation built on a steady flow of press describing the bar's pivotal role in

Journey To The Centre Of The Cramps

the genesis of punk rock. To an extent, the club's international cachet enabled it to remain vibrant, as out of town groups such as the Runaways, the Dickies and the B-52's and visiting English bands including X-Ray Spex and Squeeze, extended the sense of CBGB being a happenin' place. Often, the schedule was dominated by lesser known groups that failed to break out of the Bowery in the way in which the venue's golden genera tion had. While old faces such as former New York Dolls Arthur Kane and Rick Rivets would show up with their new groups, only regular appearances by the Dead Boys, Richard Hell, Suicide and the Cramps continued to evoke the earlier era. "We never did fit in there, except that every place we played they had to turn people away. The whole scene was really fun. I loved the Ramones and Talking Heads and Blondie. We had a good time with them," observed Lux.

Although the nature of CBGB was changing, there still remained those who chose to interpret the Cramps as some kind of hayseed novelty act. "It bugged me in the early days that people thought we were a parody of something – that we were camping it up. That's either a misunderstanding or a misapprehension of what rockabilly, for instance, was all about," asserted Lux. "Last year they called us a parody band, which we were not at all. This year we cut out some of the, I wouldn't call it satire, but we'd have some biting comments to make. Now we just go out and play straight and people say at least we used to be funny – the same people who put us down for being a parody band." Despite being unable to please everyone at CBGB, the Cramps could fill the club comfortably over three or even four nights and were attracting a committed following that not only dug what they were doing, but also included those keen on exploring rockabilly's roots. "There was this girl that saw us at CBGB and she started going out and buying Jack Scott, 'The Way I Walk', buying all these records and all of a sudden she was wearing poodle skirts and fuzzy dice and all that kind of stuff and she was saying, 'I'm going to go down there and interview some of these guys', and she came back about two weeks later saying, 'They all tried to rape me!'" recounted Lux.

Although they had risen to the top of CBGB's totem pole, the Cramps were becoming increasingly aware that they needed to extend their

The Band From Ward T

developing practice of playing gigs outside of New York in order to progress. "For a while you had to look at New York as the place to make it. Something was happening in New York and it wasn't happening in other places. But then it spread and I think a lot of people in New York didn't realise it was happening somewhere else too. It just isn't a place to depend on for success. I think that's a mistake, a waste of time," reasoned Ivy. "We could sit in New York another two years and nobody would know about us, so we have to do something about it," Lux added.

The cultural geography of America being what it is, the Cramps took the next logical step and climbed into their van for a three-day road trip for their first crack at making an impression on the West Coast. While the development of the Los Angeles and San Francisco punk scenes had accelerated due to the influence of the Ramones and an early visit from the Damned, as with its eastern counterpart, its wider genesis derived from the embers of the preceding glitter/glam milieu. This had its epicentre at Rodney Bingenheimer's English Disco on Sunset Boulevard, a hotbed of hedonistic narcissism that quickly achieved notoriety on account of the predatory nature of its underage groupies. Reporting on the venue in 1973, *Rolling Stone*'s Richard Cromelin observed, "Once inside, everybody's a star. The social rules are simple but rigid: all you want to hear is how fabulous you look, so you tell them how fabulous they look. You talk about how bored you are, coming here night after night, but that there's no place else to go. If you're not jaded there's something wrong. It's good to come in very messed up on some kind of pills every once in a while, and weekend nights usually see at least one elaborate, tearful fight or breakdown. If you're 18 you're over the hill."

This scene begat glam rock-influenced proto-punk groups such as the English Disco's resident band Zolar X, who dressed as antennae-wielding aliens and adopted stage names such as Ygarr Ygarrist, Zany Zatovian and Eon Flash, as well as featuring a vocalist by the name of Zory Zenith who introduced elements of mime and improvisational music into Zolar X's live shows. The best known of these bands was the Runaways, an all-female rock combo put together under the aegis of maverick impresario Kim Fowley, who signed them to Mercury Records in 1976, creating a

Journey To The Centre Of The Cramps

significant impact with their eponymous debut album, which followed up the low-level chart success of their ground-breaking 'Cherry Bomb' seven-inch. Fronted by the photogenic Cherie Currie and provided with significant quantities of rock'n'roll heft courtesy of guitarist and black-clad bad-girl Joan Jett, the Runaways operated at the conventional rock end of the punk spectrum. This enabled them to cross over successfully into the US mainstream and led to the band embarking on major tours across Europe and in Japan.

By the time the Cramps arrived in Los Angeles to support the Runaways at the famous Whisky a Go Go on Sunset Strip, the all-girl rockers were at the height of their popularity. Although the three night engagement represented an opportunity in terms of exposure, supporting an established band with a clearly defined audience demographic that was divergent from their own led Lux to observe that, "Playing with the Runaways this weekend wasn't a good idea as far as introducing ourselves to Los Angeles." Having become accustomed to the relaxed stage management practices prevalent at CBGB and Max's, the businesslike approach of the Whisky's personnel came as something of a culture shock. "It did seem like a job," explained Lux. "They kept calling us – 'Get down here, if you're two minutes late, we're going to cancel you.' I was told to 'Grow up and come back to the real world' by a soundman. I went over, stood on his toes and stared in his face. So he said, 'I mean professionally, of course.' Some people are not aware that there is a new style in rock'n'roll politics that is different from the old style when you just take any old shit you're given and the band does what they're told. Some people are not aware that it isn't going to happen any more."

Additionally, the overwhelming bulk of the crowds came to see the Runaways, whose orthodox approach to rock'n'roll meant that they shared little common stylistic ground with the Cramps and drew an audience that would be likely to find sudden exposure to a set of primal rockin' voodoo somewhat leftfield for their tastes. "I thought they'd have been a lot wilder than we've seen so far," Lux declared. "I have an idea that they're probably a lot wilder, but I think they're kind of studying us. When we play New York everybody is bouncing off the walls and

116

The Band From Ward T

bouncing off the ceiling – real bananas." Despite this, the Cramps' irrepressible energy and unique appeal managed to win them a few converts. "Even though they were heckling us at first, they began to accept us. Even the ones that booed like it – they worked out their aggression," observed Bryan. Although Lux further antagonised the venue's staff by climbing out onto the catwalk and breaking the glass case containing a fire extinguisher (which he found impossible to let off), the intrepid frontman declared himself willing to give the Los Angeles hotspot another shot: "If we get better treatment from the Whisky we'll be back and play real soon. It's worth the drive to play to people who appreciate it."

Subsequent shows at the Inn Of The Beginning, a former hippie hangout in Cotati some 45 miles north of San Francisco and at the city by the bay's punk hub, Mabuhay Gardens on North Beach, provided the Cramps with more enthusiastic crowds. This served to highlight the differing natures of the two main Californian scenes at the time, with San Francisco hosting a more developed punk scene than its southerly counterpart. Whereas the more conservative Los Angeles circuit caused Lux to assert that, "They've got too many hot tubs out there – too much to do besides going to see rock'n'roll bands," groups such as the Avengers, the Nuns (both of whom had supported the Sex Pistols during their final implosive concert at the Winterland Ballroom four months earlier), Crime and the Mutants gave San Francisco's indigenous punk scene a gritty edge that would soon play a key part in the genesis of the subsequent hardcore scene spearheaded by the Dead Kennedys – who were coming together at around the same time that the Cramps hit town. Additionally, San Francisco was quick in developing its own underground punk press, with the high-profile *Search & Destroy* running a full page feature on the band in its eighth issue. LA's *Slash* fanzine also published an interview with the group, as well as an early review of 'Surfin' Bird', which saw contributor Jacki Ramirez praise the single as "an outstanding effort from what looks like one of New York's most interesting bands . . . With their excellent covers of these two songs, they leave me curious as to what their original stuff is like."

A combination of the prestige attached to being among CBGB's top

Journey To The Centre Of The Cramps

attractions, the publicity generated by the Cramps' trip to the West Coast and the fact that limited quantities of their debut single had found their way across the Atlantic, resulted in the band receiving their first significant overseas press, when *New Musical Express* despatched Paul Rambali to investigate the group that summer. Generally the hippest of Britain's four weekly rock 'inkies', *NME* had a reputation for being the most responsive music paper in terms of catching hold of rising trends (although it would subsequently become a parody of itself as it sought to continue the process during the early eighties). Rambali's piece was wholly enthusiastic, describing the band as, "The kind of people you couldn't fail to look twice at were they to pass you on the street. Three guys whose taste in clothes run to fake leopard skin and leatherette, and one gal with a more sedate dress sense and a cemetery stare." Detailing the Cramps' background and influences, he identified the way in which the band had often been unfairly dismissed by New York's elitists: "Unlike seemingly any band with even a moderate level of enterprise playing in New York, the Cramps have not been the subject of endless critical lathering. While media cognoscenti will fall over themselves to sing the praises of second-rate Patti Smith/Television imitators such as the Erasers, the Cramps are regarded as at best a joke, at worst an artless conniving fraud." Running across two pages, the feature was titled 'Psychobilly and Other Musical Diseases' and served to establish both the term and those responsible for coining it in the British popular consciousness.

On June 16, the Cramps ran up against psyches of the decidedly altered kind when they travelled northeast to Napa for a concert like no other. An encounter with electro-punks the Screamers led to a conversation about an Easter dance the latter had played at Camarillo State Mental Hospital near Los Angeles. "The only other band I've heard of that did it was the Screamers," recalled Lux. "Their music was much more serious, not so much dance music. It had a depressing effect on them – they played in a more terminal ward. The people were really upset there." The Screamers had been booked on the progressive basis that their uninhibited mode of performance would represent a form of therapy for the facility's inmates. During the seventies, this sort of radical thinking was *en vogue* in certain

The Band From Ward T

Californian psychiatric hospitals. "The dance floor was rampant with bizarre, free-form techniques," recounted *Slash*'s Bob Taylor. "A girl in the front followed [Screamers frontman] Tomata back and forth across the stage while massaging her breasts. There was the semi-horizontal pogo, an old-timer went into a soft-shoe routine, another couple did a sort of rounded-out box-step (all at different tempos) and, alas, the futile Siamese-twin pogo."

Intrigued by the sheer strangeness of the idea and the Screamers' accounts of performing before an audience of the pathologically unhinged, the Cramps managed to arrange a similar event at short notice with the administrators at Napa. "We always wanted to play at a mental institution because we always had a problem with audiences not being quite what we'd like them to be," explained Lux. "We thought if we went to a mental institution, the audience would contribute – and they really did! There were male and female inmates humping each other on the ground. It was the most bizarre show we've ever done. Those people just went crazy – doing everything you'd imagine people in a mental institution would do. There were people licking the walls, people laying on each other and coming up and talking to us while we were playing, but mainly it was people dancing the weirdest dances you've ever seen." Having some degree of empathy with those who had been banished to the sidelines of society, the Cramps enjoyed the event. "They had never heard of our band and they just had a good time," enthused Ivy. "Before we did it we were concerned that they might be inactive, that they would be sedated, tranquillised, or for whatever reason withdrawn and not respond to us. But they all were just immediately spontaneous, it was just really great."

Writing in *New York Rocker*, on-the-spot reporter Howie Klein could only stand back and marvel at what had unfolded before his eyes. "I've never seen so much audience participation," he declared. "One patient went over to the superintendent and said, 'These guys look like they just got out of T-Unit'. T-Unit, the super later told me, is where they keep the 'lifers'. During an incisive 'What's Behind The Mask', one lively young lady jumped on Lux's back and held on for the whole song, screaming periodically into the mic. Later the same little honey grabbed

Journey To The Centre Of The Cramps

the microphone and made off with Lux in hot pursuit. But the greatest thing was to see all these overweight, middle-aged women holding handbags and doing totally liberated pogos."

"They were screaming 'Ward T! Ward T!' like that at us," Lux confirmed. "We found out later that Ward T is the ward no-one comes back from. No-one ever sees you again when you go to Ward T. They were saying we were from Ward T. Mostly, they weren't that strange. They just didn't know boys and girls weren't supposed to lie on each other on the ground and stuff. They hadn't quite figured out that wasn't nice to do." As the concert progressed, it became evident that some inmates were also taking the opportunity to liberate themselves as over a dozen of Napa's residents attempted to escape. "Then the people who ran the place said, 'Don't worry, we don't have to chase them. They'll come back because they don't know how to take care of themselves. They'll just come back when they're hungry,'" Ivy recollected. "Those people at Napa Hospital were less unusual than some of the crowds we've played," added Lux. "Though the guy filming couldn't point his camera at the inmates because he couldn't show them escaping."

The black and white footage of the concert shows that unlike some of the inmates the Screamers had encountered at Camarillo, there was nothing remotely threatening about those at Napa. During 'Love Me' several inmates descend on Lux to give him a group hug as he issues his pleas for affection and a small scale hoedown breaks out in another corner of the room. At one point Lux asks a female inmate, 'How do you like the Cramps so far, honey?' 'Arrrrrrgh!' she replies. "It was like playing for children," recalled Ivy. "People had no sense of space boundaries. There was a woman there who during our songs told us her uncle was an agent and thought he could take us places but she was just an inmate. There was another guy there in a cowboy hat who said he was in heaven because he thought he was going to miss punk rock because he was in Napa. He never thought punk rock would come to him. There's a video of the show with people dry humping on the ground and all that. There was very little supervision from the staff. It was very insane."

In fact, the regime at Napa was so informal that the Cramps had

The Band From Ward T

considerable difficulties in telling staff from inmates. "The administration there liked us so much they said they would write us a letter of recommendation to get us into clubs," explained Lux. "We never actually got one, but that would have been great to have a letter of recommendation from a mental institution. Everybody we met there was crazy. The people putting on the show were crazy."

Although the short-lived breakout put other psychiatric facilities off booking the Cramps, their gig at Napa State passed into rock'n'roll folklore and a DVD of the concert was commercially released in 2004. A year earlier, artists Iain Forsyth and Jane Pollard staged a pair of re-enactments of the event at London's Institute of Contemporary Arts. Entitled *File Under Sacred Music*, the performances featured a band drawn from London's garage rock scene that included Alfonso Pinto (the Parkinsons), Holly Golightly (Thee Headcoatees), Bruce Brand (Thee Headcoats) and John Gibbs (the Wildebeests). As a means of recreating the unique dynamic between band and audience Pollard and Forsyth (who had previously reconstructed David Bowie's famous final performance as Ziggy Stardust) came to an arrangement with local mental health charity Core Arts that enabled a proportion of the crowd to be made up by those suffering from psychological problems. "When we first started thinking about it seriously, we thought that maybe this is something we shouldn't do without a deep personal understanding or experience of those types of issues," said Forsyth. "But that just felt really wrong. It felt really weak to go, 'This is not something I have a close affinity with myself so I can't deal with it.' On the day, the two performances went well, "We knew it would be a challenge with the mental health patients and to see them enjoying themselves was great," enthused Alfonso Pinto, who took the role of Lux. "The second time people really got into it, so it was like, 'Let's do it.'" Footage of the event was edited and degraded to match the original film, while screenings took place across Europe and *File Under Sacred Music* was subsequently nominated for an award at the 2004 Viper Basel International Festival for Film, Video and New Media.

Back in 1978, the Cramps resumed utilising more conventional means of expanding their audiences. En route back to New York from California

Journey To The Centre Of The Cramps

the band stopped off in Lux, Ivy and Nick's old Cleveland stamping grounds to appear at an Independence Day party in the exclusive suburb of Bratenahl, which overlooks Lake Erie. The Cramps, who were joined on the bill by the Pagans and Pere Ubu, performed on a concrete path overlooking the lakeside – a situation that proved irresistible to Lux. "There was a beach there at the time and he ended the set by jumping off a cliff and kept on rolling," said Peter Ball, who hosted the party at his family mansion. The group also fitted in a pair of shows at the Real World and the Governor's Chateau. While visiting Akron, the band was reminded why they left the Midwest when they were stopped by police after cruising around a West Akron cemetery late at night. The following month saw the Cramps cross the border to Canada for two gigs at the Horseshoe Tavern in Toronto, where they were supported by local punks the Ugly, a group led by Mike Nightmare – a charismatic frontman whose manic stage presence stemmed somewhat tragically from psychological and physical damage inflicted on him when his parents took him to see a psychiatrist, who subsequently had him committed, whereupon he was forced to endure electro-shock therapy. "They burned him so bad that for the rest of his life he had scars the size of nickels burnt into each side of his forehead, on his temples," recalled former bandmate William Cork. During the concerts Lux more than matched Mike's livewire antics, ripping down the homemade sequin-encrusted horseshoe that provided the club with its backdrop. This was the Cramps' second excursion to Canada, having paid Toronto a lightning visit at the start of the year, where their show at the New Yorker Theatre had received positive press in the *Toronto Globe*. When the band returned to the city in late July, they already had a reasonable following. "In the summer of 1977, CBGB had this showcase of Toronto punk bands and even though we weren't a Toronto band we ended up headlining that showcase," explained Ivy. "So by the time we reached Toronto, we already had a following due to bands like the Viletones and just word of mouth."

After further road trips to Detroit and Philadelphia, the Cramps resumed activities at CBGB, where they recorded a brief set that was aired on the venue's new midnight slot on WPIX FM Radio, followed by

The Band From Ward T

a weekend engagement in mid-August where support was provided by arty Washington new wavers the Urban Verbs and Mike Purkhiser's garage combo, the Action. The group then set about trying out some alternative New York nightspots, appearing twice at Club 57 in St Mark's Place, and following this up with a similar two-nighter at Live 36 W on 62nd Street. Although the band's 14-song set from the Psychedelly in Bethesda, Maryland on September 8 subsequently found its way onto a succession of bootlegs, the Cramps remained no nearer scoring any kind of record deal. When interest from the tiny Scottish independent Sensible Records (who had previously released Scottish group the Rezillos' 'I Can't Stand My Baby' seven-inch, before the day-glo punks signed to Sire) evaporated, it was evident that the Cramps were going to have to continue releasing their own material. From Lux's historically educated point of view this frustrating situation was just part of the grand rock'n'roll circus that had endured since the earliest days of the form. "Specialty Records had the opportunity to sign the Beatles and they said 'Are you kidding?'" he recounted. "Little Richard tried very hard to get the Beatles signed to Specialty Records and they could have had them – the Beatles wanted it really bad because they loved Larry Williams and all the artists on Specialty Records. And Specialty Records went out of business right after that because they couldn't sell any records, but they didn't want anything to do with the Beatles because they looked too weird and it didn't sound like what was on the radio now. No one would ever be interested in that! It's just the history of rock'n'roll, it never changes."

CHAPTER SEVEN

How The Weird Can Get Started In Recording

I always thought the Sex Pistols were very sophisticated.

Lux Interior

What we attack is everything that's swell and nice and fine and easy and comfortable.

Poison Ivy

IN the continuing absence of a record deal, the Cramps' second single, 'Human Fly', was released on the Vengeance label on Halloween 1978. Although 'Surfin' Bird' had sold an estimated 6,000 copies, necessitating a second pressing, the group continued to issue their own material with reluctance, having little interest in taking part in the independent records boom that was in full flight in the UK, and gathering momentum in the States. "We don't have the time or money," Lux explained. "The Rezillos were talking to us about releasing 'I Can't Stand My Baby' on Vengeance, but we really couldn't do it right – we couldn't do a good job."

Backed by the group's blistering interpretation of Roy Orbison's 'Domino', 'Human Fly' was the first original composition that the Cramps had committed to vinyl. "It was one of our first songs and it just blew my mind the first time," said Ivy. "You don't know how good of an idea it is until you hear it and it was like 'Oh shit!'" Heralded by its now famous descending guitar scale, the track detonates early as Ivy and Bryan's malformed twin guitars combine with Nick's sledgehammer beat to produce a

How The Weird Can Get Started In Recording

savage burst of electrified energy that shudders and writhes across the balance of the recording. Sheets of serrated fuzz overlap before Lux delivers vocals that glower with perverse pride at his creature feature predicament. "Some guy had just climbed the World Trade Tower and the headline in *The Post* that day was 'Human Fly Climbs Tower'," he recalled. "I was out walking along the street at about six in the morning. It felt like *Night Of The Living Dead* the way all the people were wandering around. Somebody had jumped off the roof of the building next to ours and they were scraping him off the sidewalk. All of that made me go home and write the song."

While his lyrics splice elements drawn from science fiction movies such as *The Fly* (a 1958 cult classic starring Vincent Price that featured the irresistible promotional come-on: 'The first time atomic mutation on humans has been shown on the screen') with references to Question Mark & the Mysterians' 1966 garage smash '96 Tears', Lux's vocal is both intimate and authoritative. "It's not easy to get that sound – that 'on the edge of distortion' sound we had on 'Human Fly'. The trick is to use bad microphones," he declared. "Maybe that's what I am. All my life people have told me I was a pest, something that looked ugly, smelled bad and ought to be gotten rid of, something that spoiled everybody's planned-out fun."

'Domino' is scarcely less remarkable. Propelled by Nick's syncopation and Ivy's reverb-laden slashes, the track takes Orbison's rockin' original and imbues it with deranged danger, cementing 'psycho' and 'billy' inseparably together. Lux drawls his words as the song develops momentum and intensity, reaching a pounding peak just ahead of its perfectly executed false ending. In addition to providing evidence of the Cramps' informed ability to arrange and adapt cover versions, it also served to highlight just how good a song the 1957 'Cat Called Domino' was. "I think it would be great if we were considered the band that made people pay attention to the past again," asserted Lux. "It's the music of real crazy people, and it's different from popular music. Sometimes it becomes popular music, but it's a whole different thing."

The way in which the Cramps adapted 'Domino' to meet their own twisted ends dismissed any notions of them being some kind of revival act.

Journey To The Centre Of The Cramps

Whereas Robert Gordon perfectly preserved all the mannerisms and tropes of the original form in an impressively precise manner, the Cramps treated the source material less reverently – using it as a basis that could be moulded into something exciting and novel, while retaining the sense of abandon that many of these old songs projected. This idea lay at the very core of the Cramps' ethos. "Good rock'n'roll is always good," insisted Lux. "We're not interested in playing fifties songs – that's why we write our own lyrics – but the thing that made rock'n'roll great in the fifties, makes rock'n'roll great today; it's an urgency, it's a danger, it's a true kind of folk music based on the blues. It means something to people; it brings a certain kind of people together. It separates the squares from the cool people and pop music doesn't do that. Pop music is just for everyone's entertainment – rock'n'roll is something more than that."

The single came wrapped in a thin paper sleeve adorned with a retouched Steven Blauner photo of the band that distorts their faces in much the same, unsettling-yet-engaging way that the band mutated early rock'n'roll. The back cover featured an unfocussed live-action shot of the Cramps snapped from the crowd by one of the inmates during the Napa State Mental Hospital concert. "Someone who was there with us was handing a camera round some of the inmates and that was one of the pictures taken," explained Lux. The group had also filmed a short promotional film – which, with there being little in the way of outlets for it at the time, promptly disappeared. When I asked Lux about the clip in 2006, he explained that even he no longer had a copy. "At one time it was shown as an art movie at colleges," he added.

The Cramps saw out 1978 with a pair of shows at Max's Kansas City, which saw tables pushed back to facilitate dancing and the addition of a new song to the set, another Roy Orbison cover – this time a high-octane rendition of 'Problem Child', which originally appeared on his 1961 debut album, *Roy Orbison At The Rock House*. Although the Cramps' version of the song sounds a little like 'Mad Daddy', Lux's histrionic vocal adapts Orbison's alluring original delivery into something truly manic. Among those at Max's was Chris Spedding, an English guitarist and producer who'd recently relocated to New York in the belief that American audiences

How The Weird Can Get Started In Recording

would prove more receptive to the kind of supercharged rock'n'roll he was playing at the time. Spedding had become best known as a hired gun on the session circuit through his work with Roxy Music, John Cale and Roy Harper. Despite feeling the need to leave the UK, Spedding was nationally known, having hit the UK charts with 'Motorbikin'' in 1975 and 'Get Outa My Pagoda' in 1977.

He'd also become involved on the UK punk scene through producing an early Sex Pistols session in May 1976 and his appearance at the 100 Club Punk Festival with the Vibrators four months later. Immediately prior to his departure for New York, Chris was contacted by Sire Records co-founder Richard Gottehrer who invited him to take part in a session with Robert Gordon. These went well and Spedding was asked to join Gordon's band – in place of the legendary Link Wray, whom Gordon felt was too much of a soloist. Having taken a hotel room a couple of blocks along from Max's, Chris had started playing at the nearby venue, making his first appearance there on October 13, 1978. The following month, he was joined onstage by another English expatriate, Sid Vicious – who was the new junkie in town, having moved to New York as a means of relaunching his career following the dissolution of the Sex Pistols. "In the dressing room after the show, Sid shook my hand and I saw blood in my hand," recounted Chris. "At first I thought he was cutting my hand with broken glass, but then I saw that it was his blood, and ice, not broken glass."

When not playing or recording (Spedding's punk-tinged *Guitar Graffiti* solo album was issued by RAK Records in March 1979) Chris visited Max's on a fairly regular basis as it provided a handy hangout to hook up with other musicians and catch local acts such as the Cramps. "I saw them play when I first came to New York in 1978 and thought they were the best band around at the time," he recalls. "I offered to produce some demos for them to get a deal. They agreed, although I found out later they already had a deal and a producer, but I think they were intrigued how it would turn out. In the event, I got the band to overdub backing vocals on a couple of songs. I got the impression they thought that was selling out, but wasn't sure why. If they wanted to be true to their roots, they were only being asked to do what the original guys did."

Journey To The Centre Of The Cramps

Although his brief time in New York had brought him into immediate contact with two sides of the contemporary rockabilly coin, Spedding's adaptable playing style had seen him encompass everything from jazz to bubblegum pop during a career that stretched back to the sixties. "Rockabilly didn't register with me," he confirms. "It's all music. I didn't think they were rockabilly – whatever that may be – just a very exciting, interesting band. I wasn't familiar with the term 'rockabilly' in 1978. Robert Gordon (who I joined initially to play my tunes, but we never did) told me, 'I hope you can play rockabilly.' I asked him what he meant. He said, 'Early Elvis.' And I said, 'Oh, Scotty Moore, I love his playing!' So that's what I do when asked to do rockabilly – I try to play like Scotty Moore, one of my first guitar heroes." Moore was also a hero for Lux and Ivy, and Spedding's intuitive understanding of early rock'n'roll immediately provided the two parties with some common ground. Ivy had already been impressed with Chris' track 'Hey Miss Betty', which had been issued as the B-side of 'Get Outa My Pagoda' in 1977. "We were huge Spedding fans," she recalls. "He influenced my playing – I didn't know prior to seeing him live that if you had a smaller amp you got a wickeder tone. I saw him play and he just had a tiny amp – it might have been a 10-inch speaker – and he got this awesome sound. Now any records we make I just have this tiny valve amp."

The Cramps readily accepted Chris' offer, and in February they duly joined him for some sessions at the Hot House studios in Midtown. Five tracks were recorded on the facility's eight-track device – four of those songs ('Twist And Shout', 'I Was A Teenage Werewolf', 'Rockin' Bones' and 'Mad Daddy') would subsequently turn up on a bootleg entitled *Tales From The Cramps*. The fifth, a space-race stomper called 'Weekend On Mars', would later be recorded as a B-side for the 1983 New Rose seven-inch 'I Ain't Nothin' But A Gorehound'. "My reel-to-reel mixes sounded great," recounts Spedding. "Unfortunately, the band only got cassettes to take away. The bootleg versions of the sessions I heard were not from my reel-to-reel tape, but third or fourth generation cassette dubs. They were not representative of the band or my production. Some songs were slower or faster and some tracks were in mono – most upsetting."

How The Weird Can Get Started In Recording

Although Chris found the Cramps to be "very professional – they know what they like and always get it" and the group, in turn welcomed the opportunity to record with him, there was a general feeling that the overall mix wasn't quite right. "When Chris Spedding did those demos for us, they were technically excellent, but they ended up sounding just too thin," observed Bryan. Although disappointing, the sessions had been a positive experience and enabled the Cramps to benefit from Chris' vast experience in the music business. "In conversation with Lux and Ivy, I found that they were frustrated with their reception in New York," he explains. "Asking around, I found that they were not considered 'hip' by the New Yorkers, who seemed very insular and cliquey. Not sure who suggested it first, but the band thought that the UK might be more open to them. I encouraged them to try their luck there."

While Lux and Ivy made tentative plans to issue Spedding's cuts of 'Rockin' Bones' and 'Mad Daddy' as a third Vengeance single, further opportunity presented itself when the group were booked to open for the Clash at the 3,800 capacity Palladium on East 14th Street. Much to the Cramps' collective delight, the gig – part of the Clash's 'Pearl Harbour' US tour – would also see them share the bill with blues guitar behemoth Bo Diddley. "The Clash requested us on the bill," Ivy explains. "Joe Strummer had recently seen us at Hurrah's and told Bryan he thought we were the best American band he'd seen. We'd never seen the Clash. We liked the sound on their singles, although I have to confess we weren't very politically inclined." The packed gig (complete with swaying balconies) was a particular treat for Bryan Gregory who was a fan of the band and was becoming increasingly enamoured by their (largely gestural) political leanings. That aspect of the London quartet made little impression on Ivy, who recalls being bowled over by their live energy: "They were like an atom bomb onstage, pure white light, white heat, especially Joe Strummer. He lived up to his name. He was a frantic vibrating blur of intensity. So rockin'."

Also at the venue, where seven months later bassist Paul Simonon's act of smashing his guitar would be captured by photographer Pennie Smith for the cover of their *London Calling* album, was Clash DJ Barry

Journey To The Centre Of The Cramps

'Scratchy' Myers. "The Clash were insistent that a local and current band opened up on that first US foray," he recounts. "It was a tradition they often had in the UK. I was delighted that the chance fell on the Cramps for the penultimate gig. I'd been knocked out by and was hammering their first two singles on import and was primed up for them opening the show in New York. The Big Apple, the Palladium, the Cramps, Bo Diddley and then the Clash: what a fantastic bill and me there to link it all together! A total thrill, a realisation of dreams you couldn't even have imagined. The Cramps did not let me down. I was trapped in their web. So much so that I was caught out front, frantically calling for more — when I remembered that I was the bugger due onstage next. Fortunately they came back for an encore whilst I was still trying to flash my backstage pass at security."

A week later, the Cramps followed this up with a successful return to Los Angeles for two sold-out shows supporting the Dead Boys at the Other Masque in Hollywood that garnered positive press in the *LA Times* and *LA Weekly*. Since the previous summer's shows at the Whisky with the Runaways, the punk scene around LA had caught up with San Francisco, ensuring that both visiting bands received a lively reception at the packed-out club. After a West Coast break during which a subsequent press release claimed that the group spent 'at a trailer camp in the Mohave Desert assisting Dutch creative anarchist Paul Hessing with multimedia schemes', the Cramps travelled to San Francisco where they made a welcome return to Mabuhay Gardens, in addition to visiting nearby Palo Alto for a concert at the Keystone Club alongside country/folk singer-songwriter Dan Hicks that was broadcast live on Santa Cruz's KFAT FM Radio. This transmission later resurfaced on a curious bootleg that emerged under the title of *Nazibilly Werewoelfen*. Put together by a bootlegger who evidently suffered from both a Nazi fixation and a warped sense of humour, the 12-inch featured fascist imagery and some truly toe-curling punning in its sleeve notes, as well as giving the barrel of bad taste an extra scraping to rename the eight tracks included in ways that evoked all the fun and frolics of Hitler's pogroms (for example, 'The Way I Walk' is listed as 'The Gas I Like').

How The Weird Can Get Started In Recording

The Cramps' sold-out show at the Los Angeles Troubadour not only resulted in lengthy queues outside the venue, but also saw a higher than usual turnout from several record labels that had decided this was the time to finally wake up and take notice of the group. Any parties looking to take their interest further would now need to deal directly with Ivy, who had recently resumed managing the band after a string of shortlived incumbents, including former Blues Project frontman Tommy Flanders, had failed to work out. "We're rough on managers," she observed. "Managers are actually tough on us. They tell you they're doing things when they're not doing anything," continued Lux. "They're not coming from where we're coming from – they're small thinkers," added Ivy. "I think there are lots of levels to dig what we do. But when you talk about managers, or people doing things for us, I don't think it's easy – in the creative process – to have people help you," Lux explained. "I don't think anybody can understand us. We've become very aware of the fact that most people don't understand what we're doing and aren't equipped to understand what we're doing. So we should do it ourselves. Things have been working real good since Ivy started handling the business. We don't have half the problems we used to have."

The impact made by the Cramps' shows at the Other Masque and the Troubadour finally prompted the reaction that the group and Ivy had been hoping for since the band began gigging regularly at the end of 1976. IRS Records founder Miles Copeland offered the band a deal that included reissuing their two singles as a 12-inch EP and a tour of the UK supporting the Police, with whom Copeland's brother played drums. The son of an American CIA operative and a British intelligence officer, Copeland had grown up in the Middle East where he developed a taste for rock'n'roll and an interest in promoting events, while on his way to mastering in economics. Having cut his promotional teeth organising Beirut's first psychedelic festival and acting as de facto manager for hippie group Rupert's People, Copeland was seized by the entrepreneurial spirit and embarked on a career in the music industry that would see him become involved in promoting and managing a succession of progressive rock acts. This led to him forming British Talent Management, a combined

Journey To The Centre Of The Cramps

management agency and record label that boasted the likes of Curved Air (who also included Steward Copeland in their line-up) on its roster. BTM lasted around two years before going out of business due to the commercial failure of his 'Star Trucking '75' travelling festival, an event that featured Soft Machine and (when he showed up) Lou Reed.

Ideally situated to take note of the rising tide of new bands as punk rock and its derivatives raged out from London's clubs and bars during 1976 and '77, Miles' next move was to found another record label, Illegal, partly as a means of getting the Police onto vinyl. Encouraged by unprecedented sales of their debut single, 'Fall Out' (which exhausted its initial pressing in record time on the way to racking up 70,000 copies sold), Copeland threw himself headlong into the record business. Throughout 1977, Illegal issued a string of singles from US acts such as Wayne County and former Velvet Underground mainstay John Cale, alongside UK produce from street punks Menace and East London quartet the Wasps. Copeland also either founded, or became involved in the formation of, a series of secondary labels, which included Deptford Fun City, Step Forward, Total Noise and New Bristol Records, operating alongside Illegal under the 'Faulty Products' collective branding. In addition to issuing landmark recordings by groups such as Alternative TV and the Fall, Copeland's diverse business strategies brought him into contact with a wide range of musicians and industry executives, which in turn enabled him to tie up a distribution arrangement with A&M Records.

In 1979, Copeland had formed IRS as the stateside arm of his Illegal organisation, allowing him to release records in the US as well as providing the opportunity to license foreign material for the American market, as he subsequently did with several Buzzcocks records. While the Cramps accepted Copeland's offer to reissue their existing singles and tour the UK, they were keen to record an album, and as a means of convincing IRS of the project's worth, later recorded a set of demos in Ohio with Alex Chilton. These sessions subsequently surfaced on various bootlegs that appeared from the mid-eighties onward. Alternatively titled *All Tore Up* or *Ohio Demos 1979* the albums feature around half of the cuts that ultimately made it to the Cramps' debut LP, the balance being made up of a trio of

How The Weird Can Get Started In Recording

songs that would appear on *Psychedelic Jungle* ('Subwire Desire', 'Jungle Hop' and 'Rockin' Bones') and works in progress including 'Uranium Rock' and 'Twist And Shout', as well as 'I Can't Hardly Stand It', from the lyrics of which *All Tore Up* derived its title. Rated as one of the better Cramps bootlegs, the bulk of the songs clearly indicated that the band had sufficient material that had been developed to a degree that it was more than ready for release.

After a trio of sorties to Washington and a gig in Bryan's native Detroit during April and May, the Cramps played a pre-tour warm-up gig at New York's Irving Plaza on May 25 before travelling to Britain for a month of gigs which would also see them joined on the Police's bill by Scottish rocker Bobby Henry, who'd recently recorded a pair of singles for A&M. Despite having received a smattering of press in the UK, the Cramps were largely unknown when they stepped out onto the stage of Glasgow Apollo at the end of the month. As had been the case when they first visited Los Angeles, the fact that they had very little musically in common with the Police tended to ensure a lukewarm reaction from audiences that had turned out for an evening of undemanding, reggae-infused pop-rock. Reporting on the concert for *New Musical Express*, Glenn Gibson appeared equally ambivalent to the Cramps: "If the Cramps were any older they'd probably have been in Andy Warhol's films – one of them even looks like a fibreglass model of Joe Dallesandro with half of Human League vocalist Phil Oakey's hairstyle in aluminium dye," he wrote. "You also get a post-Nico, vacant blonde and a singer who likes to slink around like a half-reptile vampire slave with epilepsy. Punkability voodoo, the punk is New York attitude and mainly visual; the ability is the music – see the band, borrow the records; the voodoo is redolent of adverts for bat-shaped savoury snacks."

However, the following night's show at the Edinburgh Odeon was covered by *Record Mirror*'s Johnny Waller, who was far more enthusiastic: "The Cramps, well, they were a-mazing. Try and imagine a weird fusion of the Rezillos and the Ramones (well, try then), topped off with a heavy sixties R'n'B influence and Addams family visuals. Occasional NY Dolls echoes filtered through and large sections of the audience felt alienated. If

Journey To The Centre Of The Cramps

the Cramps didn't exist, someone would have to invent them – stolen riffs, tacky image and all. I loved every moment."

Undaunted by the lack of enthusiasm from sections of the Police's crowd, Lux took the direct route toward breaking down the barriers between audience and performer, launching himself off a 14-foot high speaker stack to swan-dive head first into the bemused gathered below. "Sometimes I kind of hypnotise myself when I'm up there and it's as if I'm mentally invulnerable to physical danger. But if it's a good show I'm putting on, why would people want to hurt me anyway? Only if I'm doing it badly should they get really angry," he observed. "It's more dangerous walking down the streets of New York than it is being in this band."

Unlike Blondie's British tour debut, where they had been compelled by headliners Television's management to play in a restricted area of the stage and denied soundchecks, the relationship between the two very different bands was largely friendly. "They were real nice to us, that was a fun experience," confirmed Lux. "Yeah, there weren't any horror stories. I guess since we were a band from New York they kind of treated us good," added Ivy. "It was such a thrill for us, and the Police were incredibly nice and hospitable and let us have soundchecks, which I've heard is not typical at all. I've heard in this business you're really lucky if people are nice to you. And their audience found a facet to us that was entertaining, whether it was morbid fascination, or whatever."

The Cramps hit England for the first time on June 2 for a set that saw Lux respond to hostility from sections of the crowd by treating them to a demonstration of confrontational performance that would have done Alan Vega proud: "Lux gets bored and decides to shake things up a bit," wrote *Melody Maker* journalist Jon Savage. "He quickly moves to the front of the stage and starts climbing over into the stalls: the guard – well, this isn't the sort of thing – restrains him. Lux pats his shoulder, wonders whether to deck him and brushes past to take his theatre to the goggling audience: the number winds down, he whips around, whips the mike round the bouncers head and shoulders: 'This man wants a word with you.' While the bouncer fumbles, exeunt Cramps."

How The Weird Can Get Started In Recording

Unlike many of those who'd travelled to the Empire for a night of Policing, Savage (one of the UK music press' more dynamic commentators) understood where the Cramps were coming from. "The Cramps present the nightmares of the fifties, as today's heroes (think about that), and lost music as stylistic rebellion. It'd be easy to write them off as a kitsch-obsessed writer's wet dream – their ability to be simultaneously menacing, danceable and very funny knocks that one on the head."

On June 5, the Cramps took advantage of a gap in the Police tour schedule to headline their first London show at the compact-but-legendary Marquee on Wardour Street. This resulted in a glowing review from *NME*'s Max Bell, who'd coincidentally spotted the group at a screening of Werner Herzog's recently released *Nosferatu The Vampyre*, the previous night. Bell added to the growing mound of critical acclaim, declaring: "Everything about the Cramps is perfect, from their swinging light bulb and voodoo incantations right down to their backline rockabilly maelstrom. London has not witnessed a classier New York export since the Ramones."

This growing buzz intensified as a thunderous set in Birmingham the following night almost blew the roof off of Digbeth's Civic Hall, while a sparse crowd at Manchester's Free Trade Hall on June 8 got a close look at Lux as he embarked on another of his seat-climbing excursions. Among those who witnessed the show and stayed to view the spectacle rather than recoiling to the bar in horror (as many did) was future Smiths frontman Steven Morrissey, then a prolific letter writer to the UK's music papers. Morrissey, who had previously lionised the New York Dolls, Sparks and doomed glam 'superstar' Jobriath, was equally taken by the latest American export to land in his hometown. In a missive published in *Record Mirror*, he enthused "They are the most beautiful, yes beautiful group I've ever seen. The fact that they exist is enough. Meanwhile Manchester will never be the same again (Thank God)." A second letter, to *Sounds*, echoed the comparisons between the Cramps and the Police that had also been a feature of Jon Savage's *Melody Maker* gig review. "The Cramps are worth their weight in gold for making the Police seem like a great big sloppy bowl of mush. The Police, hardly dabbling in degrees of the unexpected,

Journey To The Centre Of The Cramps

presented a farcical imitation of their *Rock Goes To College* thing – several people clapped, but then, I suppose someone has to. The Cramps were enough to restore faith in the most spiritless. They have it all, and their drummer is the most compelling in rock history."

Following a further eight shows that had the Cramps zig-zagging up and down the country in support of the Police, and included two showcases at London's Lyceum ballroom, Miles Copeland made good on the second part of his initial agreement with the group by issuing *Gravest Hits* on Illegal Records. In addition to rounding up the group's two Vengeance singles, the 45 rpm 12-inch also included a bonus cut in the form of a haunting cover of 'Lonesome Town', which had been a Top 10 US chart hit for Lux's hero Ricky Nelson in 1958. Like the other four tracks, 'Lonesome Town' had been recorded by Alex Chilton at Ardent in 1977, and the sparse, reverb-laden production bears comparison with some of the material found on Chilton/Big Star's *Third* LP. A departure from the Cramps' customarily high-octane approach to adapting classic rock'n'roll, 'Lonesome Town' got the David Lynch treatment, as Nelson's gently crooned original is mutated into something menacing, with Lux's fairly faithful reproduction of Nelson's delivery juxtaposed against a radical rearrangement that reduces Nick's drums to a heartbeat, while Ivy's repetition of the melodic motif is strafed by discordant shards launched across Bryan's crepuscular backdrop. While it initially shifted only in moderate quantities, *Gravest Hits* provided many Cramps fans with their introduction to the band. Reissued around a dozen times, the EP sold steadily for several years, briefly returning to the independent chart as late as 1983, around the same time its five tracks were included on IRS' *...Off The Bone* compilation. To support the release of *Gravest Hits*, the Cramps stayed on in England to play a series of smaller clubs that included more prestigious venues such as London's Nashville, Manchester's Factory and Eric's in Liverpool alongside the likes of York's Pop Club and the Rock Garden in Middlesbrough.

With these shows serving to further enhance the band's growing reputation, Ivy declared herself pleased with her introduction to gigging in the UK, noting that, "We were fortunate that we got the tour and were

How The Weird Can Get Started In Recording

critically acclaimed." Being far more compact than the US, it was possible for the Cramps to make an impact very quickly, as the intensive nature of the weekly music press and the influence of disc jockey John Peel's BBC Radio show was able to spread the word nationally almost overnight. "I'm not surprised English kids like us. We're very, very American and English people have always found that exotic," Lux observed. "I think the English scene is real great. I really like that a lot. I think it's great the kids are back to rebelling again. I'm sure it's time we need that sort of thing. The bands in New York all sound different. They're all going in different directions. There isn't a lot of unity in New York like there is in London."

Certainly, the mostly positive press and the unpretentious nature of the audiences the Cramps encountered in England was the complete opposite of the way in which the group had been ignored and marginalised by New York's hip elite two-and-a-half years earlier. "Americans think we're too silly," Ivy asserted. "In England it seems like rock'n'roll is a religion, but in America they just think, 'Oh, that's just rock'n'roll.' And they're mystified by us in America too. A lot of writers are. They don't understand what we're doing, so they attack it. It's a natural reaction to attack what you don't understand."

'Scratchy' Myers caught up with the band he'd been knocked out by at the Palladium in February, DJ-ing for the Cramps at the Marquee. "I also put up with the Police, who I loathe, so that I could do the Lyceum shows with them," he recalls. "I was already a fan of the Nuggets-type garage bands, but the Cramps' love of an even trashier aesthetic unearthed a much deeper treasure trove of sounds that I'd previously not come across. It was they who led me to great forgotten rock'n'roll antiheroes like Andre Williams, the hillbilly and garage caterwauling of Dave 'Diddle' Day or the Trashmen and put masterful one-offs like Ronnie Cook & the Gaylads 'Goo Goo Muck' on my turntables. And I want to thank them for that."

By 1979, the British equivalent of CBGB's original coterie of hierarchically inclined, credibility-conscious hipsters had moved away from the punk scene and were now either busying themselves carving out careers in the industry, or mining history's dressing up box at clubs such as Billy's and Blitz as the new romantic scene gathered its achingly self-conscious

Journey To The Centre Of The Cramps

momentum. In turn, this meant that the rock'n'roll-derived strain of punk's legacy had been embraced by the ubiquitous kids on the street, who were generally far more concerned about having a good time than they were with scoring credibility points with their peers. This suited the Cramps just fine, as Nick Kent surmised in his high-profile *New Musical Express* feature on the group, "The Cramps are out on their own but their music has spiritual connections with similar maverick and under-marketed works by the likes of the incredible Roky Erickson and Captain Beefheart. And more than anything else, these outfits are creating a new music that doesn't need to rely on synthesizers and all manner of self-conscious crap to be termed 'no wave'. I truly hope they break out and shake things up before rock gets swallowed by this Orwellian wishful thinking jive."

The critical enthusiasm that had greeted the Cramps' first visit to Britain (and had included front page coverage in *Melody Maker* and *NME*) provided Miles Copeland with sufficient encouragement to sign the band to an album deal. From Ivy's perspective, this represented another box ticked on the path to mainstream success. "We're shooting for the limit – we don't want to be a cult band. I consider us a totally commercial band. It's a matter of bending people our way. It's not doing what they already have and want more of, yet it's equally commercial," she declared. "We don't want to be huge in a Madison Square Garden sense, but huge value-wise. We went to become unforgettable. Gene Vincent was never huge, but in a way he's the biggest," added Lux.

Like the Ramones, who had the bulk of their first three albums written and road-tested before they recorded their eponymous debut, the Cramps' corpus of available material had reached such proportions that there was a wealth of songs available from which they could select tracks for inclusion on their first album. "We've been playing for three years and we're still playing the same songs with basically the same arrangements," Lux explained. "We may have added a lead guitar here or there, but we haven't changed our sound in three years and I don't really expect us to change in the next three years. Because we're biased, and the music we listen to all the time, and the music we listen to when we're driving in the car or when we're sitting at home, is not what is coming out today. I'm

How The Weird Can Get Started In Recording

always listening, but I don't hear much stuff I like." So far as Lux was concerned, recording an album simply presented the Cramps with an opportunity to continue doing their own thing. "I don't believe in musical progress, I think that's crap," he insisted. "To say that there's some kind of standards that I have to live up to because the rock audience has decided we must do something is a load of crap. I don't have to do anything I don't want to do. We're all doing what we enjoy and a lot of people enjoy what we're doing. So we're gonna keep on doing it."

Having little interest in tinkering with the formula they had been fine tuning since the band's inception, the Cramps opted to continue having Alex Chilton handle their production. "We had already promised Alex that we would do it with him when we finally did get some kind of record deal," explained Lux. Unsurprisingly, Chilton again chose to record the Cramps in his hometown of Memphis. However, rather than book into Ardent Studios, the decision was taken to hold the album sessions at Sun. "I think it makes them feel good to be in Memphis, down here where all the music that they have collected for so long and liked so much came from. I think that being here in Sam's studio makes them feel great," Chilton reasoned. "There was a feeling in that studio. That's why we did it there, to get away from the music business," said Ivy. "Sam Phillips is wonderful, I mean he's really responsible for that sound and he wasn't just a businessman, he was the recording engineer at those sessions. He was the one who recognised that something special was happening. There's a very famous recording of him with Jerry Lee Lewis, where Jerry Lee Lewis wants to stop recording in the studio because he's also very religious, he says 'I can't do this, this is the devil's music' – it's a very famous conversation and you hear Sam Phillips speaking over the speaker to him, convincing him that it's worth doing and it's not a contradiction to his religion to do this 'devil's music'."

Like Ivy, Lux was similarly enthusiastic about recording in the cradle of rock'n'roll. "It had to be an inspiration for us. In the South, rockabilly has overtones of fire and brimstone. It's a fusion of country, R&B and holy-roller fundamentalism, the same way it was for Elvis. Those people drink strychnine and handle snakes and they also play Stratocasters – those

Journey To The Centre Of The Cramps

are their rites. We're coming from another territory, that's all," he explained. "We used Sam Phillips' studio because it's very basic and very cheap," added Nick. "The wooden walls and sound-screens suit our sound well."

Given that the Cramps were recording a set of songs that had been in a state of readiness for some time, accompanied by a producer with whom they were familiar and in a studio environment that they found inspirational and suited to their technicalities, it would be logical to imagine that the progress would be brisk. However, in keeping with the kind of misfortune that would resurface intermittently throughout their career and which Lux described as an "Egyptian curse", getting the album down on tape kept the band off the road until August, when they left Alex to get on with the mixes before America forgot who they were.

Much of the blame for the delays can be laid at Chilton's door. "Regardless of what you may have heard about him, he really is completely totally out of his mind," revealed Lux. "We kept having to wake him up all the time because he was too stoned to stay awake . . . It cost us $18,000 to record, but that was Alex Chilton – he goes to Paris by way of China."

Often in an addled state, Chilton embraced a whimsical form of perfectionism, making the group record multiple takes in the hope of capturing something unspecified that only the producer was apparently able to discern. "Chilton made us do the songs over and over again until my singing got bad enough that he would accept it. He just kept us going as long as he could," recalled Lux. "Why not?" added Ivy. "He figured the longer it took to make the record, the longer he had a job to work – I'm not kidding!" In addition to Alex's idiosyncratic methods, the Cramps found themselves in the frustrating position of having to return to square one after a technical hitch rendered the first batch of songs useless. "We were plagued with bad engineers. The first one – we'd just had four days of performances that were really hot and then he discovered that all the tapes had distortion on them."

Once the Cramps had again recorded the songs to Chilton's satisfaction, the mixing process opened up a whole other can of worms deriving, in

How The Weird Can Get Started In Recording

part, from the poor relationship between Sun's studio engineers and the wigged-out producer – who threw out one mix that nobody else could see anything wrong with. "We did the backing tracks in about five days, but it took three months to do the mixing," explained Bryan. "We couldn't find any engineer that could work with Alex. They wouldn't let him touch the board cos they're the engineer. We didn't get any respect by the studio. They'd look at us like we weren't a serious recording act. They wouldn't really cater to us," Ivy recounted. "The mixing was a problem too cos we couldn't get any engineers that could stand to listen to this music. They'd sit there and say, 'How can you listen to this distortion all day?' And any time Alex wanted to put his hands on the board to move the faders, it was 'How dare you?'"

With the album scheduled for a September release and a string of gigs booked for August, band and producer resolved to cut out the middlemen and take a form of direct action. "We finally threw out all the engineers and Alex, Ivy and I went in, did all the plugging in of cords, all the engineering. What we came up with is probably an engineer's nightmare," remembered Lux. "That's part of the Cramps – nothing's a big deal. Recording studios aren't a big deal. Technology isn't a big deal. Today, most things are like exercises in technology. It seems like a real bad period right now. People don't make good things any more."

Even at the very end of the extended recording and mixing marathon, it seemed that Alex was still searching for that indiscernible (by anyone else, at any rate) *something*. "We had the album done, in exactly the form you hear it in now if you go buy a copy at a record shop, and we were all going, 'Oh yeah, great!'" recounted Ivy. "But Alex is never happy with anything, so the night before it was going to be mastered, he was calling us up and saying, 'Look, instead of paying me the rest of my advance, let's use it to re-record everything. We'll fly Nick and Bryan down here tonight, and I'll mix it at the same time we're recording it.'"

In the interests of their own sanity, the Cramps declined Chilton's generous offer and it came as something of a relief to the group when they resumed performing with their first US show since May with a one-off appearance at the Boomer Theatre in Norman, Oklahoma on August 2.

Journey To The Centre Of The Cramps

Despite their studio ordeal, both Lux and Ivy continued to enjoy spending time in the South. "It's a very soulful, very spiritual, very sexual place. As opposed to the North for instance. So the reality of the situation is different from what you hear people saying it is. Sometimes when people say 'hillbilly' it's one more snooty thing, where they say, 'Oh those hillbillies' describing someone as white trash, just because they're sincere people," observed Lux. "The Midwest in America is a lot worse than the South is. That movie, *Easy Rider*, has got people thinking that the south is just a bunch of stupid, horrible people. Yet segregation was mainly confronted in the South in the fifties and sixties – although it was everywhere in the country – not just in the South. Yet the South gets a bad rap for that."

The Cramps announced their return to the Union side of the Mason-Dixon Line with a show at the Bookie's Club 870 in Detroit on August 11. They then picked up where they'd left off in New York, coming back to Irving Plaza for a concert that was broadcast live on FM radio, and subsequently showed up on a number of bootlegs, as did recordings from the first of their two-night engagement at Club 57, which commenced the following evening. While the mixing of their debut album dragged on, it seemed that everybody with a tape recorder was taking advantage of the growing demand for Cramps songs. The group's Friday and Saturday night double header at Philadelphia's Hot Club toward the end of the month (which saw support from Destroy All Monsters, whose line-up included former Stooge Ron Asheton) also later fell prey to the bootleggers. With further delays caused by studio payment issues and Chilton working on his own material, the release of the forthcoming album was put back to January. As a means of keeping the pot bubbling while these issues were resolved, Miles Copeland despatched the Cramps for a national tour supporting the Buzzcocks on a bill that also featured British agit-rockers Gang of Four that coincided with the US release of *Gravest Hits*. Copeland had licensed the Buzzcocks' *Singles Going Steady* compilation and the Cramps joined the tour for much of its run, in addition to fitting in some gigs supporting Iggy Pop, the Clash and the Police during October and November. After a break the following month, they resumed gigging with the Buzzcocks at the start of December, wrapping up their

How The Weird Can Get Started In Recording

most intensive year of touring with a show at the Stardust Club in Los Angeles, two weeks before Christmas.

1979 had been a remarkable year for the Cramps, they'd toured at home and abroad, increased their following and established a reputation as a spectacular live act and signed a record deal. However, the year had one final kick in it: "At the end of December, Alex told us we needed to remix it cos the drums were out of phase, which means you can hear them on each side but as soon as you walk into the centre of it, they disappear. And, as we had time, we presented them with a plan which would only delay the release by two weeks." Illegal rejected this plan on account of the difficulties it would present in marketing the disc and organising tours to support it at relatively short notice. Instead, early the following year the label announced that Chilton had finally reached the end of his mixing desk odyssey and that the album was now mastered for a March release, with tours of the UK, Europe and North America to follow.

CHAPTER EIGHT

The Bad Stuff

I turn into a werewolf when I go onstage. I think that's who I really am, not this.

Lux Interior

It's like the damned playing for the doomed.

Sting

JUST over a year after the Cramps had first encountered Miles Copeland in Los Angeles, the IRS and Illegal Records founder released their debut album on both sides of the Atlantic. The long-awaited arrival of *Songs The Lord Taught Us* was accompanied by a succession of single releases that teamed 'Garbageman' with a variety of tracks. Whereas in the UK, Illegal issued the Cramps' rockin' endorsement of the trash aesthetic as a double A-side that also featured the band's insidious cover of Eddie Cooley and Otis Blackwell's 1956 standard 'Fever', the US edition matched 'Garbageman' with 'Drug Train', a cut not included on the album that had developed from 'Twist And Shout'. A further French pressing saw 'Drug Train' supplanted by 'TV Set'. With these singles coinciding with the tours Copeland had set up in support of the new LP, it seemed as if there was a sudden glut of Cramps vinyl emerging from the Faulty Products empire.

With the exception of 'Fever', a track ill-suited to the ebullient nature of the Cramps' live set, the remainder of the sonic coven of 13 songs included on *Songs The Lord Taught Us* was drawn from the band's established set list. In addition to road-tested favourites such as 'I'm Cramped',

The Bad Stuff

'TV Set', 'Sunglasses After Dark' and 'The Mad Daddy', tracks culled from the fringes of the band's substantial corpus of songs also made the cut. These included 'Zombie Dance', a twisted, churning satire on the way in which New York's hip elite had been too cool to cut a rug even when confronted by a band that made them want to dance, and 'Rock On The Moon', Jimmy Stewart's 1959 space-age cut. The Cramps' escape-velocity adaptation of the original featured some impressively well picked lead from Ivy, while the sultry sax found on Stewart's cut is replaced by Bryan's white noise excursions. Including 'Rock On The Moon', *Songs The Lord Taught Us* included four fully accredited cover versions ('Sunglasses After Dark' being credited to Lux and Ivy as well as Link Wray and Dwight Pullen) and three tracks that referenced material from the fifties and sixties: 'I Was A Teenage Werewolf' drew upon the Shades' sax-infused instrumental 'Strollin' After Dark', 'What's Behind The Mask' subverted Dale Hawkins' 'Tornado' and 'I'm Cramped' revisited another instrumental adorned by a lead saxophone, the Busters' 1963 surf hit 'Bust Out'. "We don't get ideas from regular sources," explained Ivy. "We'll get ideas for guitar parts from the saxophone parts on a record, things that aren't obvious. I love sax, you know? We've never had one in our band, but I love sax. I don't *play* sax, but I like it as much as guitar to listen to, like fifties rock'n'roll, the really obnoxious kind of sax."

The manner in which the balance of *Songs The Lord Taught Us* tilted toward material that had been drawn from Lux and Ivy's ever expanding collection of classic rock'n'roll served to reinforce the ideas presented within the lyrics of 'Garbageman': the Cramps adapted source material discarded by the mainstream of popular culture to construct something new and exciting while maintaining or enhancing the rebel spirit of those originals. "If we don't do these songs, nobody ever will. Nobody will know what great songs came out back then. If some revival band does the songs nobody will pay attention to it," asserted Lux. "I'm just hoping we will bring attention to that. 'Wow! What a weird song – you sure you didn't write it? It sure sounds like you did. Who the hell could have written that?' And then they'll find out who did."

However, this imbalance between new and secondary material was not

Journey To The Centre Of The Cramps

entirely to the liking of the band, who expressed a degree of discontent about the way that Alex Chilton had selected 'Rock On The Moon' and the cover of the Sonics' 'Strychnine' rather than 'Drug Train' because he didn't think it fitted in. Similarly, despite Chilton's multiple attempts to mix the album to his satisfaction, Ivy felt that the Memphis maverick had failed to completely capture the group's raw essence. "Even though the production on that is fascinating, it didn't showcase the Cramps for what we are – which is a tough rock'n'roll band," she insisted. "It didn't get what we do live, which is rock. It didn't really capture that. It definitely had a creepy atmosphere, and that has a certain kind of appeal to it."

The breadth of this appeal manifested as the album made a more than respectable impact on the UK Independent Chart, where it spent 18 weeks, climbing to the top spot in the process. The British single release of 'Fever' fared less well, hitting number 12 in an Indie Chart topped by Birmingham pop-reggae combo UB40. The British press maintained their enthusiasm for the Cramps with the already converted Paul Rambali leading the charge to praise the album. "Play this record and you step into the twilight zone," he enthused in *NME*. "The Cramps are an entity unto themselves and the normal rules don't apply . . . Get this album while it's still warm and let a loud, depraved influence into your life." *Melody Maker*'s Penny Kiley was similarly keen, describing the Cramps as "an isolated pocket of brilliance in a directionless world", before adding that "covers and originals are so much in sympathy with each other that the only distinction lies in the subject matter", while David Hepworth praised the "aggression and savage wit" of the band's "demented debut set" in *Smash Hits*, where he also observed that, "The Cramps sound like a haunted jukebox cranking out voodoo rock'n'roll that fairly rattles with intensity."

Back home, *Creem*'s Robert A Hull also highlighted the way that the Cramps adapted their influences: "What's so captivating about this band is their willingness to junk everything (musical ability, the record's mix, fame and fortune) in favour of the elusive shudder of primitive rock'n'roll. With the discernment of genuine trash aesthetes, they combine the sloppy ineptitude of a mid-sixties garage band with the mental derangement of an

The Bad Stuff

American rockabilly Dixie-fryer." In common with a number of other reviewers, Hull also drew specific attention to the Cramps' evocation of horror movies: "Along with their image, the Cramps' musical carnage is explicitly concerned with horrific content," he noted. Wary of seeing the band labelled as some kind of horror-rock novelty act, Lux was quick to address the media's emphasis upon this perception of the Cramps. "We all dig horror movies, but I don't want that to get out of hand. Some songs we write are based on that but it has to do with American culture and we're not trying for that image. People have also called us a rockabilly band and that's not completely true either. We have also been accused of being comedy, of being a parody, just because I say some unfunny lines onstage." Although the Cramps' dark humour represented an aspect of the horror tradition that infuses a hefty slice of the genre's cinematic history, the manner in which rock'n'roll had been sanitised and traduced in films and on television also served to generate misconceptions about where the Cramps were coming from. "Our show onstage has given people the wrong impression," observed Lux. "It's kind of an intense thing. Some people tend to look at it as comical and theatrical, but it's just rock'n'roll. If those same people saw Jerry Lee Lewis in 1957, they would have said he was comical and theatrical."

The frontman was also less than thrilled by the manner in which IRS had allowed A&M to promote the album in the States: "They described us as 'a cult new wave band' who'd just recorded an album in Nashville. That really insulted us. Apart from the fact that we made the record in Memphis, to be labelled a cult group is so horrible, it implies an elitism that we don't want." Despite these niggles, Lux remained committed to his and Ivy's avowed mission in life. "I can't see us making a lot of money out of this, but that's not the point," he observed. "I wouldn't choose to do any other thing. I think the hottest thing you could be in the universe is to be in a rock'n'roll band. If rock is dead then I don't care because we're unaware of it. If it's dead then I don't care to convert the people who think it's dead. If they get converted and listen to our music that's great, but we don't care to convert anybody. We're not championing any cause; we just do what we like to do and the only thing we know how to do."

Journey To The Centre Of The Cramps

Similarly upbeat, Ivy declared herself pleased that the long-delayed album had finally seen the light of day: "I don't think *Songs The Lord Taught Us* could have come out on another label. I think most of the major companies would have tried to place us with a producer who'd try to give us a sound that'd sell."

The Cramps arrived back in the UK in early March, kicking off their trans-continental tour with a show at London's King's College that immediately demonstrated that their previous visit and the subsequent dissemination of *Gravest Hits* had gained them the kind of wild following that was wholly in keeping with the Cramps' untamed spirit. Reviewing the show in the following week's *NME*, Neil Norman noted that "before they were halfway through their third number, 'Caveman', the crowd had turned into a pulsating blob; weaving, jumping and spilling onto the stage despite the efforts of the hapless student bouncers." At times, this enthusiasm went a little too far, as the small King's College stage was repeatedly invaded by growing numbers of attention seekers vying for a moment under the lights. Lux scarcely seemed to notice, getting down to his underpants while delivering the set's final songs without dropping a stitch. "I was having a real good time up there," he recounted. "It was out of control and it was fun. But then I'd think to myself, 'Oooh, there's these people out there that can't see what's going on and they can't hear it' cos people are standing in front of the amplifiers. And I'd keep going back and forth like that."

The touring party then headed north for concerts in Liverpool and Leeds, before a late-starting show at Nottingham Boat Club that saw Lux tear down chunks of the ceiling and *NME*'s Lynn Hanna declare: "The Cramps have stripped down sound to rock's garish dawn and then pulverised it so that past and present implode to produce a primal, fiery, perverted progeny." After a gig at Sheffield's Limit Club on March 11, the Cramps took a day off before crossing the border to make a return visit to Scotland, where they had made their British debut nine months earlier. Instead of playing the larger Edinburgh Odeon as they had while supporting the Police, the Cramps' second time in Scotland's capital saw them appear at the Astoria, where the vigorous nature of those who had

The Bad Stuff

gathered to mainline rock'n'roll's sweet nectar caused the anxious club owner to attempt to cut the power. To the delight of the crowd and the dismay of the straining bouncers, Lux fended him off.

Support for the Cramps was provided by Manchester mavericks the Fall, who at the time were operating under the Faulty Products umbrella, having had several singles issued on Miles Copeland's Step Forward label, before decamping to Rough Trade in mid-1980. The two groups had elements in common – the Fall's mainstay Mark E. Smith was also a rockabilly and garage enthusiast, which the band mutated into new forms of their own devising. After the Edinburgh show, Smith – in typically blunt fashion – took Lux aside to advise him that he, "Shouldn't bother with all that Kiss theatrical shit. You don't need it." This hardly went down well with the Cramps' frontman, not least because it attacked the very core of the band's determination to put on a show. "How can anyone tell me it's theatrical? I'm sorry that we used the stage. That's what the stage is for. I admit we're still in love with a nonsense life, that we're remnants from a time we took acid and never came down, but I hate making sense all the time," he raged.

From the Cramps' perspective, the notion of putting on a show did not mitigate against any kind of authenticity, whereas the Fall's approach to rock'n'roll came wrapped in an avowedly anti-fashion, do-it-yourself aesthetic that had its roots in aspects of the UK punk scene. "Don't you think all that shit sounds synthetic?" retorted Ivy. "Have you ever heard a voice like Lux Interior, besides Lux Interior? No. That's a real person and not synthetic . . . It's going back to something real. Real rock'n'roll – that's what we take seriously." Just as Jerry Lee, Little Richard or Elvis dressed flash and acted cool as part of an overall performance, the Cramps' live show represented the visual counterpart to the way that the group adapted classic rock'n'roll. The idea of there being any kind of hierarchical separation between band and audience was anathema to Lux, who was demonstrating this, up close and personal, on a nightly basis. "When we go onstage wearing rhinestones and gold paisley jackets, and things like that, it's not saying, 'We're stars and we're better than you so we get dressed up.' It's saying, 'We're all stars and you can get dressed up too and

Journey To The Centre Of The Cramps

everybody is in this together.' A lot of people know we never played instruments before, so it's saying 'Anyone can do this'," he explained. "I think those people who accuse us of putting on this show, or something like that, are people whose lives are so boring that they think no one could be like this."

While punk had introduced notions of authenticity and credibility that had gained currency with certain bands, journalists and fans, so far as the Cramps were concerned this was a moot point – they weren't attempting to *be* anything, they were simply being themselves. "They think that people don't really act like this and that there's nothing natural about acting this way. They can't conceive that it could be for somebody," observed Ivy. "I see somebody walking down the street in a brown three-piece suit or something, or any kind of stereotype you like, it looks fantastic to me," added Lux. "I can't believe that someone's life is actually like that. To me that's fantastic, that someone could be that boring."

After three more gigs that exposed Scotland as a hotbed of fervour toward the Cramps, the touring party (which also included new wave synth combo Fàshiön Music, who'd signed to IRS the previous year) headed marginally closer to the equator with a trio of shows in the major population centres of Manchester, Birmingham and London. The UK leg of the tour wrapped up with a gig at Derby's Ajanta Theatre, where the Cramps were supported by Gloucester punks the Dead Airmen, cult combo 23 Jewels from nearby Nottingham and local alternative outfit Egyptian Kings. In just over a fortnight, the Cramps had further enhanced both their reputation and their following (a dynamic that would be further progressed by the formation of a UK fan club, the Legion of the Cramped, the following month) and seen *Songs The Lord Taught Us* spread the lord's word further as it ascended the Independent Chart.

"I liked England, but every time we play there I'd get cuts all over my body and they'd turn green," revealed Lux. "They turn off the water at 11 o'clock at night, in every hotel, from the best to the crummiest – I don't know why. When I'd come offstage, I'd look like Al Jolson – covered in black from head to toe. That, coupled with the cuts gets me infected every time. Scotland was even worse. When we played in Glasgow, we went to

The Bad Stuff

a hospital to try and get some antibiotics, and there were all these cops over there going, 'Hmmmm . . . how did you get like this?' We'd look out in the waiting room and there were the fans who'd gotten smashed up from being in the first row. I said, 'Just give me some antibiotics and let me take a shower,' and they told me, 'If we let you take one, then everybody'll want one.' And this was a hospital."

Aside from the NHS' reluctance to allow bleeding rock'n'rollers to freshen up on their premises and an aversion to Mark E Smith's singular brand of pep talks, the only other aspect of the successful tour that Lux found disagreeable was the way in which the vibrant nature of the British live circuit came to resemble a conveyer belt once one was aboard it. "You begin to feel that you're in a slot," he explained. "Somebody lines up 30 dates and you go play them. Yours is the next group at Wally's Fish Bar, the one after 999 and before XTC. I liked being able to do things like play at mental institutions, but now we're working with people who just know how to set up normal things."

Before leaving England, the group took the opportunity to film a promo clip for 'Garbageman', appropriately enough in a crypt, near Shepperton Studios, where many of the Hammer and Amicus horror features were made. The simple, quickly shot footage is surprisingly effective, depicting the band lurking menacingly within the crypt's ground, and features an irresistible performance from Lux, who comes across like some manner of crazed preacher.

The following week provided Lux with the novelty of visiting France for the first time, where the Cramps played half a dozen shows that demonstrated their popularity had spread across the channel onto the European mainland. "They act like it's Saturday night and they just got paid," enthused Ivy. "I think they do, oddly enough, understand the background of our music. Europeans seem to know more about American culture than Americans do, so they recognise the roots that are influencing our music. Whereas maybe Americans just judge it for the moment, and that's cool."

As the band racked up the miles around France, crammed into their rental van, Bryan studied such esoteric literature as George Hay's *Necronomicon: The Book Of Dead Names* and Lux formed ideas about the

Journey To The Centre Of The Cramps

specific nature of the European mindset: "In Europe – I mean the rest of Europe more than England – I felt that there's always the threat of war and of being vulnerable to war. America wasn't really hurt by the war – Europe was gutted. People there seem to have more of a sense of what they are, and how short life is, or whatever. They had a different attitude towards appreciating things. It's just a totally different attitude about life altogether." Looking at European attitudes from a perspective originating on the eastern side of the Atlantic, Barry 'Scratchy' Myers observes, "I think we need to consider something that for us, in Europe, came second-hand, was an integral part of growing up in the teenage culture of the States during the fifties and sixties. Where the UK punk scene came out of the clash between our love of rootsy rock'n'roll and the realities of our socio-political-economic situation, the bands that emerged across the pond, like the Ramones who were perfectly encapsulated in the cartoon-style of John Holmstrom, the raucous poetry of Patti Smith and the Cramps' gore-fest, were quintessentially American."

Like the English, the French had taken groups such as the New York Dolls – who were largely overlooked in their home country – to their hearts. France also had its own punk scene, with groups such as Metal Urbain and Stinky Toys emerging to make an impact overseas. This was all part of a healthy rock'n'roll subculture that was particularly evident in Paris. "It's great, we seem to have something that they want over there," declared Lux. "I think it's just the fact that we're very American and we all love America and this is real American music we play and they've loved that for years over there in France. You go into any mall in France and all the Gene Vincent, Eddie Cochran albums are in stock, right now, in any big record chain stores. I think all the people from Holland and France came over here in about 1964 and took all the rockabilly records back to Europe with them."

The Cramps also benefitted from a healthy slice of media attention, with Paris' *Rock And Folk* magazine subsequently running a feature that served to enhance the group's legend. "We have this really good friend Philippe Garnier and he used to write for *Rock And Folk* magazine. Later on he became a writer about films, but in an article there, as a metaphor he

152

The Bad Stuff

called me 'daughter of Duane Eddy' and people took it literally and they thought I was Duane Eddy's daughter – I loved it. I didn't say anything," explains Ivy. "They believed it," added Lux. "So we've been feeding that over there and a lot of people think she is."

The Cramps then travelled across the Italian border for a trio of gigs supporting the Police in the north of the country that provided both groups with a graphic introduction to the nature of local crowds and the methods used to control them. Covering the concert for *Melody Maker*, Allan Jones described the scenes as Lux attempted to face down 10,000 baying Police fans at Milan's Palalido on April 2: "An orange bounces off Lux Interior's forehead and the Cramps' singer dives into the crowd. Someone bites a chunk out of his shoulder, hands claw at his naked back. He's thrown back onstage, covered in blood. The audience want nothing to do with him. More fruit flies at the stage, splattering against the equipment." This failed to amuse Police guitarist Andy Summers, whose main concern was for his group's expensively assembled amplification. As Lux disappeared under yet another barrage of missiles, Summers complained, "This is absolutely marvellous – we pay a fucking fortune for the best PA we can assemble, hand it over to this shower and watch it reduced to ashes before we even get to use it." The following night's concert at the Palasport in Reggio Emilia ended up in a full blown riot as fans who had forced entry into the arena were tear-gassed by armed police who also attacked them with batons and shields. A third Italian concert, in Turin, passed off without any major civil unrest as the group played before an estimated 16,000 people for a show that was broadcast live on local radio.

The Cramps wrapped up their debut European jaunt with a short burst of one-off shows that included a gig in Brussels and a return to London for a concert at the Venue in Victoria billed as 'The Last Supper', which saw them supported by locally based garage rockers the Barracudas and climaxed with Lux, who'd stripped down to his leather briefs, diving off the stage onto a table of record label executives, sending glasses and bottles flying in the process. Excerpts from the Cramps' performance later surfaced on a bootleg EP, most notable for the inclusion of the band's version of 'Louie Louie'.

Journey To The Centre Of The Cramps

After a short break and a warm-up gig at Club 57 in New York, the Cramps kicked off the final, US section of their tour with two shows at the Whisky. These were followed by concerts in San Francisco and Berkeley, after which Bryan Gregory unexpectedly quit the group. "We smoked opium. I said goodnight, went to bed, and next morning he was gone," recounted Lux. In addition to leaving the group without a founding member, Bryan's moonlight flit also deprived the Cramps of much of their equipment, which Gregory apparently drove away with. Although the nature of his departure was unexpected, it soon became evident that he had been becoming increasingly detached from the collective dynamic for some time. Part of this stemmed from his own insecurities, which were amplified considerably by his increasing use of heroin. With Nick also having something of a junk habit, this served to create the kind of tensions within the band that customarily arise whenever folks opt to shift their focus toward shooting up. This, combined with a tendency to become beguiled by whatever the latest trend happened to be, led to his progressive disengagement from the rock'n'roll mission as defined by the group's other two founding members. "What wasn't known publicly was at that point we wanted to finish off the tour and then say no more Cramps," revealed Ivy. "We had a hopped-up vision of the Cramps and we weren't changing – and still haven't – but he was."

Bryan's carefully constructed badass public image belied the fact that he was prone to oversensitivity. "I told him some day his insecurity was gonna be the end of it all," recounted Lux. "The first time he came over to our house, the buzzer didn't work, so he thought we weren't answering the door on purpose, pretending we weren't home." This was not a characteristic that combines well with any kind of serious junk habit, and it's easy to see how Gregory was prone to becoming paranoid. Additionally, he saw himself as a superstar in the making and having decided that performing feats of sonic alchemy with base material inspired by early rock'n'roll and garage rock was probably not going to help him achieve his due status, he began looking to switch direction. "He was really grossed out by us. He kept saying, 'Don't you want to make it, don't you really want to make it?' It was all fashion to him," recalled Ivy. "Bryan always

The Bad Stuff

thought of himself as the new Brian Jones," observed Lux. "He collected pictures of him, idolised him. His whole thing was pretending to be Brian Jones. I once told him that Bryan Gregory was bigger than Brian Jones, because he was alive. But he just wasn't satisfied being Bryan Gregory."

Given that the nature of the Cramps as defined by Lux and Ivy was pretty much non-negotiable, any suggestions from Bryan concerning stylistic changes would have been futile and antagonistic. "He wanted us to do political songs because at that time the Clash had *Sandinista* out and they were big," said Lux. "This is somebody that couldn't read a label on a bottle of ketchup, but he thought this was what you do to make money." Bryan's penchant for latching on to the next big thing indicates a certain degree of suggestibility on his part. "Whoever Bryan was hanging out with, he would listen to and believe what they said," Lux explained. "In the final analysis, Bryan didn't understand us; he didn't know what was going on in our heads and it freaked him out. I tried to be his friend for as long as I could. I was for a long time but he just got to hanging around with individuals who were doing too many different kinds of things and he just didn't know what was going on any more. We would never do anything to Bryan. He just got paranoid about everyone around him." Bryan's developing interest in the occult could also be interpreted as in keeping with his suggestible, faddish mindset. While his malevolent stage presence served to stoke a mystique that added additional menace to the Cramps' overall image, it was basically an act. In person, Bryan was socially awkward, quietly spoken, bitchy and slightly camp. Ivy had already observed that "he was more girl than me", while former *Melody Maker* editor Allan Jones recalls Gregory whispering "growl for me" into his ear. While his 'nun's bones' necklace inspired a roaring trade in similar jewellery constructed from leftover chicken remains among the stalls of Kensington Market, Bryan was an unlikely magus. "It was a bunch of crap. At the time, the record company thought he was going to have a solo career, so they were making up all this stuff about him being a witch. I mean, he can't even read. It's very difficult to be a witch if you can't read," asserted Lux. "There is no way you can read those books he was reading, that black magic stuff, and be into the temporary rock'n'roll anti-culture

Journey To The Centre Of The Cramps

that the Cramps is all about. He just didn't understand what the band was about in the end."

With Bryan's focus flitting between ideas of becoming the next Brian Jones, the new Mick Jones, or another Jim Jones, while simultaneously feeling increasingly paranoid and alienated, he began to struggle with life as a Cramp. A couple of months touring overseas in the constant company of the group scarcely served to improve matters. "He despised touring because of his fear and hatred of foreigners. He thought rockabilly was goofy, but said we made it work for us 'cos you're so weird,'" explained Ivy. "We went into the studio to record 'Voodoo Idol' in England as our next single and when we got to the studio he couldn't remember how to play the song. We've been doing that song almost two years and he forgot how to play it." While in England, Bryan's paranoia was further stoked by the intensive nature of the music press. "He was afraid to read our press clippings in Europe," confirmed Lux. "In England when the paper said 'Bryan was visibly shaken' [in reference to an audience stage invasion] he got scared and stopped reading our press. He didn't know what he was playing onstage, we were doing 'Human Fly' during a soundcheck and the part where he comes in with a bunch of distorted noise, well he's just strumming two strings – he didn't even remember how to play. He didn't like us, he didn't like the sound we had, he had no idea what was going on. He was just burning incense and listening to the Pretenders."

With Bryan requiring regular encouragement to play his guitar leads and showing signs of turning into the Cramps' very own Syd Barrett, his relationship with occultist Andrella Canne provided another source of friction. "He was just stupid. He chose between a girl and the band," declared Lux. "Without a passion for and understanding of the fundamental forces influencing the Cramps, a combination of too much hard work, chemical haze and backstage leeches drove him to the next bright, shiny object in his path," Ivy explained. Stating his case in the October edition of *New York Rocker*, Bryan rejected Lux and Ivy's observations: "They're trying to say that, but they don't know how I felt a year or so prior to even meeting her. Things were pulling away personality-wise within the band for a long time. They wanted Nick out too. They tried to kick him out

The Bad Stuff

twice, but I didn't want Nick to be kicked out and there were frictions with that."

Once back in the States, it seems probable that with another lengthy spell on the road with the group stretching before him, Bryan experienced some kind of anxiety attack, panicked and fled. "I know what happened to him at that point was that he didn't have the integrity that we have about rock'n'roll and what the Cramps are all about," stated Ivy. "He liked the initial energy of the band, like when we were first playing CBGB and it was just fun, but he just began taking himself so seriously and wanting us to become a heavy, serious thing." From Bryan's point of view, the Cramps simply hadn't got big fast enough to satisfy his ambitions. "When we started that many years ago, we were way ahead, but we kept missing and everyone else kept catching up. We were out way before the B-52s, but two weeks later they got signed and their record is out," he explained. "I just got to feeling that I was in just another band, one of many. It just seemed that if we didn't get pushed all the way then it wouldn't be worth it and there wasn't enough pushing."

Whereas Lux interpreted Bryan's ambition as a desire to get rich quick – "Like a lot of people, he got a little bit of success and it went straight to his head and he just wanted to get rich – that's all he thought about" – Bryan's conviction that the Cramps' continuing adherence to their rock'n'roll mission was inhibiting his rise to stardom led him to cite the careworn 'musical differences' as the reason for his abscondment. "A lot had to do with taste in music. My tastes are changing, I started liking Public Image more than Johnny Burnette." In turn, this cut little ice with Ivy: "Eighty percent of that he never said to our face. That we were stuck in the fifties, or that we wouldn't let him listen to Iggy records – that was ridiculous. He was second guessing us in his head without saying anything," she declared. "Bryan was great for whatever he was, but he didn't really understand what we were doing," added Lux. "It bothered him and he would keep telling us that it bothered him."

Ultimately, Bryan's widening dislocation from the core ideas that made the Cramps what they were served to create a gulf between himself and Lux and Ivy, and as that widened, Gregory found being in the group

Journey To The Centre Of The Cramps

increasingly onerous. "There was a lot of ill feelings within the band, too much hostility toward each other and I didn't want to deal with that," he explained. "We were getting to the point where it was getting good, but it was no longer worth it. Our personalities had changed and I decided that I didn't want to do this for the next few years if everybody hated each other."

Reasonably enough, Bryan's chosen method of leaving the Cramps – disappearing in the dead of night while the group were on the road – left Lux and Ivy feeling let down and bitter. "He was just a money-grubbing creep, is what he turned into. He wasn't when we met him, he was just a kid," raged Lux. "He barely played on any of our records. I hate to destroy it for fans, but the guy was fighting us the whole time. He was a dumb glue-sniffer from Detroit, and that's all it amounts to. Not that I've got anything against glue-sniffers or Detroit." Ivy was equally forthright in expressing her anger, declaring that "I never want to see him again." However, despite the simmering rancour, Lux and Ivy's first reaction on discovering Bryan's disappearance had been one of concern. "We were freaked out when he first left on account of Brian Jones leaving the Rolling Stones," admitted Lux. "I was sure he was going to be on the bottom of a pool somewhere."

After the initial furore had died down and sufficient time had passed to enable more reflective opinions, both Lux and Ivy recognised that Bryan had played a unique role in their group. "I enjoyed the first line-up, which a lot of people love because Bryan was in the band," said Lux. "Actually, the Bryan and Nick Knox line-up wasn't the first, but I consider it the first line-up. They're all really great memories. Bryan could just do so many weird things. He was just such a weirdo at first. Later on, he became more of a rock star, unfortunately. But at first he'd go out onstage, fold himself up in the yoga lotus position, and run around on his knees. Then he'd spin around on one knee and jump into the audience, which was so dangerous. He really frightened people. That band was a real four-pronged attack."

"We had a brief, intense relationship, and I don't think any of us knew what hit us," observed Ivy. "At one time we all wanted to be in a band that people were afraid of offstage. He was a true DMF – Detroit Motherfucker."

The Bad Stuff

As the Cramps frantically tried to work out how they were going to fulfil their touring commitments without their one-man white noise maelstrom, IRS attempted a little damage limitation, capitalising on Gregory's mystique by implying that he had quit the band in order to join some manner of occult cabal. "A lot of that initial thing was hype from the record company, when they thought they still had him signed as a solo artist, and they were trying to hype a solo career because they thought he'd want to have one," Ivy explained. While this rumour and another that he had committed suicide turned out to be patent hokum, Bryan's ambitions of becoming a superstar were to remain unrealised. Having resurfaced to explain himself to *New York Rocker*, he became increasingly elusive, with rumours of him forming a band with ex-Dead Boy and fellow junk enthusiast Stiv Bators proving to be little more than speculation. In 1982, Gregory re-emerged in a band with the suitably Crowleyesque name of Beast, who also included Andrella on vocals. Featuring a sleeve photo that depicted Bryan wearing something akin to a cow-print body suit, Beast's debut single, 'Possessed', had little that distinguished it from the output of any number of goth rock bands that were around at the time. The following year's follow-up 'Love In A Dying World' was similarly unremarkable, and after a third single, 'New Moone', also failed to make any kind of impact, Bryan quit the group on the eve of a planned UK tour, leaving the rest of the band to form the Veil, another similar combo who released three singles and an album, *Surrender*, before breaking up in 1986.

In the wake of Bryan's departure, Lux and Ivy decided to move quickly. Rather than run the risk of losing a whole summer of gigs as they had two years ago after Miriam had left the group, and needing to re-book the tour's remaining shows to avoid becoming blacklisted or sued by promoters, they opted to take on a replacement on a temporary basis and make a final choice later. The band duly approached Julien Hechtlinger, the guitarist in New York punk combo the Mad. A more conventionally competent musician than her predecessor, Julien picked up the stage name of 'Grindsnatch' and quickly assimilated the basis of the Cramps' set, ensuring that the group were back in action by mid-July, resuming their delayed US tour with a show at JB Scott's in Albany, New York State.

159

Journey To The Centre Of The Cramps

Although Lux observed that, "Like a good Christian fuzztone rock'n'roller, she carries her weight," *New York Rocker* seemed less convinced of Julien's ability to adequately replace the charismatic Bryan Gregory: 'Strapped in the unenviable position of supplanting the person whose dripping sinisterness [*sic*] best embodied the Cramps image, the former member of the Mad was a visual shrug, barely drawing any eyes from the hold of Lux Interior, Ivy Rorschach and Knox. Although spewing occasional snatches of good white noise guitar, Julien's weary rendition of a Kate Pierson cum Alice Cooper black-eyed beachnik showed just how far her size seven foot has to grow to fill the size twelve boot vacated by Gregory.'

Julien remained a Cramp just long enough to fulfil the remaining 10 dates of their US tour. Despite her brief tenure with the group, she made it onto the big screen when footage of the Cramps' performance in Santa Monica was included in Miles Copeland's *Urgh! A Music War* movie. An unadorned compilation of live performances featuring a diverse selection of acts that included synth-poppers Orchestral Manoeuvres In The Dark and Wall Of Voodoo, and British reggae groups Steel Pulse and UB40 alongside a sizeable contingent of punk and post punk artists such as John Cooper Clarke, the Gang of Four, XTC, 999 and the Au Pairs, the movie was accompanied by an A&M soundtrack album that omitted the Cramps' rendition of 'Tear It Up'. "I hate that video, because someone talked me into getting a little wave in my hair the night before," Lux recalled. "Because of all these beauty parlour people that made us come there, I got a little wave that turned into an Afro. So I hate the way I look in that movie." By September 1980, Julien had decided that the Cramps, and life on the road in a rock'n'roll band in general, were not for her. "Julien left because she was real young and had a boyfriend," explained Lux. "It's real simple; she thought she wanted a rock'n'roll life – travelling and everything at the beginning – but she didn't understand what in the world we were doing."

Increasingly upset by the way in which the rock'n'roll lifestyle took a toll on her peers (three former members of the Mad having died prematurely), Julien withdrew from the scene altogether after returning home. "While it was fun to be in the music scene in New York back in the

The Bad Stuff

seventies, there is a lot of pain in thinking back to that time," she subsequently explained. "Think about it for a moment and realise that many of the people who were alive then didn't get to live to be true adults. They were all creative people who had their lives cut short by drug addiction, mental health issues, and HIV. Not to be trivialised nor romanticised . . . there were many deaths around 1980. I would appreciate it if fans of the time period understood this reality. I don't like romanticising the past."

Once again, the idea that being a Cramp required just the right sort of weirdo appeared to be holding true. "It's hard to be in our band," Ivy affirms. "We are demanding, but what we're trying to do is special. It seems like we've always had this one member, kind of flaky, who's just not into the music. Anybody can be a Cramps fan, but they don't always understand the music that influences the music that we make. They might not like Jack Scott, but they like our version of 'The Way I Walk', but we need people who like Jack Scott to be in our band. To make our music, you've got to take it back that far." Before the Cramps could entertain any notion of further tours, let alone recording a follow-up to *Songs The Lord Taught Us*, Lux, Ivy and Nick would have to kiss a few frogs before they found their prince. "It seems like we can't get anybody to work with us who doesn't want to put the guitars through an octave-splitter so it'll sound like we have a bass or to take music lessons so that we'll play better or something," Ivy opined. "It's hard for us to think of ourselves as some bizarre revolutionary band, but I guess we are because we just go through people like water trying to find somebody who understands us."

As a means of maintaining the Cramps' profile while they were searching for a permanent replacement for Bryan, Illegal Records released 'Drug Train' as a part of a three-track EP at around the same time Julien left the group. Having been a late omission from the album, the version issued in the UK and Europe was one that had been recorded with Gregory and Alex Chilton in Memphis the previous year. The EP also rounded up two more covers that had failed to make the cut earlier in the year: 'Love Me' and 'I Can't Hardly Stand It'. With regard to the former, both Lux and Ivy were longtime fans of the Phantom's one and only hit single and duly expounded on the song's provenance with enthusiasm. "It's an old

Journey To The Centre Of The Cramps

rockabilly classic, really wild," declared Lux. "He wore his hair in a ponytail in the fifties, when he was famous," adds Ivy. "He was on *American Bandstand*, the whole thing. Used to get down on his knees in the middle of the set and start sobbing. 'And when I left', he would say, 'There was a little pool of tears on the floor and all the girls were crying.'" Still being used to advertise Southern Comfort liqueur more than 50 years after its initial release, the Phantom's original cut of 'Love Me' resonates with the kind of unrestrained abandon that ensured it was perfect source material for the Cramps. "He drove off a cliff when he was drunk one night, Ivy explained. "He said, 'When I first found out I was paralysed, boy was I pissed.' He's really nuts – all old rockabillies were that way, and that's what it's all about, period. These people were too wild to be controlled, so they drove off cliffs – and that's rockabilly." Opening with Lux's customary shriek, the Cramps' adaptation ups the lunacy ante in all respects, with Ivy's circular lead patterns evoking a tangible sense of a descent into psychosis. "He only made one record and both sides of it are just amazing," enthused Lux. "You couldn't do it better, so you just do it different."

Lux's maxim held equally true for the recorded version of 'I Can't Hardly Stand It', which, like 'Love Me', was a long-established part of the group's live set that had developed into a shuddering, antic version of Charlie Feathers' strangely plaintive song. "All of his songs are a little spooky. Charlie Feathers also claims he taught Elvis everything he knows, but he's been caught fibbing about things," said Ivy. "He taught Elvis plenty, I'll bet, because Elvis had his ear open all the time," Lux interjected. "Charlie was at Sun Records before Elvis was. He could do 'A Whole Lotta Shakin' Goin' On' so you wouldn't recognise it – it's just the things he does to make a song his own." Fractionally assisted by the Phantom's alter ego, Jerry Lott, sending 10 dollars to England for two copies of the EP, 'Drug Train' made number five on an Independent Chart dominated by the varying punk stylings of Killing Joke and Zounds.

The period that Lux and Ivy were temporarily denied access to the treadmill of recording and touring that they had climbed on the previous summer gave the couple the opportunity to take stock of their situation. Having returned from a trip to the West Coast to discover that their

The Bad Stuff

apartment had been reclaimed by the lettings agent in their absence, they took this as a sign and headed straight back to Los Angeles. "We ended up driving a 1980 Grand Prix out there for some courier service and hitched up a U-Haul to it, which we weren't supposed to do," Ivy remembered. "We wrote 'California Or Bust' on it," added Lux. With CBGB's glory days now a receding memory and many of those who had played a part in creating it now elsewhere, it seemed an opportune moment for the Cramps to base themselves in fresh pastures. "Right now it seems like New York is concentrating on British bands or out of town bands. It's not like that in Los Angeles. There's a great local scene there, and that doesn't seem to be happening here any more," Lux declared. "For five years we lived in New York and we lived there during the glory days of New York punk rock," explained Ivy. "We'd written songs, so we just literally moved to New York to have a band and play CBGB. It really happened – it was like a dream in a way. So we were there for five years and that scene really died. Now in New York it's just dance clubs, there's really just no scene there. We didn't move to LA because the scene was in LA, it was because there was no scene any more that there was no reason to stay in New York.

"When something dies, it's time to move on – and something did die here," she concluded.

CHAPTER NINE

The Magic That You Do

Drugs and a crazy way of life is good for some people and bad for others, but there has to be somebody speaking out for that side of things.

Lux Interior

There are so many ways to initiate people and drugs aren't essential – but sex and rock'n'roll, it's a whole different thing.

Poison Ivy

ALMOST exactly five years after they had arrived in New York to participate in the Big Apple's burgeoning rock'n'roll underground, Lux and Ivy arrived in Los Angeles just as California's second wave of punk rockers were defining the parameters of the US hardcore movement. The half decade that the couple spent in New York had seen the most apolitical of bands rise to prominence while the punk scene from which they had risen had become increasingly politicised. As the Soviet Union invaded Afghanistan and the final years of premier Leonid Brezhnev's reign saw the Cold War approach a nuclear boiling point, America and Britain's media stoked public concern, which resulted in both nations electing right wing administrations that promised to oppose the perceived threat of Soviet expansionism. By the end of 1980, UK prime minister Margaret Thatcher had also embarked on a series of radical policies aimed at addressing the country's economic problems, which led to the dismantling of Britain's industrial and manufacturing infrastructure and unprecedented levels of unemployment that led to widespread civil unrest the following year. On November 4, US voters returned former B-movie

The Magic That You Do

actor Ronald Reagan to the White House with a decisive majority, his policies promising to take America along a similar path as that of Britain. As the Conservative government organised the distribution of a booklet to every household in the UK explaining what measures should be taken in the event of the increasingly anticipated nuclear strike on the country, those opposing the regime became more vocal.

These societal shifts were reflected within the punk movement, just as the Clash's well-intentioned but naively gestural approach to politics had been superseded by the more considered militancy of groups such as Crass and the Poison Girls. In America, Californian bands including the Dead Kennedys, Black Flag and the Circle Jerks were indicative of the way in which stateside punk had also become more political. As Los Angeles punks increasingly embraced this culture of opposition, the Cramps again found that they were swimming against the zeitgeist. "We're different from that in that our music isn't political. Our lyrics aren't political and that's just not what we want to do. I think [hardcore] is a platform for political ideas in their lyrics," Ivy observed. "We very deliberately avoid politics in our lyrics. We figure that our lifestyle is enough of a statement and a comment on politics or anything else. We don't vote, but we feel like we vote with our behaviour, we vote with how we spend our money – because money is the main thing that gives power to something. If you don't want something to exist, then don't back it up by buying certain things."

Whereas the Cramps embodied the unholy trinity of sex, drugs and rock'n'roll, the American hardcore scene possessed a puritan streak that would subsequently result in the curiously ascetic 'Straight Edge' movement, whose advocates refrained from alcohol, drugs, tobacco, sex and caffeine, often with such shrill self-righteousness that it became difficult to distinguish them from religious fundamentalists. "It's kind of like 1977 Sex Pistols. I used to think it was crazy to revive that, but now I understand it comes from the same frustrations. Not from having no future or no money, but from having too much," declared Lux. "Bands that are really political, it always seems really insincere to me, like it's just an act – it's a way of getting seen, 'You gotta stop this' and 'the government' and all this kind of stuff – it seems so insincere, it seems glaringly insincere to me most

Journey To The Centre Of The Cramps

of the time. But hardcore, I like the underground-ness and I respect that and everything, it's just there's no groove to it usually."

Feeling little connection with the incoming punk tide, Lux and Ivy took up residence in a primarily Mexican East Hollywood neighbourhood and set about planning the Cramps' next move. As the couple settled in to their new surroundings, they took advantage of California's ongoing attachment to the internal combustion engine to resume their practice of taking long drives while listening to rock'n'roll. "I think this place has a lot more to do with the Cramps than New York ever did. You can drive around in fast cars here. You can play tapes real loud," Lux asserted. "Before we started the Cramps, we'd got one of these new gizmos called a cassette player. It was battery operated and we'd set it on the seat and we'd be listening to the Flamin' Groovies' *Grease* and *More Grease* EPs, cos they were on drugs and they're just a 90 miles an hour amphetamine thing, and we'd just drive and listen to that mixed with driving rockabilly songs and stuff. When you're in a car, there's some way that you can tell that this is a dud, or 'Wow, this is great – this is the best thing that ever happened.' You can tell." In addition to providing the couple with a valuable means of evaluating music, it renewed their passion for cars that would later underpin the *Flamejob* LP. "We hear it in different ways," Ivy explains. "At home we don't hear the detail that we hear when you're in the car, when you're right there in that small space with it, there's all kinds of stuff going on. I guess when you're home, you're messing around doing things and you don't hear everything."

Far removed from the growing *froideur* that was slowly embracing their former base, Lux and Ivy found that the open roads and warm California sun were not the only advantages of their new environment. "It's a lot cheaper to live in Los Angeles," observed Ivy. "We lived [in New York] for about five years, which is the longest I've lived any place, but it was too long. I mean, there was a reason to be in New York a few years ago." With their car loaded with groovy tapes, the couple began exploring their new home state, which in one instance saw them make an unsuccessful attempt to visit the Disneyland theme park in Anaheim. "We even abided by the dress code, but they wouldn't let us in," Ivy recalled. "I did wear an

The Magic That You Do

earring," admitted Lux. "But they said Ivy was wearing too much make-up, too. I really wanted to go. They were having the Ventures, the Surfaris and Annette Funicello. Even one of the guys from the Surfaris couldn't get in." Added Ivy: "I guess they already had their quota of crazy people in there that day." Happily, their journeys of discovery to Los Angeles' vinyl vaults provided the pair with a more successful method of maintaining their vintage rock'n'roll habit. "It's a great place for finding records," enthused Ivy. "When you live in different regions, you find out that there's certain musics that only hit those regions. LA's great for finding really great instrumentals, and that's fun."

With their cross-country move now out of the way, Lux and Ivy again began to consider how to bring the Cramps back up to full strength. With a healthy selection of unreleased material available for their second album, it would be vital to find the right guitarist for the recording and subsequent touring schedules. For her part, Ivy was clear on what was required: "Just that they have total, unshakable faith in rock'n'roll. And have total faith in what the band is, [that it] is bigger than any individual." In addition to sharing Lux and Ivy's commitment to the Cramps' mission, the new group member would need to have a passion for rock'n'roll that came from the heart. "Anybody can dig a good rock'n'roll song to be in this band," explained Lux. "But they don't have to know what the matrix numbers are on Elvis' second single on Sun, or stuff like that."

Ivy, in particular, has always been a great believer in chance, and this belief was reinforced as she and Lux began showing up at concerts featuring local bands as a means of seeing if there were any likely candidates on their doorstep. Fairly quickly, fate intervened to set recently formed Los Angeles quartet the Gun Club before them. Having come together as the Creeping Ritual in 1979, the group had recently undergone some line-up changes that had resulted in founding members Jeffrey Lee Pierce and Brian Tristan being joined by former Bags rhythm section Rob Ritter and Terry Graham. Led by the charismatic Pierce, the Gun Club set out on a stylistic path that drew on the same blues-based influences as the Cramps. "Jeffrey gave the band a tape of songs he was interested in to influence the band," Tristan explained. "The tape had different things on it like Bo

167

Journey To The Centre Of The Cramps

Diddley and Marvin Rainwater, Marty Robbins' murder ballads, old Little Richard, some blues stuff – and that really solidified what direction the band would go. We did our homework and listened to these records and started making it. It was kind of a natural thing."

Given this shared ground between the two bands, it was scarcely surprising that Lux and Ivy took a shine to the Gun Club, who in turn were Cramps fans. "We were playing a lot of live shows and one of our big hits was our song 'For The Love Of Ivy' because everyone knew we were singing about Ivy from the Cramps," Brian recalled. "I made up the first set of lyrics that I took from a book I had, called *1001 Insults*. Because the song, although it turned into a tribute to Ivy, was not always that – it was just a good title because we loved the Sidney Poitier film *For The Love Of Ivy*. I can't remember what all the '1001 insults' were but they were really funny and really scathing but we decided just to change it to use some very blues imagery and steal different scathing blues lines . . . It became our tribute to hunting down Ivy – because we wanted to have sex with her." When asked about the song soon after, the titular object of desire seemed a little bewildered by the attention. "I'm probably as mystified by it as you are," said Ivy. "It was printed in an English paper that one time onstage he got real gone and started ranting and raving about how he wanted to murder Lux! That's all I know. I'm afraid to ask him about it."

Despite Jeffrey's passionate declarations, Gun Club drummer Terry Graham's then-girlfriend Lois Kimmerle recalls his trepidation at what Lux's reactions to the song might actually be. "The first set of lyrics instead of the ones they put on the album, it was, I can't remember all of it, it was basically the same, but it was really bad lyrics about Ivy. I mean, he didn't hate, he loved Ivy. But Jeffrey was afraid Lux would kill him, so he changed all the lyrics. 'Your face is cracked just like a liberty bell,' and he said all things like that. And he had heard that Lux got mad at someone for saying something bad about Ivy. Just making a remark about Ivy. And he beat him up, so Jeff changed all the lyrics. He was like mortified he was going to get killed. 'Well, we can't put that on the record, we have to change these.' But it didn't have the same impact that it did when he originally sang it. I don't know, maybe people didn't notice. He wrote great lyrics."

The Magic That You Do

Brian's passion for both Ivy and her band was longstanding. Having visited New York several times, he'd relocated there in 1978, where he shared a Lower East Side apartment with Bradley Field and Lydia Lunch. "That's when I was really introduced to the Cramps," he confirmed. "I made friends with a lot of the kids that were around – a lot of bands you don't hear about like Little Annie & the Asexuals and the Student Teachers, and it was a very fertile time." Tristan's method of introducing himself to the Cramps initially took the form of shouting at them. "He came up to us before a gig at CBGB and yelled, 'Hey Cramps! Can you get us in tonight? We're from California," remembered Lux. "He was real obnoxious," added Ivy. "He was real fucked up until I hit him in the face with a mic stand that night at CBGB," grinned Lux. After his sojourn in New York, Tristan returned to Los Angeles where a chance meeting with Jeffrey Lee Pierce at a Pere Ubu concert sowed seeds that would bring forth desert flowers in the form of the Gun Club. Although Lux subsequently joked that, "They rip us off everything they do," he instinctively recognised that "the Gun Club is a really great Los Angeles band – one of the best bands down there", while Ivy noted that "they were amazing". After some encouragement from a mutual friend in the form of Mumps' keyboard player Kristian Hoffman, they made contact with Brian and invited him to join the Cramps. "I asked them if they wanted me to audition, they said 'No'. I asked what they wanted to know, and they asked 'Well, what are you willing to sacrifice?' and I said, 'What? My band, or school, or moving somewhere?' And they said, '*No*, like . . . a finger!' and I told them I would put it under consideration."

This offer presented Brian with a dilemma – in addition to taking college courses in journalism and Spanish, he was committed to the Gun Club and particularly loyal to Jeffrey, but an opportunity to join the Cramps was of the golden variety. Jeffrey, having served time as president of the Blondie fan club and modelled his hairstyle on Deborah Harry, understood the passion of the hardcore fan and duly encouraged Brian to seize the chance. "I thought about it and I went to Jeffrey and told him that the Cramps just asked me to be in their band, and he was like, 'Are you crazy? The Cramps? That's incredible! You should do it. I would do it

Journey To The Centre Of The Cramps

in a minute!' I called them up and said I would do it – and that was that," recalled Brian. "I quit everything, threw my shoes in the air and my books out the window and said, 'I'm going with you!'"

In terms of live or studio experience, Brian was a relative novice and once his initial excitement burned off, he felt some pressure at joining one of his favourite groups. "I was a bit frightened. I didn't know what would happen. To us, the Cramps were big rock stars – a real band that made real records and really played live," he admitted. "I wasn't sure that I could cut the mustard." However, Lux and Ivy reassured Brian that he was good enough for them and his initiation into the group began with a crash course in the Cramps' sprawling palette of influences. "Before, it was very much about certain records and certain types of records like rockabilly, like garage rock – stuff I was already into," explained Brian. "But now, I was going to have to dive much deeper into this world. The B-movie world – the horror movie world. Another chapter in learning about subculture started."

As had become customary, Brian would need to have a suitable stage name. He initially suggested the voodoo-inspired 'Brian Gris Gris', but having already had one Bryan in the group, that was rejected. Similarly the literal 'Mr Tristan' and 'Thing', which owed its provenance to the *Addams Family*'s helpful hand, were also found wanting. Finally, the solution came courtesy of Ivy's Santeria candles, which came with a legend that read, 'When you light this candle, Congo powers will be revealed to you.' Thereafter, 'Congo Powers' was spliced to 'Kid' (reflecting Brian's status as the youngest in the group) and Brian Tristan had his new identity. Kid Congo Powers also underwent an image makeover, getting a tattoo, growing his hair and putting together a wardrobe based around his gold Lansky Brothers blazer. "I started to focus on kind of an 'anything goes' kind of look," he remembered. "Really mix the feminine with the masculine and make it sexy. The Cramps were so much about sex. Almost more than anything. So it had to be a sexy look. I think at first I wore a turban and wraparound sunglasses – that was my first look. I thought that was pretty great."

Having established a name and a look, the Kid also had little difficulty

The Magic That You Do

assimilating the Cramps' outsider mentality. Unlike Bryan Gregory who often played upon his innate campness to create confusion about his sexuality, Kid Congo was gay. "I used to hang out a lot with the Screamers from LA and they were straight out of a drag scene from New York. So that was never an issue but at the time, no one ever spoke about it," he recounted. "It was something that was there, everyone knew it but . . . labels were taboo, labels were just not good for anything." In a similar manner to the way that the Cramps had been just too different for the hipsters at CBGB, Kid Congo's aesthetic and musical otherness separated him from the mainstream of California's gay scene. "I think that created a kind of weird confusion in a lot of gay people and also feeling so much outside of gay culture and such a freak, a monster outside," he explained. "There was not going to be any acceptance of a crazy person, you were not attractive to gay culture at that time."

Not wanting to waste any further time, the Cramps set about a period of intensive rehearsal aimed at bringing their new guitarist up to speed with their established set of originals, their corpus of cover versions and the new material earmarked for the forthcoming album. "I wasn't a really proficient guitar player at the time," recalled Kid. "The good thing is that Ivy taught me a lot about rockabilly rhythm and blues scales because I had to play things with a lot of bass lines. So I practised a lot. I remember thinking, 'God, these songs are so hard – how am I ever going to remember all of them?'" Having been a fan of the way that Bryan Gregory had used low-end fuzz to fill in the sonic gaps caused by the absence of a bass guitar, Kid Congo set about experimenting along those lines. "They gave me my first fuzz pedal," he explained. "I'd never used a pedal before – I just played straight into the amplifier with the Gun Club. I started learning songs and trying to add my own version of what I would like it to sound like. They were going through a period of more psychedelic than 'burn-them-out' rockabilly and they were also quite oozy and sexy. There was no bass guitar. I went for that really fat 'rrrrr' kind of sound. It was all about having the beat come down and then slide some and then go into the next one. That's what I decided to make my root bassiness."

Kid Congo's live debut as a Cramp came at London's Lyceum on

Journey To The Centre Of The Cramps

December 14, a one-off show that came about as a result of persistent requests for the band to return to the UK, where the continuing sales of *Songs The Lord Taught Us* and 'Drug Train' served as an indication of their increasing popularity – a fervour that was spread by their very active UK fan club. Supported by East London post punks Wasted Youth and straight up rockabilly revival act the Polecats, the Cramps gave their new member a flying start, blasting through an 18-song set that included 'Weekend On Mars', 'Louie Louie', and revived one of the band's earliest covers, 'Hurricane Fighter Plane', alongside a mix of old and new material. Although the group received a heroes' reception and Kid Congo was greeted warmly despite many present having been Bryan Gregory fans, the performance was, at times, a little rough around the edges. "I think we were probably very under-rehearsed," admitted the Kid. "I really didn't know about having sound at concerts and stuff. And even though we made it through the concert and I was a big hit with the fans and the London press, it was kind of a diabolical concert."

Having survived one baptism of fire (he'd get another later in July at the Roxy), the Kid found himself pitched from frying pan to furnace as he joined his new bandmates to record the Cramps' second album at the outset of 1981. This time around, in the hope of avoiding the whole circus of hassles that accompanied Alex Chilton, the group would self-produce the album with an assist from studio engineer Paul McKenna. "We didn't know much about production," recalls Ivy. "We were limited by budget restraints." Rather than return to Memphis, the Cramps capitalised on IRS' relationship with A&M and booked into that label's Hollywood facility. "It was my first recording experience. So that was a pretty posh thing – a big recording studio," remembered Kid Congo. "We had a lot of amps and a lot of different things and I learned a lot fast. That's when I really had to pay attention to Ivy and she was actually a really good teacher. She showed me what to do. They knew I had no experience when they got me in the band, but I think they liked having a slave in their band. They knew they could make me a slave – and I was more than willing." With the Kid duly in their thrall, the Cramps made rapid progress. "It was a piece of cake," Nick declared. "It was much easier than

The Magic That You Do

working with Alex," added Lux. "Ten days and mix it and everything. It was $9,000 what we did it for – pretty cheap. We spent the rest on drugs."

Continuing the practice initiated with *Songs The Lord Taught Us*, the Cramps unearthed and adapted a succession of under-recognised rock'n'roll gems for a new generation. Half of the album's 14 selected tacks would be covers. "Sometimes we get accused of stealing things from other people, or doing things because we don't have original thoughts, but we look at these things as magic. We're not saying, 'Hey, we invented this guitar lick', or 'We invented this line', but we love them," explained Lux. "If we hear a song and think, 'God, that's as good as any song we've written' and we feel like it's expressing us even though someone else wrote it, and in addition to that if we feel like we can do an equally exciting version, then we'll cover it," Ivy expounded. "Sometimes we won't touch a song, because it's been done so well originally that we don't have an idea of doing it better. But if we can do something – I hate to say better, because most of the originals are pretty exciting too, but they're different – but if we can Crampify it."

In keeping with the title of *Psychedelic Jungle*, the balance of those cover versions veered momentarily away from rockabilly and toward the esoteric end of the garage rock spectrum. Two of the tracks selected for Crampifying, the Groupies' 1966 raw blues-influenced proto-psychedelic 'Primitive' and 'Green Fuz', the eponymous debut single by a group of Texan teenagers in 1968, had come to Lux and Ivy's attention via the *Pebbles* album series, which represented a vast stash of 'Original Artyfacts from the First Punk Era' across a lengthy series of compilation releases that had begun in 1978. "There's about 10 of them on release in the States right now," explained Ivy. "'Green Fuz' was by a band called the Green Fuz and it was the trashiest sounding thing I ever heard in my life. For years I thought it was beautiful and wanted to do it."

Aside from their versions of 'Rockin' Bones' and 'Jungle Hop' that had been in the Cramps' set for over three years, Lux and Ivy's devotion to the cobweb encrusted corners of rock'n'roll's past saw the band record a creepy, slithering cover of Ronnie Cook & the Gaylads 1962 sax-driven

Journey To The Centre Of The Cramps

rumbler, 'Goo Goo Muck'; 'The Crusher', Minneapolis garage quartet the Novas' 1964 tribute to wrestler Reginald Lisowski; and an unforgettably menacing take on Jim Lowe's 1956 number one hit 'Green Door' (which was subsequently covered far more conventionally by Welsh rock'n'roll pop star Shakin' Stevens, who scored a chart-topping hit for himself in the process). Although these tracks each bore the hallmark of the Cramps' mad-scientist approach to cover versions, this process was muted in comparison to the treatment given to many non-original cuts on both *Gravest Hits* and *Songs The Lord Taught Us*. To a degree, this can be ascribed to the necessity for Kid Congo to assimilate a lot of new material in a relatively short space of time. Whereas Bryan Gregory would have simply laid down slabs of noise and distortion, the Kid had a more orthodox technique and duly utilised that to set up low rumbles and bass drones that filled in the bottom end of the group's sound. Although he plays little more than a bassline on 'Green Fuz', 'Jungle Hop' and 'Green Door', several of *Psychedelic Jungle*'s original tracks provide clear indications that the Kid was developing his own take on the 'misdirected noise' approach established by Bryan. This is particularly evident on 'Caveman' where Kid's nasty fuzz effectively combines with Ivy's lead during the song's middle eight. "What I really always loved about *Songs The Lord Taught Us* and *Gravest Hits* was Bryan Gregory's guitar solos," he explained. "They were just pure weird sound. So with 'Caveman', I got to make a sound like a caveman – and I think quite successfully."

Although the haunting 'Voodoo Idol' and 'Natives Are Restless' are atmospheric, it is the remaining original compositions that provide indications of where the Cramps' sound may have been heading, in addition to providing *Psychedelic Jungle* with much of its fizz. "We did lots of different weird experiments like taking lots of speed so we would be like ghosts when we played," recalled Kid Congo. "I think that worked sometimes – but I don't remember because you really can't remember things when you're on speed." The creeping bump and grind of 'Can't Find My Mind' becomes increasingly unhinged and mesmeric as the number gathers intensity through repetition. "I was really happy with the sounds," Kid declared. "I really like 'Can't Find My Mind'. Maybe we did become

The Magic That You Do

ghosts because you could hear these really weird overtones and things in my guitar and every time the guitar stops you could hear these breaks – you could hear these amazing sounds."

'Don't Eat Stuff Off The Sidewalk' marks the point at which *Psychedelic Jungle* truly lives up to its title, as the trip kicks in hard. Notable for the absence of any orthodoxy, the Kid's weird guitar noises combine with Ivy's mutated Duane Eddy and Link Wray licks to provide a platform upon which Lux can deliver his authoritive, twisted vocal. "I think people bought a Doors album and then decided, 'Ooh, I'm gonna get moody and heavy, and that'll be really intense.' I was around during the psychedelic days and it doesn't remind me of what was going on then at all," asserted Lux. "'Psychedelic' means 'mind-manifesting' and to me that means living and optimism, not depression or gloom."

Similarly lysergic in tone, 'Beautiful Gardens' is again gloriously un-orthodox, as Kid Congo delivers more nasty distortion that adds to the unsettling tone and is exacerbated considerably by sheets of discordance, noise and a backward vocal section. "'Beautiful Gardens' was a totally improvised song. I kept playing this crazy riff and again, that was one of our ghost songs where we completely improvised the song. So we would play a riff and a beat and then Lux would go off and it went wherever it went," recounted Kid. "At one point it fades out and comes back in and you hear this backwards weird sound and it's Lux saying, 'If you knew what I knew about this record company, this place would be a parking lot.'" The tripped-out lyrical brilliance of the song is matched by Lux's calmly crazed performance on 'Under The Wires', which finally made it to vinyl having been a part of the Cramps' set since 1976. By degrees intense, claustrophobic, unsettling and hilarious, the song in its final, real-ised form is revealed as one of *Psychedelic Jungle*'s standout tracks. Both 'Under The Wires' and 'Beautiful Gardens' benefit from the manner in which the group's own production served to bring out Lux's vocals far more clearly than Alex Chilton had. "I actually think it's a little too clean. I like the sound of our *Gravest Hits* EP. *Songs The Lord Taught Us* was too muddy. I like something in between," observed Ivy. "I think it's more accessible sounding, without us going out of our way to sound that way –

Journey To The Centre Of The Cramps

just because it's clearer sounding. *Songs The Lord Taught Us* was so murky sounding that you really had to dig deep to hear a lot of it. Immediately, you can hear Lux's voice on this one – where on the other one, people would ask, 'What's he saying?'"

Despite the cleaner sound, *Psychedelic Jungle* has plenty of texture, as Kid Congo's more adventurous contributions combine with Ivy's customary precision to produce overlapping layers of guitar that float and slither above Nick's solid rhythms, while liberal use of reverb adds mystery and strangeness to the sonic gumbo. "It's an instant gimmick," Ivy explained. "Like every record I ever liked when I was a kid, if it had an echo, it just sounded famous immediately; beautiful and religious. Just by flipping a switch. That's the main problem we have with engineers. They tell us that we can't use echo that way; it's too gimmicky." Equally mysterious was the fate of the message that Lux and Ivy had added to the album's run-out: "We were gonna scratch 'Elvis was murdered' onto the vinyl of our new album," Lux revealed. "It was on the acetate, but never made it to the final version. It kept disappearing and reappearing. Then we were gonna put it on the single, but it never did come out. Strange . . ." The inscription did, however, show up on some US pressings of the LP.

With *Psychedelic Jungle* in the can, the Cramps made their first appearance at CBGB in well over a year as part of a short burst of one-off shows aimed at giving Kid Congo some additional live experience ahead of several months of British, European and US tours that were being arranged to coincide with the album release. Depending on where you were in the world, *Psychedelic Jungle* hit the shelves in late March or early April. The album was plucked from those shelves at roughly twice the rate of its predecessor, helped in part by any early review from *NME* heavyweight Charles Shaar Murray declaring that "nobody does it better, nobody does it worse, nobody does it *period*", before adding that "there is nothing like this music anywhere, unless it's on other Cramps records." On the album's official release shortly after, *NME* ran a second review that saw Edwin Pouncey award *Psychedelic Forest* [sic] an unreserved five stars: "The album taken as a whole eats like a parasite into your subconscious," he enthused. "To try and remove those nagging little hooks that dominate

The Magic That You Do

the music would either mean a thorough brainwash or extensive surgery, because once this record has got its rabid fangs under your skin, you're infected and there's no cure except to play it again, and again, and again, and . . ." Almost as enthusiastic was *Smash Hits'* David Hepworth, who awarded the disc eight out of 10 while observing that: "The songs are stronger here than on their debut album but the atmosphere is no less demented." While some shared Ivy's opinion that the LP had too much clarity, Kid took the opposing view: "It got a great reception from all parties involved. Everyone involved was like, 'Oh we don't miss Bryan Gregory' or 'The Cramps made a great album.' Some people thought it was a bit too clean for them, but if you listen to that now – it's no clean album. I'll tell you – it is one dirty album." Inevitably, those who still insisted on perceiving the Cramps as a latter-day Bobby Pickett & the Crypt Kickers chose to carp about the way the band had sidelined the monster motif in favour of even wilder weirdness. "We've been accused now of trying to play down the monster thing that we 'used to do'. We never did 'used to do' anything different from what we do now. We're not playing it down," Lux retorted.

With a good deal of the praise lavished upon *Psychedelic Jungle* emanating from the UK music press, further proof of the Cramps' developing popularity became immediately apparent by the sheer force of the demented reception that their British fanbase met them with. "They were some crazy magic voodoo shows and Lux did incredible things onstage that were so dangerous and crazy, from jumping off of speaker stacks, swinging a microphone with the lead so long that you thought he was going to decapitate you – but he never did," remembered Kid Congo. "He would tie my legs together with the mic cord and drag me around the stage while I was still playing – during 'Surfin' Bird' usually." Support on the 13-date tour was provided by two sides of Britain's recently minted rockabilly coin: South London psychobillies the Meteors and Glasgow's more conventional, skiffle-influenced Shakin' Pyramids. While the latter were agreeably rockin', they were essentially revivalists whose material resembled a busked version of the kind of songs the Stray Cats had made popular. The Meteors, on the other hand, stood at the vanguard of the UK's

Journey To The Centre Of The Cramps

nascent psychobilly scene – their stripped down, aggressive approach to rock'n'roll owing its provenance in equal parts to the badass end of the fifties rockabilly boom, punk's sulphate-fuelled velocity, and the Cramps. Led by guitarist/vocalist P Paul Fenech, who developed a reputation for spitting chicken blood into the crowd, the trio had made an instant splash with their recent *Meteor Madness* EP. Adorned by Fenech's impressive mastery of rockin' lead and Nigel Lewis' powerhouse stand-up bass and unique vocals, the four track disc featured tracks such as 'Maniac Rockers From Hell' and 'My Daddy Is A Vampire', which extended the line of influence from Screamin' Jay Hawkins that the Cramps had been contributing to for some time. However, the Meteors did their own thing, accelerating rock'n'roll past escape velocity, while effectively emphasising the 'never say die' rebel spirit (as encapsulated by the *Meteor Madness* track 'You Can't Keep A Good Man Down').

Although some purists dismissed the Meteors as a 'punk band', they quickly developed a rabid following known as the Wrecking Crew, whose unswerving loyalty to the group has ensured the band's continuation (with Fenech enduring as the band's driving force) up to the present day. A trip down the front at any Meteors gig was not for the faint of heart, as the Wrecking Crew, stripped to the waist and filled with psychotic abandon, were liable to chew the unwary up and spit them out in a manner that led Lux to declare, "I wish kids would learn a more sexual form of dancing." Unsurprisingly, there was considerable crossover between the Cramps' and Meteors' audiences and the presence of Fenech's band on the tour added much to the kinetic nature of attending those shows. "Fights would often erupt in the audience, girls' clothes came off, and then Lux would be wearing them," Kid recounted. "The audience would pull Lux in the audience and Nick would jump from behind his drum kit and jump in the fray. It was pretty wild. If something bad was happening, Ivy would snap her fingers and point and we'd have to go beat someone up. It was like being in a gang – like a juvenile delinquent band – and it was great."

While the Meteors originated the UK psychobilly subgenre that not only incorporated a cornucopia of rockin' bands such as the Guana Batz, Demented Are Go and King Kurt but would also be exported to the US

The Magic That You Do

later in the decade, Lux and Ivy remained ambivalent regarding the Cramps' influence on this developing subculture. "It's flattering that people say that and I think it's true to some degree, but none of those bands really sound like us, either," observed Lux. "I have heard people say 'this Cramps-influenced band' and 'that Cramps-influenced band' and most of the time I can't hear it. I think that they're more influenced by all the things that we kind of stand for. It kind of spawned a bunch of bands that like the same things that we do and have the same ideas about some things that we do and then make a little bit different kind of music. So that's good, I think that it's made for a richer musical horizon out there than might otherwise exist."

Similarly, Ivy felt that although the Cramps had coined the phrase 'psychobilly' and provided many of the bands that were subsequently part of that subculture with varying degrees of influence, there remained a clear distinction: "There seems to be a style of music called psychobilly now and I think it's defined by a stand-up bass, a very speeded-up pace which we don't do. I think our songs have a more sensuous tempo. I'm not sure what exactly defines psychobilly but it seems to have taken on a life of its own. But it's not quite what we do." Essentially, the core of this distinction lies in the fact that whereas the Cramps drew upon a smorgasbord of influences that included R&B and doo-wop, the psychobilly groups tended to eschew blues-based influences and splice rockabilly to a punk template that hadn't existed back when the Cramps got started.

Regardless of these differences, while there were some psychobillies that didn't dig the Cramps, to many they were godparents to a scene they had no direct part in creating. Like the Cramps had done and continued to do, the Meteors were adapting rock'n'roll for a new generation, and the vitality with which this was done ensured that they, and many of the subsequent psychobilly groups, were of far greater merit than the continuing succession of revival acts. "I couldn't believe all those bands that came along during the rockabilly revival. All those original rockabillies were really nasty, aggressive, intense men, who had one thing on their mind – or maybe two or three things at the most. Then all these cutie-pie bands came along in the late seventies singing about hubcaps and soda shops and

Journey To The Centre Of The Cramps

stuff like that. I never could believe that when the modern age went back to rockabilly, that's how it would interpret it," Lux marvelled. "I think it misses the point," added Ivy. "It does rockabilly a disservice," insisted Lux. "You can discover the skull of the missing link and then you've got something, or you can make one out of plaster of Paris and say 'This is what it looked like'. Rockabilly happened back then and it was something special; to try and imitate it now seems dangerous. People are going to think that's what rockabilly really is – the music where they wear those silly clothes."

In comparison with the kind of anodyne rock'n'roll that groups such as Matchbox and Racey had been having UK hits with, psychobilly represented a welcome antidote. The Meteors would subsequently be rightly credited with spearheading the movement, and in P Paul Fenech it had a suitably maniacal figurehead. "I'm surprised that there haven't been too many great rockabilly bands that have featured really depraved, crazy, scary people," observed Lux. "It's all this kind of cutie-pie thing, a lot of them are pin-up material, and then there are the purists who insist on a dogmatic approach to the music. I always thought the original artists who played this music were just crazy, really fucked-up crazy people, way ahead of everybody else."

After the British leg of the tour came to a premature end when a booking foul up led to the cancellation of a gig at Birmingham's Cedar Club on May 28, the Cramps headed for the continental mainland. As in England, the Cramps' French fanbase had grown in both size and fervour. "We're like the Beatles in France, we go to France and it's incredible. You just wouldn't believe it," Lux marvelled. The epicentre of this Crampsmania was located in Paris, where they appeared at the Palais des Arts on June 7. "When we're in Paris, there's riots when we play. That's how it should be," declared Lux. "We played a place that could hold 1,000 people, but when the band played the city before, they twice sold out this place that could hold 2,000," explained Kid Congo. "So a lot of people didn't get in. There were so many people outside that they broke down the big plate glass windows. There were people climbing through windows and by the second song the entire stage was just completely invaded."

While the Kid took this in his stride far more readily than Bryan would

The Magic That You Do

have, the whole band was shaken by events after a gig at Club 54 in the northern city of Rouen. "They kept on applauding for 45 minutes after the lights went on. They didn't stop, and all of a sudden they started to literally tear the place apart. We were afraid they were going to physically drag us back onstage, but there was no stage left," recounted Lux. "This girl explained to us why everyone was so crazy. She took us to this art school that at one time was a cemetery. The fence around the place was like 20 feet tall and made of timber, and in between the wood is cement. Every once in a while you'd come across this little round hole with a little piece of glass, and when you'd look inside it you'd see these bones of people, or of animals that they walled up alive inside the wall. She told us, 'This is a magical place and we see the magic that you do.'"

In addition to 10 gigs in France, the Cramps also nipped across the borders for gigs in Belgium, Luxembourg, and further afield to the Netherlands. "Holland's real fun," declared Lux. "All the people just lay on big pillows and take drugs. They sell drugs at the clubs – they sell all kinds of hashish there. A lot of them had their eyes very open, but they stay very still. They just stare at the stage laying on their backs. It's a real strange place to play, it's like playing in an opium den or something."

The remixed 'Goo Goo Muck' had been released as a single by IRS in May. Available on both sides of the Atlantic on attractive transparent yellow vinyl, the track had been reworked in order to be more representative of the Cramps' current status. "*Psychedelic Jungle* is not the direction we're going in," Lux explained. "It's something we did, but it isn't the direction we're going. If anything, in the future we're more likely to sound like *Gravest Hits*. Like our singles have always sounded more like *Gravest Hits*. We've remixed 'Goo Goo Muck' to sound more like that." 'Goo Goo Muck' was backed by the Cramps' remarkable cover of Hasil Adkins' already terminally unhinged 1964 hillbilly masterpiece 'She Said'. Describing the aftermath of a disappointing one night stand in an almost incomprehensible Virginia drawl, Adkins' original features dynamite lines such as 'she looks to me like dyin' can of that commodity meat'. "Lux, to get that correct Hasil Adkins sound and phrasing, he stuck a whole styrofoam cup in his mouth and sang the entire song chewing on [it],"

Journey To The Centre Of The Cramps

remembered the Kid. "So this is where I was learning what recording technique was all about. And then we just ran around throwing ashtrays and screaming."

The success of the UK leg of the Cramps' tour and healthy sales of the single and album it was convened to support led to a few additional gigs being tacked on to the end of the schedule as June reached an unusually sweltering end. Among these was a riotous climactic concert at Hammersmith Palais on June 22, which saw support from post punk combo Red Beat, sixties shock rock legend Screaming Lord Sutch (who made his customary entrance via a coffin) and the Meteors, who were fast becoming a staple of promoters Straight Music's London bills. After Lord Sutch had caused widespread mayhem by detonating pyrotechnics in industrial quantities, and the Wrecking Crew had turned the front of stage into a no-go area, the Cramps' performance ended their European tour on a triumphant valedictory note as Lux made several excursions into the churning mass of bodies before him. Among those who witnessed the show was Ace Records managing director, record producer and Rock On Records honcho Roger Armstrong, a long-time friend of Lux and Ivy. "There was this huge crowd and I was standing at the back. Lux came off the stage and ran through the audience, and as Lux was running he was gathering these guys, who were hanging onto guys, who were hanging on to guys and I remember the crowd parted in front of Lux and he just looked at me and went, 'Hi Rog!' It was so cool." Following the climactic, sweaty rendition of 'She Said', Lux made his own way backstage by ripping a hole in the stage floor and dropping through it. "I think that's a real aspect of rock'n'roll," he explained. "It's real important – destruction, violence – all the kind of things that parents are afraid of. A lesson for teenagers and a warning for adults."

The Cramps returned to the US for a less intense burst of touring that commenced in Trenton Gardens, New Jersey on June 26. This show, like their Mudd Club performance a few days later, was filmed (the latter for a cable TV show called *Paul Tschinkel's Inner Tube*) and later showed up on several bootleg DVDs. After snaking their way around the northern half of the country, the Cramps wrapped up their *Psychedelic Jungle* gigs with a

The Magic That You Do

show on home turf at LA's Roxy on July 25. "We had candles onstage and Kid's hair caught on fire, going up like a torch because he wears so much hairspray. What a scream! It really stunk," remembered Ivy. "I had a lot of hair spray and a giant bouffant of hair and we had candles on our amps," explained the unfortunate Kid Congo. "We were doing 'Sunglasses After Dark', where we go and put on our sunglasses and there are candles there and they're making a feedback, and I went like this [leans forward] and the whole hair just went 'whoosh'. Luckily I had a lot of lacquer on it so just the outside of it went up in flame but the audience screamed. I never had so many girls screaming for me!"

While the band (and Kid's hair) recovered, IRS kept the Cramps' UK fans happy by issuing a 12-inch single of 'The Crusher', backed by two new songs – 'Save It', a cover of Hargus 'Pig' Robbins' 1959 single that cast Lux as a mad scientist in a rock'n'roll laboratory and churned with innuendo-laden lust, and 'New Kind Of Kick', a storming original adorned by Ivy's Link Wray lead and featuring a savage and shuddering extended guitar break from Kid Congo. "We hit another psychedelic thing. That was one of my proudest guitar moments to this day," he recalled. "It's actually a duet between me and Ivy. And it's me playing the guitar and Ivy was switching switches like on and off faster and slower, so it sounds like it's going backwards and slowing down and up – and it's one of the wildest sounds. I've never been able to recreate it, nor have I heard anyone else recreate it – this kind of magical sound."

'The Crusher' sold in healthy quantities in the UK, largely on account of its two unreleased B-sides. It would be the last record that the Cramps released for two years.

CHAPTER TEN

Cramped

We tend to move away from things when other people start doing it. I don't think you can cause trouble any more if people know it's coming.

Lux Interior

I never heard anyone call the Rolling Stones a 'blues band', but they brought a lot of attention to Howlin' Wolf.

Poison Ivy

AT the beginning of 1982 *Billboard* announced that the Cramps had filed a million dollar lawsuit against IRS, Illegal and Miles Copeland. The band's dissatisfaction with their label dated back over a year and there were even suggestions that the recording of *Psychedelic Jungle* was hastened by the Cramps' growing desire to fulfil their contractual obligations and get off the label. An alleged failure by IRS to pay the group the sum of $10,000 that had been agreed as part of their original deal in July 1979 provided the meat of the legal action, while claims that the label had failed to supply copies of the fully executed contract and made 'erroneous and fraudulent deduction from record royalties' were also made. "We weren't getting our money . . . people think we sued them for money, but the only thing we wanted was off the label," Lux recounted.

"They were really unhappy with the record company for whatever business reasons they had," explained Kid. "They felt misunderstood by them, they felt cheated. They felt like they weren't getting legal statements that were correct and law suits started to try to get all the correct information." Additionally, the band had been unhappy by the way in which

Cramped

'New Kind Of Kick' had been included on their recent 12-inch single. "That was only supposed to be a demo," Ivy asserted. "We'd written the song the day before. We were in the studio and it didn't really belong to IRS Records but because we did it at A&M's studios they just took it and they put it out and it was half baked."

In general, the Cramps were also irked by what they perceived as a lack of promotion from the label, as well as IRS' failure to submit sleeve art for their approval. From Lux's point of view, these shortcomings were indicative of the label's high-handed treatment of his group. "They hate their acts," he asserted. "We've noticed this with record companies, even though they want to be in the business, they feel jealous of their acts and they hate their acts. If you want anything a certain way, then they act like spoiled brats because you're trying to make your career go right or something. Many times record companies ask you to do things that are just impossible to do and then put a photo session where they want close-ups at the end of the day after you've answered questions for 10 hours or something – this kind of thing where they just have no idea, where someone that had been in a band would know more the way it's supposed to be." The reduced budget allocated for the recording of *Psychedelic Jungle* in relation to *Songs The Lord Taught Us* also provided a further bone of contention, particularly when viewed in the light of the more generous amounts of money that had been spent on all-girl new wave group the Go Gos' recent debut album *Beauty And The Beat* (ironically, the Go Go's would later initiate their own lawsuit against IRS).

For the Cramps, the immediate implications of embarking on this litigation were profound – they had entered into an adversarial situation, immediately ensuring that any support from the label was withdrawn. Until the action reached some kind of resolution the band would have to organise their own tours and fund any studio time out of their own pockets. Conversely, there would be no question of the Cramps recording new material for release by a label that they were involved in a legal dispute with, nor anyone else while they remained under contract to IRS. While the band had a certain amount of money in the kitty – thanks in part to a lucrative one-off gig in Leeds the previous September where the

Journey To The Centre Of The Cramps

Cramps were flown in from LA to appear at the Futurama two-dayer alongside the likes of Echo & the Bunnymen, Bauhaus and Theatre Of Hate – they were scarcely in a position to fund a national tour, let alone trips abroad or to the studio. "We had to put a hold on recording," confirmed Kid Congo. "So there wasn't a quick follow-up record or even the writing of songs. So we started playing live a lot to live and support ourselves."

IRS, having far greater resources available, could afford to let the legal action drag on, embroiling the Cramps in a war of attrition that may possibly lead to them backing down. However, any thoughts that the label may have been entertaining along those lines would have grossly underestimated the strength of Lux and Ivy's resolve. Between April and July, the Cramps undertook several short bursts of regional live dates that enabled the group to keep going. "Copeland just thinks we're so hardpressed, without a nickel, without any resources," said Ivy. "Without a nickel – it's so true! But without any resources; we still have our fans and our friends and our gigs are still financially productive."

However, the passion of the Cramps' fans for the group would prove to be something of a mixed blessing; while it enabled the band to get by from week to week, the growing demand for new Cramps recordings led to the steady trickle of bootlegs becoming a torrent. "We know of about 60, so I figure if it's 60, if it's like cockroaches – they say for every cockroach you see there's 500 more," speculated Ivy. "It's horrifying. It amazes me that there are bootlegs out of soundchecks, of us just talking in a room with somebody where somebody has taped it. I think it's horrible, especially as they go for twice as much as a regular record." In addition to taking food from the Cramps' increasingly threadbare table, these bootlegs often featured lo-fidelity recordings and misleading packaging. "A lot of it is pretty bad quality," asserted Ivy. "They re-title songs because we have fans that'll collect everything. So they change the title of a song, and our fans take the records home and they'll call 'Psychotic Reaction' something, like on one they called it 'A Walk Down Broadway'. So the fans think, 'Well I never heard them do that song, I guess I'd better plunk down all my dough and buy this.' Then they take it home and it's 'Psychotic

Cramped

Reaction.' It's mean." So far as Lux and Ivy were concerned, the sole redeeming feature of this proliferation of bootlegs was some of the more oddball releases. "Some are really slick and have bar codes, and you can tell it's just there to hustle money, and then another one will be like a real crazy looking fan thing by some psycho, and that's kinda more interesting," observed Ivy. With no means of releasing their material, the danger of new songs being bootlegged before the band had the chance to properly record and release them led to the Cramps increasingly basing their live sets around cover versions and songs from their back catalogue.

By late summer the Cramps were off the road completely on account of Nick requiring eye surgery due to what was officially described as a 'rare infection'. In reality, Nick's continuing junk habit was the root cause of his hospitalisation. "The only person who ever shot me up was Nick Knox," admitted Ivy. "He lost his eyesight in one eye from doing dope. That kind of scared everybody. We didn't do it any more." However, while Lux and Ivy may have been dissuaded from any further dalliances with heroin by Nick's plight, Kid Congo was finding that drugs served to fill the increasing periods of enforced inactivity. "The morale of the band started to get down," he explained. "I started to get estranged from the band. I was going on with my life – and my life included doing a lot of drugs – a lot of hard drugs and hanging out with Jeffrey a lot more." One advantage of the Kid being around his old bandmates was that the Cramps were able to borrow Gun Club drummer Terry Graham to fill in while Nick was recovering from his operation.

As a means of dispelling the gathering sense of depression that was enveloping the Cramps, newly appointed manager Art Fein persuaded them to record some demos. The latest in a lengthening line of short-term Cramps managers, Fein had previously looked after the interests of Californian blues rockers the Blasters and subsequently became established as a journalist, author and broadcaster. While Fein never adequately explained to the group why he thought recording the demos would be profitable, it at least gave the Cramps something to focus on other than their progressively restricted and difficult circumstances. The three tracks that emerged from the sessions, surprisingly convened at A&M's Hollywood

Journey To The Centre Of The Cramps

studios, were largely unremarkable. Apart from two fairly faithful covers they had been playing live – versions of the Third Bardo's 1967 garage classic 'Five Years Ahead Of My Time' and Tommy James & the Shondells' chart topper 'Hanky Panky' from the previous year – the main point of interest was provided by 'Call Of The Wighat', Lux and Ivy's tribute to Ghoulardi that incorporated exaggerated semi-autobiographical elements inspired by the Animals' 1965 cut 'The Story Of Bo Diddley'. While Terry Graham's emphasis on snare and lighter approach to the toms and bass drum meant that all three songs lacked the Cramps' trademark pounding rhythms, 'Call Of The Wighat' evokes the wild hucksterism of Ghoulardi and is also notable for some spectacularly effective subsonic sawing from Kid Congo. Graham would subsequently play just over a dozen gigs with the Cramps before returning to the Gun Club at the start of 1983.

Although the Cramps played at CBGB in November 1982, it would be their last appearance at the venue for over a decade. With hardcore bands such as Washington leviathans Bad Brains now pulling in a very different kind of crowd to that which had witnessed many of the Cramps' earliest performances, their New York gigs increasingly took place at the Peppermint Lounge on West 45th Street. "It seems like in the old days, a New York audience was from Manhattan," observed Lux. "Now it seems that a New York audience is from New Jersey or Queens. The prices have gone up so much that the kind of people who live down on the Bowery can't afford to go to these clubs any more."

With Nick back in the fold, the group arranged their sets on February 25–26, 1983 to be recorded for later use on a projected live album. Given that everyone else seemed to be taping the Cramps' live shows for their own ends, it made perfect sense that with the group unable to record a studio album they took a leaf out of the bootleggers' manual. "They were saying 'What the fuck are we doing? What do we do now? What do we do next?'" recalled Kid. "The Peppermint Lounge record was kind of like I was saying – we couldn't record a studio record any time soon because of all the legal hassle still going on, so that was the way around it they decided to come up with some new songs." Despite having got some good quality

Cramped

live recordings from the two shows, the ongoing legal wrangle precluded any notion of an early release, so the band returned to gigging as a means of supporting themselves, mostly dividing their time between short runs of shows in California or in and around New York. Additionally, when the opportunity arose to mix the tracks back in Hollywood they found that Kid's sloppy performance rendered several of them unusable, which resulted in Ivy having to overdub his guitar parts. With Kid Congo becoming increasingly unreliable, Lux and Ivy came to the conclusion that his tenure with the group had run its course.

Unlike his bandmates, the Kid was not bound by the IRS contract and was therefore free to record. "I was talking to Ivy and she was like, 'I don't know what we're doing, I don't know what's going to happen.' And the Cramps were the type of people to be like, 'You're in the Cramps and you can't play with anyone else.' And I was kind of itching to record with Jeffrey and I wanted to be a musician and do different things," he explained. "I asked Ivy, 'What would you think if I went ahead and did something with Jeffrey?' Because we were thinking maybe I should do a solo record or a weird project. She said that it was probably a good idea because she didn't know what was going on with the Cramps." As serendipity would have it, Jeffrey Lee Pierce was stranded in Australia with bassist Patricia Morrison where he had been compelled to borrow drummer Billy Pommer Junior and guitarist Spencer Jones from support band the Johnnys after Terry Graham and Jim Duckworth had made a last minute decision not to make the trip down under. "He called me up and asked me to come," recounted Kid. "I was like, 'I just quit the Cramps and I'm free.' So the next day I got on a plane to Australia and I was in the Gun Club again."

To an extent, Kid Congo was a casualty of the Cramps' ongoing legal wrangle with Miles Copeland, although as he subsequently admitted, "I was on so much heroin it wouldn't have mattered to me anyway." Although his departure brought the band's touring to a dead halt, the parting of ways was undramatic and amicable. "It was a better situation for him and a good time to leave. He really shines in the Gun Club and not as a Cramp, particularly his guitar style," Ivy observed. "He plays really

Journey To The Centre Of The Cramps

beautiful slide guitar in the Gun Club, which we just didn't have a place for," added Lux. Opting to retain his Cramps-given name, Kid Congo Powers remained with the Gun Club until the end of 1984, when he, Morrison and drummer Desi Desperate quit to form Fur Bible. After that group disintegrated in London, he travelled to Berlin where he joined Nick Cave's band, the Bad Seeds, where he remained until the early nineties. He subsequently made albums with the likes of Magazine bassist Barry Adamson and indie-rock singer/songwriter Mark Eitzel before recording his own *Solo Cholo* LP in 2005. Most recently he has enjoyed a long run and significant critical acclaim with his group Kid Congo & the Pink Monkey Birds.

As if to add insult to the injury that Illegal/IRS had inflicted upon the Cramps through its continuing, vigorous contesting of the lawsuit, the label cashed in on the band's undiminished popularity by releasing the *...Off The Bone* compilation in May 1983. Rounding up the *Gravest Hits* EP and the tracks that graced both sides of the four singles the Cramps had recorded for the label, *...Off The Bone* sold like crazy, spending an impressive 71 weeks on the UK independent chart. "The less we do, the hotter it seems to get over there," Lux observed. "*...Off The Bone* was number one on the alternative lists all summer. They're bugging us like crazy to go over there now." The album was also issued as a picture disc with the additional carrot of the unreleased 'Uranium Rock' included to attract completists.

While the Cramps would be due royalty payments on the disc once the legal dispute was resolved, *...Off The Bone* was released entirely without their blessing. This came as a surprise to Graham Humphries who provided the album's eye-catching anaglyphic sleeve art. "I'm such a fan, I listen to their stuff so often, it's really bad knowing I couldn't do anything for them," he declared. "I was told they had okayed the whole project – I thought it was just the release of back catalogue material. I was just hoping they'd like the sleeve." The following year, IRS cashed in still further with the release of *Bad Music For Bad People*, a skimpy 11-track singles compilation that offered the Cramps' cover of 'Uranium Rock' to fans as an incentive aimed at getting them to fork out for a further 10 tracks they

Cramped

already had. A *Sounds* review aptly nailed the money-grubbing strategy: "Miles Copeland's IRS label pick the carrion of their former label mates even cleaner by releasing a watered down version of the *...Off The Bone* singles collection that was released in the UK . . . The music's still great even if the scheming behind *Bad Music For Bad People* stinks of decay and corruption."

The healthy sales of *...Off The Bone* provided continuing evidence of the Cramps' popularity in the UK. However, many of those fans were disappointed in September when Lux and Ivy took the decision to compel Lindsay Hutton, founder of their British-based Legion Of The Cramped fan club, to close the operation down. Hutton, who had previously been responsible for the lively *Next Big Thing* fanzine, had started the fan club (alongside Steven Morrissey, who subsequently quit to concentrate on his developing career fronting kitchen-sink nostalgia quartet the Smiths) as an extension of his passion for the band. In addition to a snazzy membership card, Lindsay also produced *Rockin' Bones* – a fanzine that served as a Cramps newsletter, which continued for several issues focussing on other groups after he had received a letter from Lux and Ivy requesting him to cease his Cramps-related activities. Although the Legion Of The Cramped had served to sustain interest in the band, Lux and Ivy felt uncomfortable with being represented by a third party. "It was just becoming a thing on its own, where we had this life – our lives – which might or might not be the lives of stars, but what the fan club ended up representing – I think partly through us being on ice for two years – things were being generated that had nothing to do with reality," asserted Ivy. "The thing about not having a fan club is I think we're real loners as a band in a way; we just didn't want to be defined. I mean, people will always define us in the press or whatever, but the fan club was being taken as a source of information, a mouthpiece of the band and it wasn't really representing us. It couldn't."

"Our fans are our fans, [and] that has nothing to do with the Legion Of The Cramped. That was a fan club that we hoped would be a good thing and it just didn't turn out to be exactly what we wanted it to be," Lux explained. "We stopped it because that was just one guy and he was kind of deciding what we should be, or we felt it was this way." In part, Lindsay

Journey To The Centre Of The Cramps

Hutton's enthusiasm and goodwill collided in an unfortunate way with Lux and Ivy's implicit adherence to the 'No Club, Lone Wolf' outsider ethos. "I can't define the Cramps, so I don't know how anyone else can. And we're just uncooperative as far as a fan club, because we're not the type to write letters," declared Lux. "It's just that I get tired of being told how we are. This guy was making himself out to be a martyr to us; he said he was spending six hours a night writing letters to fans about the Cramps. I mean, what did he write about? He didn't have any contact with us, so how could he know what we were doing? All we did for a year was go into lawyers' offices where the carpet was so thick you get a shock if you touch a window frame."

Although this was harsh on Hutton, who had put in considerable time and effort in establishing the Legion as one of the most vibrant fan clubs around, Lux and Ivy's request that he shut the club down again has some connection with the Cramps' ongoing lack of activity. "Another reason we stopped was because we didn't know how long this lawsuit with IRS was going to go on," stated Lux. "For two years we weren't doing anything except playing music, and we didn't want publicity. The more we talked to people the more they said things like, 'You've got to get a record out' and it just added to the pressure." Despite this, both the Legion of the Cramped and *Rockin' Bones* are fondly remembered by many fans and Hutton's evident talent enabled him to carve out a niche as a music journalist of some note. "I never (to this day) fully understood why the LOTC was canned when it was – but for me, it was pretty much over anyway – people who claimed to like Bauhaus were joining," observed Lindsay. "I have had no contact with the band since August 1983 when the termination letter arrived. There was never any intention for this tail to attempt to wag said dog and despite some uncharitable mumblings toward me in the period that followed, I felt let down but let the chapter slide. *Rockin' Bones* continued for a few issues and was a little more expansive. It covered the emerging worldwide garage rock explosion, which in many ways the Cramps almost single-handedly ignited."

In October, just short of two years after the Cramps had initiated their action against IRS, the slow, self-serving wheels of the legal system finally

Cramped

ground to a halt as both parties reached an agreement. One of the terms that IRS stipulated as part of the settlement was that any revelations concerning the precise nature of the arrangement that had been reached would be forbidden, and while it remains vague whether the band received any remuneration in regard to monies that they had claimed were owing to them, it was abundantly clear that the group had achieved their aim of getting off the label. "Our main objective with that lawsuit was to get off the label – which is what we ended up with," confirmed Lux. "It was hell, it just destroyed us for a long time but we ended up getting off the label. There was nothing else we could have done, we couldn't stay on the label, there was no decision or anything – it was the only possible thing we could have done."

This resolution removed a massive psychological, emotional, and financial burden from Lux and Ivy, who had been compelled to divide their energies between keeping the Cramps going and maintaining the legal action. "We had a lot of pressures on us for the last couple of years, trying to keep things going and deal with these lawyers and everything. We couldn't sleep at nights because we worked, like, 24 hours a day. We'd be working at night and we'd work in the morning," Lux recounted. "The only reason it took so long was because it's his bunch of lawyers against our bunch of lawyers and they all have a good time while us two just sit on the sidelines and buy each other hot dogs while we wait for it to finish."

The successful outcome of the lengthy dispute with IRS served to validate Lux and Ivy's enduring belief in doing their own thing in their own way. It was this ethos that had driven them to relocate to New York and form the Cramps seven years earlier and had underpinned many of the decisions that the couple had subsequently made. "It was valuable; it made us understand how to do things. More importantly, we learned to stay out of the music business as much as we possibly can because the fact is that it is the most corrupt business on the face of the earth," Lux declared. "For two-and-a-half years we couldn't make records. It was like a hex. People we're calling and writing us constantly, but it was something that we had to do. A lot of people understand what we've been through and what we went through might have been completely unique." With the necessity to

Journey To The Centre Of The Cramps

deal with legal matters now consigned to the past, Lux and Ivy were again free to devote their full energies to doing what they did best. "We hope that we can record real soon, we've got a lot of songs written that only need final arranging and we hope to get a new deal together because we're free to do a new deal and I think it's important to do another studio album now," asserted Ivy. "We love recording, we love playing live too, but recording's special to us, maybe because we do collect records and love records, I think they're really magic. We've been frustrated for a long time."

From now on, Lux and Ivy's understanding of what worked best for the Cramps would become the sole guiding principle on which the band would operate. The lessons learned from the lengthy legal process had only served to strengthen the couple's resolve to continue their mission in life. "He can tell you about how much trouble we are," declared Ivy when asked about the dispute with Miles Copeland. "He fought us as hard as he could but we're still here," added Lux. The Cramps' experience with lawyers, managers and fan clubs had led them to resolve that any agencies outside the group should be avoided as much as possible, and to this end Ivy again assumed the role of band manager. "I don't know what I'm doing," she said. "To me, what it feels like more is if you meet a little kid and their mother's a junkie or something, so they're like a seven-year-old that's a little bit more mature than they should be. It's kind of like by default."

In order to get the Cramps back on the road, the group kept things in the family by recruiting Nick's cousin Mike Metoff, who had previously served time in Cleveland punk quartet the Pagans and garage combo the Clocks, both of which had issued a pair of independently released singles. "We want to keep it a nice incestuous relationship," explained Lux. "He's used to playing in bands in Cleveland and getting this thrown at him." Nick initially set his cousin on the road to rock'n'roll damnation by giving him some of his old sixties singles. Although Mike was asked to leave his first teenage group on account of his poor musicianship, Nick again provided the inspiration that encouraged his younger relation to keep at it. "At this time my cousin Nick was playing in a band called the Electric

Cramped

Eels," recalled Mike. "When I heard their tape I realised that you don't have to be good to play this stuff. So I started my own band called the Transducerz. We played a lot of pre-punk, Iggy, Lou Reed, Patti Smith, New York Dolls, and early Ramones and Dictators songs along with some sixties garage covers." After a spell playing local gigs at roller rinks and community centres, Metoff decided he was ready to progress to bigger things and auditioned for a more established local band called the Wild Giraffes. Although they were unimpressed with Mike's abilities, they recommended that he hook up with the Pagans, who shared the same garage and punk influences. The group took him on immediately and under the name Tommy Gunn, he contributed to their ultimate graduation to CBGB. However, any illusions that the band would follow in the footsteps of Cleveland buddies the Dead Boys proved to be shortlived. "At first we thought we had a chance," Mike recounted. "Then we got to New York – that woke us up real fast."

The Pagans slowly broke up – "We just stopped calling each other and going to practice – and Mike became a founder member of the Clocks, who formed at the end of 1979. After their debut single, 'Ticktockman', received some positive press, the Clocks added keyboard player Chas Smith to their line-up, which led the group's sound to drift toward the new wave. "Probably because of this, we became one of the top local club acts in the summer of 1981," remembers Mike. "That was a great time. We got our picture in *Rock Scene* magazine and had one of the best shows ever opening for Iggy Pop at the Cleveland Agora. But, of course, the good times were short lived." The Clocks broke up in much the same manner as the Pagans had, at which point Mike reformed his previous band. The Pagans resumed playing at CBGB and scored some high profile gigs supporting the Ramones and ex-Dead Boy Stiv Bators' post-punk supergroup the Lords of the New Church (which also included former members of the Damned, Sham 69, and the Barracudas), as well as recording the Pagans' debut LP, *The Pink Album*, before they again went their separate ways during the late summer of 1983. Mike's availability and family connection to Nick made him an obvious candidate to become the latest incumbent of the Cramps' fourth-member hot seat. "Someone was

Journey To The Centre Of The Cramps

needed to go on tour," Mike explained "Both the Pagans and Clocks had opened shows for the Cramps so we were somewhat acquainted. Anyway, I got the call and for a short time I became 'Ike Knox'. I arrived in Los Angeles on the same day the Three Stooges got their star on Hollywood Boulevard. Maybe that was some kind of omen."

Tall and leanly muscular, Mike shared his cousin's dark hoodlum looks and slotted in to the second guitarist role well when he made his live debut as a Cramp at the end of October. "I kinda consider it a north eastern Ohio band now," observed Lux. "He's been thrown in this in rather traumatic circumstances," added Ivy. "There's been line-up changes, but the Cramps'll never change. Usually when a band has line-up changes it's because they're changing direction, but with us – we get rid of the ones who change and we keep it pure."

"The wimps fall through the strainer," grinned Lux. "We've got along with Nick for six years and he's impossible to get along with."

With the Cramps back on the road playing a nine date mini-tour of northern population centres that also saw them make a one-night flit across the border into Canada, Ivy's next move was to find a label that would release the live set that the group had recorded at the Peppermint Lounge eight months earlier. Turning to somebody she trusted, Ivy contacted Roger Armstrong to see if he would be interested in issuing the six-track 12-inch in the UK. "That was kind of my first managerial stunt. I got a book about how to do licensing. He told me later that he found it unusual to talk to the artist," she recalls. "I didn't know what I was doing but we'd been burned by everyone that said they'd take care of us. Some people think that we've had bad luck, but the truth is that we haven't – every artist, they've all had equally bad luck; the difference is they packed in – we didn't. They let it get to them and it kills their vision. It wasn't like, 'If we do this we'll get signed and get some money . . .' it was always kind of nebulous. We didn't think about it, it was more organic." In addition to setting up a deal for the mini-album to come out on Armstrong's Big Beat label in the UK, Ivy also arranged the licensing for a US release on Californian independent label Enigma and with Patrick Mathé and Louis Thévenon's New Rose Records in France, which also issued the

Cramped

album (along with an additional track, 'Weekend On Mars') as an attractive box set of four different coloured seven-inch singles.

Released on November 11 with the fragrant title of *Smell Of Female*, the six-track 45rpm disc opened spectacularly as Lux's introduction and a gong ushered in 'Thee Most Exalted Potentate Of Love', an expansive triumph that featured Ivy's live guitar and subsequent overdubs meshing magnificently to create both a demented sand-dance-style lead and some truly mesmerising distorted rhythm. The song was one of four originals on the mini-album, which also featured 'Call Of The Wighat', 'You've Got Good Taste' (a thunderous, churning number dedicated to 'all you Gucci Bag carriers out there') and the exploitation/horror move inspired 'I Ain't Nuthin' But A Gorehound'. The group also dug into their extensive library of classic B-movies for a cover of 'Faster Pussycat', the theme song from Russ Meyer's sex and violence 1966 cult classic *Faster, Pussycat! Kill! Kill!* "I think mixing violence with glamour goes really good together . . . That's what a lot of our music's about. His music is the best sex and violence together, not sex here and violence there," asserts Ivy. "That's one very strong influence," added Lux. "But there are a million directors like Russ Meyer who were really great – Russ Meyer was one of the best technically, he made some really great movies." *Smell Of Female*'s second cover was an established live favourite, the Count Five's 'Psychotic Reaction'.

"I think this record is closer to the core of what we're all about. It's less confusing than some of the other records we've done," declared Lux. "Like on the first album we'd done 'Teenage Werewolf' and 'Human Fly' and *Gravest Hits* and stuff, so a lot of people said we were a horror movie band, period. Then we'd do some rockabilly songs and people would say we were a rockabilly band, period. It wasn't a conscious thing when we were doing this record, but it kind of seems that way now it's done; we're focussing in – we're trying to get rid of the extraneous details that don't have anything to do with anything. Just because I like some movie, I don't stick it in there any more." In addition to its provocative title, *Smell Of Female* came wrapped in a sleeve that featured a sexy image of Ivy in full burlesque apparel taken by Lux, who was developing a keen interest in

Journey To The Centre Of The Cramps

photography. "There were certain camps at the time that we're calling us 'teen fun' and whatever and we were like, 'We feel very adult, so we need to reinforce that.' And I think that may have pushed us toward *Smell Of Female*," explains Ivy. "I don't think people realise how real we are, and how different. Therefore, we don't feel like our music is for everybody. It's music for others who can identify with being a hoodlum, an outsider. Those who would call it kitsch or camp can't begin to know the world, the reality that this represents." Lux viewed the album art – which also featured another half-dozen sizzling snaps of Ivy on the back cover – as being in the grand tradition of groovy, sexy record covers. "That's the way I bought every album I ever got during the sixties – this is costing me $2.49, it better be cool," he observed.

With their rabid British fans having been starved of any new Cramps material for what had seemed like an eternity, it was scarcely surprising that *Smell Of Female* stormed to the pinnacle of the UK Independent Chart where it spent the next two years moving up and down. Writing in *NME*, where he gave the disc a five-star review, Edwin Pouncey declared that the six-track set "proves to be much more than just a treat for the fans – it's proof positive that *real* rock'n'roll has got to have guts to sound this good, real men's guts." Similarly, Ivy declared herself delighted with finally getting some new material released and the new release's licensing arrangements. "Big Beat is wonderful, they like old things too. They know what rock'n'roll is and I think they know what the Cramps are, that we are a rock'n'roll band and not some kind of weird thing," she enthused.

Despite this sudden detonation of positivism around the Cramps, normal service was resumed when Ike Knox quit the band in December. "Ike has this girlfriend who told him that if he didn't go home she was going to throw all his stuff out of the window in the snow in Cleveland. We auditioned a lot of people, but no-one was cool enough for us. We're looking for someone special, cos we're like a gang," Lux explained. "Outside the three of us, anyone else seems a stranger. There's no way round it." Among those auditioned was Kim Kane from Washington DC group the Slickee Boys, Surf Punks co-founder Drew Steele, and Click

Cramped

Mort – an untried guitarist who joined the group for less than a month before being found wanting. Mort subsequently resurfaced later in the decade as part of Los Angeles garage rock combo the Loafin' Hyenas, which also included former Gun Club bassist Rob Ritter, who had also been in the Bags. Surprisingly, Bryan Gregory made a tentative enquiry to see if he might be welcomed back into the fold he'd abruptly deserted. "He thinks we stink because he phoned Nick and asked him if he could join the band again but we said no. We wouldn't go within a hundred miles of him now," insisted Ivy. "He's so square; he's living in Cleveland now with a 40-year-old woman doing a really boring job like being a clerk or something." With the band again reduced to a trio, a projected three-date visit to the UK was shelved as their search for a new guitarist dragged on into 1984. In the end, Ike was persuaded to return in order to get the Cramps' medicine show back on the road.

After three relatively local warm-up shows in April and three further gigs in Portland, Seattle and Costa Mesa, the Cramps kicked off their longest bout of sustained touring since 1981 in Minneapolis on May 7. "People didn't forget about us when we were away," announced a delighted Lux. "We're four times as big in the States now as we were before. Maybe people think this is the last time they'll get the chance to see us." After a three concert mid-month return to Canada, the band played a New York showcase at the Peppermint Lounge before flying to England where they reintroduced themselves to the nation with an appearance on Channel Four's Friday evening TV music show *The Tube*. The band then set about working their way south from *The Tube*'s Newcastle studio, stopping off in Leeds, Manchester, Leicester and Birmingham before playing four sold out nights at Hammersmith Palais across May 27–30. Supported by two London glam/goth outfits, Specimen and Sex Beat, the Cramps' set list included two new covers: 'Sinners', a 1961 cut by Freddie & the Hitch-Hikers that would subsequently show up a decade later on the *Flamejob* album, and Andre Williams'1957 R&B hit 'Bacon Fat'.

By 1984, the British weekly music press had begun its long, apparently terminal, decline and while the Cramps' return generated coverage in

Journey To The Centre Of The Cramps

NME and *Sounds*, several features chose to concentrate on the band's influences and penchant for horror movies, topics that had been thoroughly forked in the past. "Everybody's got influences," sighed Ivy. "Maybe the difference is we mention our influences, while other artists pretend what they're doing is new, like they totally made it up themselves. What should I say – 'Link who?'" Additionally, sections of the press seemed disappointed that the group had turned up without either Bryan Gregory or Kid Congo Powers in tow. "The British press were definitely convinced that I didn't belong," explained Ike. "In England they're really repressed, they're just so uptight about everything and everybody's got their heads up their asses," observed Ivy. "The critics there just drive things into the ground."

The Cramps then hopped across the English Channel for a pair of typically riotous gigs at the Eldorado in Paris in early June. Although the venue wasn't demolished this time around, some serious damage occurred when the headstock of Ivy's Louis guitar was snapped clean off. "There was this riot, and a security guy grabbed it really fast," lamented Ivy. "Actually, what broke it was him falling down the stairs with it." Having played the solid-bodied instrument for several years, Ivy subsequently opted to switch to a vintage 1958 model 6120 Gretsch guitar, which would lead to a significant development in her technique. "It totally just changed my playing," she explained. "Part of the reason why is that it's a hollow body so I really got into feedback on a different level."

Being new to the band, Ike was amazed by the fervour of the Cramps' French fans and still has fond memories of his first trip to Europe as a professional musician. "The touring was wild, very rock star, especially in Europe," he recalled. "Major interviews, TV shows, four star hotels, and big concert halls. Like nothing I've ever done before or since. Of course, it didn't last long. I had a difficult time with commitment in those days. Looking back, I'm not so sure I fit in all that well with what they were doing, the lifestyle and everything. After all I'm pretty much just a dumb guitar-playing slob from Ohio." Ike's penultimate experience as a Cramp came after the band had returned to the US, where they finished up the tour with three Californian gigs – the first of which, at Hollywood's

Cramped

Palladium on June 16, provided some indication that their American following was catching up with its rabid European counterparts. "We were in the news," recounts Ivy, "and what did they call us – 'the Crabs' or 'the Craps' or something. They showed all these cops and punks running around and throwing rocks at cops and said, 'This is at the Crabs concert.'"

"Dangerous punks were attacking the police last night . . ." added Lux. "But it was the other way around," continues Ivy. "Dangerous police were attacking the punks." As the dust from the tour settled, Ivy refocused on the unfinished business of finding a label that would fund a studio album. "Everything we wanted to do we've had to finance ourselves. So we're limited to a certain point . . . So a studio album will have to wait 'til we can spend a little more on it," she explained. "We learned the lesson about not getting involved with anything like that again. There's plenty of places to record cheaply, so we decided to pay for our own recordings and license records to labels. So that was the lesson – stay away from the music industry," said Lux.

With Lux and Ivy being understandably wary about committing to anything that had the potential to develop into a re-run of the nightmare that they had endured with IRS, the Cramps' first new studio recording since 1981 emerged on the soundtrack album to Dan O'Bannon's forthcoming zombie movie *The Return Of The Living Dead*. The band had been invited to submit a track by Enigma, which had released the Stateside edition of *Smell Of Female* and was one of the label possibilities being considered for the next Cramps album. Working as a trio, with Ivy playing bass for the first time on record, the band rustled up 'Surfin' Dead', a suitably brain-hungry stomper that presaged the kind of four-string bump and grind that Ivy would later bring to *A Date With Elvis*. Written and recorded in just three days, the track was the standout cut on the 1985 album that also included contributions from the Damned, former 13th Floor Elevators maverick mainstay Roky Erickson, Californian hardcore group TSOL, and ex-Meteors double-bass titan Nigel Lewis' new group the Tall Boys.

While the year had begun with some promise following the resolution of the IRS lawsuit, after Ike made his swansong appearance with the

Journey To The Centre Of The Cramps

Cramps at a spectacular double header alongside Screamin' Jay Hawkins in October, it seemed very much as if the group were ending 1984 back at square one. Regardless of this apparent lack of progress, Ivy remained positive: "I'd love to have a hit single, I don't think we have to change a thing to do that either, because we really are just rock'n'roll and not one of these weird cultish things"

"We're going to write a single just like 'Billie Jean' by Michael Jackson and call it 'Rockabilly Jean'," Lux added. "Change the words around a little, change a note or two – I think we can make it."

CHAPTER ELEVEN

Adult Kicks

*The difference between us and a lot of artists now is that their influences are
only two weeks old.*

Lux Interior

There's kind of a square revolution amongst young people.

Poison Ivy

THE Cramps may have been off the road until a fourth member was
recruited and a new record deal arranged, but Lux and Ivy were
scarcely confronted with endless empty hours to fill. As would generally
be the case when circumstances necessitated a hiatus in band activities, the
couple retreated into their private world, immersing themselves in a rich
culture of forgotten music, cult movies and forbidden pleasures. As a
group that assimilated and adapted influences drawn from the dustier
corners of rock'n'roll's archive, any time spent exploring the mammoth
collection of vinyl that occupied ever increasing space within their East
Hollywood home could potentially bear strange fruit. "They're stacked up
in boxes all over the place," said Lux. "We've got some great stuff. We've
got all the Sun Records 45s and 78s, except for a few. There are like
maybe six or eight of the early blues numbers that we don't have. We have
them in alphabetical order, like we have all the rockabilly in one place, all
the rock'n'roll instrumentals in one place, all the surf instrumentals in
another place, R&B in another place, blues, you know . . ."

Lux and Ivy's passion for rock'n'roll ensured that there was usually
something on the turntable, as the couple plucked discs from their resting

Journey To The Centre Of The Cramps

places, using connective thinking and whimsy to compile pick'n'mix playlists on a daily basis. "Over the years you get to know them just like they're friends," Lux explained. "Like friends you have on your mind, and you think, 'Oh, I wanna listen to that,' and you just go grab it. When you've got a lot of records, it's more fun, because you can just go looking through them, and you always find something that you don't remember what it sounds like, and you rediscover something you haven't heard in 10 years."

Just as this constant exposure to rock'n'roll, garage, surf and assorted exotica served to fuel the creativity that enabled the Cramps to conflate and combine this music in new and exciting ways, Lux and Ivy's passion for cult cinema provided lyrical inspiration. "A lot of sexploitation [movies], just even titles, influence our songs," confirmed Ivy. "The dialogue from a lot of those movies is in our songs: 'Hot Pearl Snatch' is the name of a movie, 'All Women Are Bad' is the name of a movie. They're powerful titles to us enough that we felt like writing songs about them. Also they're in lines of our songs." The kind of films that the couple enjoyed were drawn from a broad basket of cinematic sub-genres including horror, science-fiction, exploitation and underground foreign movies. As cineastes, Lux and Ivy tended to explore similar outsider territories to those they focussed on as record collectors. "I think those things are like little nightmares, they're usually made by one or two people who had the idea and filmed it, and most of the time they don't make any sense on normal people's level, but they make so much sense," observed Lux. "It's like looking at some kind of Dada or surrealist painting or something. On some other level it makes much more sense than anything you encounter in normal, everyday life."

The notion that films released on the margins of the movie industry contained a far more meaningful interpretation of reality than more mainstream fare stems from economic necessity – many of these movies were shot on such meagre budgets that, despite their often extreme or exotic subject matter, there was generally more *vérité* than could be found in Hollywood blockbusters. "You're actually seeing people that can't act very well, so you see them as people, and they usually take place in

Adult Kicks

somebody's real house and on real streets, when all the other movies were being made on sets," Lux explained. "There's a slice of reality that you don't get in regular movies with those. I don't know what it is; once you've developed a taste for those, you can't go back somehow."

As had been the case with their musical influences, the Cramps were never shy about citing the movies and directors that inspired them. This led to a stream of features in the music press that detailed the band's taste in films and, in turn, often led to speculation about the visually striking group appearing on the big screen. Although both Lux and Ivy regularly declared their desire to feature in or make movies, this ambition remained un- realised as a series of projects were mentioned and then abandoned. At the beginning of 1985, there was considerable speculation concerning Lux and Ivy taking part in a sequel to cult director Herschell Gordon Lewis' 1963 shocker *Blood Feast*, which Lux regularly cited as being among his all time favourites: "You've got to love *Blood Feast* just for the line with the two detectives – they're standing there looking at each other and then one looks down – he's supposed to be looking at the desk – and he says, 'Looks like another long hard one.'" Although the Cramps would be linked with *Blood Feast II* well into the next decade, nothing actually materialised and a Cramp-less sequel crept out in 2002 to little excitement. Similarly, as time wore on there was often talk of a film being made about the Cramps, with actors such as rubber-faced comedy giant Jim Carrey and underground scream queen Erin Brown mentioned as possibilities for the principal roles. Again, these projects failed to reach fruition and, to date, the recreation of the Napa State Hospital show remains the sole cinematic depiction of the band.

Aside from their well-publicised passion for obscure music and movies, Lux and Ivy also numbered cars, photography, cats, fashion, art, design, gardening and, perhaps most sensationally, serial killers among their mutual interests. "It's always interesting, because I think anyone's poten- tially a serial killer," asserted Lux. "I think everyone's basically completely weird, even the most normal looking person, if the truth be known, is probably pretty weird." This interest was by no means passive – in addi- tion to visiting the home of recently executed murderer and body snatcher

Journey To The Centre Of The Cramps

Ed Gein in Plainfield, Wisconsin, Lux conducted a lengthy correspondence with John Wayne Gacy. Known as 'The Killer Clown' on account of his strategy of dressing as a clown in order to gain access to children's parties from which he sourced his victims, Gacy was executed in 1994 for the rape and murder of 33 boys and young men. "I really like the guy. I don't care if he killed 33 people. But there are people I like who didn't kill 33 people. And there's people who didn't kill 33 people I can't stand," insisted Lux. "I've written to him quite a bit. He writes very interesting letters back and painted a picture of me that I like very much. But I heard he wrote a book which published a couple of my letters. I thought we had a kind of sacred thing going."

The book, an anthology entitled *They Call Him Mr. Gacy*, was published by McClelland Associates/Grindhouse Graphics in 1989 and includes several of Gacy's primitively unsettling paintings alongside his collected correspondence. "He did one of me, it's a beautiful painting. It's a Polaroid somebody took of me and my chest is all cut up from onstage and he said, 'I did this painting and all the other convicts say that you look like a corpse,'" recounted Lux. "I was creeped out by that! He did a barroom scene – this has got like twelve figures in it or something, it's got a girl dancing, doing a high kick on a table and all these guys – that's a really great one. And Peter Pan – I loved to be Peter Pan – my mom made me a Peter Pan outfit, I'd run around the neighbourhood with my cape."

This fascination with serial killers was again indicative of Lux and Ivy's wider interest in people who exist on the extreme margins of society. Although Lux subsequently lost interest in the lives and personalities of murderers, at the time it connected to his ongoing curiosity about alternate interpretations of reality and the subversion of mundane existences. "That's what I liked the best, the ordinary ones like Ted Bundy, that's kinda interesting, the people that looked really ordinary," he explains. "For me, I would think Ed Gein," mused Ivy. "It sounds strange, but in a way he was just culturally different from the people in his area. He was reading a lot of books about cannibalism and headhunters and other cultures. The things that he did are actually common practices in some primitive cultures and in other countries, or maybe in another era."

Adult Kicks

More conventionally, Lux and Ivy used the break from band activities to make their debuts producing music by other groups. This took the form of *Music For Men*, a six-track mini-album from New Jersey quartet the Mad Daddys, which emerged on the local PVC label in 1985 before being licensed for European release on New Rose, which also subsequently issued their 1987 *Apes Go Wild* EP. The suitably rockin' cuts were mixed by Lux and Ivy at A&M Studios in Hollywood and in addition to featuring future Cramps drummer Slim Chance, the disc was adorned with a sexy cover shot of Ivy wearing little save a fishnet body-stocking.

As had been the case with *Smell Of Female*, the French New Rose label was one of a number of record companies with whom Ivy negotiated licensing deals for the Cramps' next album as the year progressed. With Roger Armstrong's Big Beat imprint representing a reliable means of providing the disc's initial launch in the UK, she also made arrangements for the LP to be released in Australia, New Zealand and Scandinavia, although American fans would have to score an imported copy, or wait for years for it to finally come out on Enigma. In order to get the ball rolling a little faster, Lux and Ivy accepted an approach to join their group from Tim Maag, formerly the bassist with South California hardcore combo D.I.. However, after involving Maag with the initial *A Date With Elvis* sessions in September and giving him the suitably Crampy stage name of Touch Hazard, he was deemed surplus to requirements and joined the lengthening list of those who would have brief tenures in the band. Hazard's sole notable appearance as a Cramp came when he was pictured with Lux, Ivy and Nick on the back cover of their album-heralding 'Can Your Pussy Do The Dog' single, which saw the light of day in November 1985.

Having had the experience of re-recording a number of Kid Congo's guitar parts for *Smell Of Female*, Ivy realised that she could fill in the group's bottom end as well as any outsider, and the band resolved to make the album as a trio. "It evolved in a real natural way on *A Date With Elvis*. We didn't have a fourth band member, and I had already done that song, 'Surfin' Dead', for the soundtrack of *Return Of The Living Dead*. We were still between members at the time that we made that, so I just made a wall

Journey To The Centre Of The Cramps

of guitar and included bass," she revealed. "The bass I played with was a Dan Electro six-string, and I also played a little bit of Fender VI on *A Date With Elvis*. I only played a real bass on one song, but I kind of dug it. It seemed even more prehistoric to me."

While the decision to record the album in this way came out of practical considerations, it resulted in an album that came closer to the Cramps' pure essence than any of its predecessors, as almost every aspect of *A Date With Elvis* – from the cover art through to its production – was done by the group. The sole outside input came from engineers Mark Ettel and Steve McMillan, who finessed Ivy's production. "I lose my mind in a week," says Ivy who, as a rare female producer, joined an overlooked lineage. "There are also several women producers who weren't famous," she recounted. "Cordel Jackson was a producer in Memphis, and she played guitar. We were able to meet her when we recorded our first album in Memphis. She had a label called Moon Records. There was another woman producer named Mira Smith who had Ram Records out of Louisiana and she also played great guitar. So, these are kind of some of the semi-unsung heroes of mine. There aren't a lot."

Similar to the way that Ivy had drawn inspiration from the work of Link Wray, Duane Eddy and a cornucopia of lesser-known guitarists, she adapted some of the production techniques used on early rock'n'roll, R&B and surf records as her studio technique developed. "A lot of it just comes from listening to old records. They have such weird production on a lot of them, things people don't do any more. They had real good accidents that are worth figuring out," she explained. "I love making records. They're magic and I hope that the accidents always happen." As the digital age of studio recording gathered virtual steam, the Cramps typically swam against the tide, favouring the more tactile benefits of analogue technology. "There was fire heating up those tubes," Lux declared. "When you yelled into a microphone or played a guitar, it would heat up a fire and that's what made it so wild-sounding. Now you've got those little cold pieces of clay called transistors, and that's what recording is."

The 11 songs selected for inclusion on *A Date With Elvis* contained the lowest number of cover versions of any Cramps album thus far. Aside from

Adult Kicks

an emotional, exaggerated rendition of Charlie Feathers' 'It's Just That Song' and an adaptation of 'Chicken' (based on a traditional song previously recorded by the Spark Plugs for a 1960 novelty cut, the track saw Luxhorn Leghorn and his band invent poultrybilly as Ivy's pecking lead and distorted bass chords drove the track along at fast food velocity), the remainder of the album comprised new material. While Lux's lyrical wit infuses many of the tracks with energy and humour, *A Date With Elvis* can reasonably said to be Ivy's album. Right from the reverb-laden extended opening chord of 'How Far Can Too Far Go' she is everywhere – supplying glorious discordant guitar breaks, her trademarked precision leads and even providing siren song backing vocals to the bongo beat exotica of 'Kizmiaz'. Fittingly, the track's mystic island lyrics were composed by Lux in suitably wet'n'steamy conditions. "He disappeared in the shower for 10 minutes and came out with this whole damn song," exclaims Ivy. "It's all zees, everything 'z', and he comes out with this insane song – he does that a lot."

Perhaps unsurprisingly, given that the band had never utilised a bass guitar prior to 'Surfin' Dead' and that Ivy understood the musical structure of the Cramps' songs better than anyone, she hooks into Nick's rhythmic base to spectacular effect. This is particularly evident amid the growling bump'n'grind of 'The Hot Pearl Snatch' where she combines with her own Duane Eddy-influenced lead to produce a form of sonic 3-D. Another track that owed its lyrical provenance to Lux and Ivy's fascination with cult cinema, the gloriously salacious 'What's Inside A Girl' incorporates lines from the 1975 revenge shocker *The Love Butcher*. "It's hard for us not to use these lines because we're just kind of submerged in these movies. We think that way. They don't sound like dialogue to us," Ivy observes. "If you'd allow me to get a little artistic about it, I'd say our songs almost get like collages sometimes," added Lux. "We have so many references to other things. Not that anybody needs to know any of that to enjoy our songs, but for some reason we seem to need to do that. I don't even know why. We just love these things for some reason."

Featuring a vocal contribution from the 'McMartin Preschool Choir' (a quintet of high-register vocalists archly accredited as being attached to a

Journey To The Centre Of The Cramps

daycare facility that was at the centre of an ongoing investigation into sexual abuse and Satanic rituals at the time), 'People Ain't No Good' finds Lux employing his slapback technique to fine misanthropic effect, while Ivy generates overlapping layers of churning guitar. Lux is in similar fine form throughout the innuendo-laden 'Can Your Pussy Do The Dog', a number loosely based upon Rufus Thomas' 1964 Stax single 'Can Your Monkey Do The Dog'. In addition to featuring a savage section of distorted guitar noise that sees Ivy out-weird Bryan Gregory, the song provides a concrete indication of the Cramps' R&B influences. "It's strange; no one ever comments on it," mused Ivy. "Everybody says we do garage punk and psychedelic and rockabilly, but there's all kinds of sixties and seventies soul in our songs, too, and definitely rhythm and blues, and blues. 'Can Your Pussy Do The Dog,' that was just like a sixties soul song. Most of our albums have that influence, but it seems like nobody ever brings that up. We love soul music."

A Date With Elvis' bucolic subtext is extended by the barnyard blast-off of 'Cornfed Dames', another track that finds Ivy taking sonic experimentalism further than Bryan ever did as she cuts loose with vicious Link Wray-style slashes again and again, particularly during the instrumental break during which the track seems to teeter on the edge of implosion. With lyrics that evoke a randy version of the Beverly Hillbillies, the song's title comes from a comic strip sent to the band by their friend Dave Stuckey, who was half of hillbilly revivalist duo Dave and Deke and who had been a serious contender for the vacant fourth spot in the group. "I came out and rehearsed for shows, but ultimately decided not to take up their offer," he recalled. "We remained good friends – I've had some of the best times of my life record hunting with Lux, he turned me onto many great records – and I did wind up recording with them on their *Cry-Baby* demos. I really can't say enough nice things about those guys."

The album was rounded off by 'Aloha From Hell' and '(Hot Pool Of) Womanneed', the latter a frantically rockin' bubbling cauldron of desire that neatly showcases Lux's ability to preach forbidden scriptures and Ivy's mastery of rockabilly bass. Like several of the self-penned tracks on *A Date With Elvis*, '(Hot Pool Of) Womanneed' was packed full of the kind of

Adult Kicks

libidinous innuendo that replaced the anticipated lyrical themes of horror and psychosis. For Lux, this cheeky use of *double entendre* was a more imaginative approach to representing rock'n'roll's sexual subtexts than any direct form of expression. Like burlesque, it was a tease: "It's much better to leave a little for the imagination, it's more surrealistic that way – leave something for people to visualise," he asserted. "I think what we do is natural," declared Ivy. "Sometimes I see bands being so blatant, I think they're trying to be outrageous. We don't try to be outrageous. We're just expressing ourselves in a natural way. I think that's why a lot of blues songs can appeal to me now, something that was from the fifties. Because of that same kind of innuendo that you're talking about. It's sexy, rather than confrontational. It's just more seriously about getting it on, rather than getting in a fight."

Of course, once *A Date With Elvis* was released in February 1986, lyrics such as 'Sugar and spice is just a bluff / You can tell me baby, what is that stuff?' were interpreted as sexist by sections of the British music press too tied to their socio-political dogmas to entertain any frivolous notions of fun. "It's just kind of weird, because they'll also say we're sexist, but they won't even comment on my playing as being unique, which I find pretty sexist," reasoned Ivy. "The kindest thing that's ever said critically is that I can play as tough as the men. That's a pretty sexist crack. I play unique, innovative, original. I produce this band, I manage this band and anyone who says we're sexist is blind and uptight." Reasonably enough, Lux echoed Ivy's dismissal of such facile criticisms, seeing them as being indicative of a dull worthiness that ran contrary to the spirit of rock'n'roll: "We like to bring a little more of the sick humour back to rock'n'roll, rock'n'roll's just way too healthy these days. It's horrible, it's obnoxious – all these rock stars doing good all over the world and everything – oh my god, enough is enough."

A similar storm in a tea cup developed around the album's title and its cover image, which depicted a platinum-blonde-wigged Ivy resplendent in devil horns and snakeskin basque, on a background of golden satin and surrounded by the kind of accoutrements one might expect to have found had they been invited to visit Elvis during his final days – The Bible, various

Journey To The Centre Of The Cramps

quasi-spiritual books such as Cheiro's *Book Of Numbers* and a generous selection of high-calorie toasted sandwiches. Some quarters, presumably ignorant of the band's influences, chose to interpret *A Date With Elvis* as an insult to The King. "It's a tribute, but it's also what a date with Elvis would really be like," said Lux. "If you had a date with Elvis, what would really happen is that he would give you pills and stuff like that, he would read to you from religious books. A real date with Elvis was a sick deal. It wasn't a convertible ride or anything like that." In addition to being titled in homage to him, the very nature of the outsider rock'n'roll produced by the Cramps was wholly consistent with Elvis' legacy. "This is the guy who started making white kids go crazy about rhythm and blues. It was such an important, dastardly, violently extreme thing he did. I mean – wearing mascara to high school in the South, in the fifties. This was wilder than most people can begin to imagine and he was that way his whole life."

With *A Date With Elvis* recorded and mixed, the Cramps recruited guitarist Jennifer Dixon to complete their line-up for tours that were being arranged subsequent to the album's release. "I became friends with Nick Knox after he started coming to Hollywood Hillbilly's shows," she recalls. "My bandmate/boyfriend Gary and I hit it off really well with Nick and before long he suggested to Lux and Ivy that they should come to one of our shows and they did.

"The Hollywood Hillbillys were pretty wild, live chickens and a rooster named Elvis onstage, a hillbilly-surf-biker musical extravaganza. We played anything from Conway and Loretta duets to the Lonely Surf Monster and Wild Angels instrumentals. Gary was really into Link Wray. Our 'Yakety' Sax player Jack Ruby would cross-dress for Flatt and Scruggs' anti-hippy seventies song 'Can't Tell The Boys From The Girls' in our Day Glo out-house that we always had onstage. There was lots of Day-Glo straw too. Pretty crazy. I met Lux and Ivy, and Lux started dropping hints that I would be a great addition to their line-up. He'd stand behind me at Club Lingerie after we played while I was watching another band and he would whisper in my ear 'join our band . . . join our band'. It was really wild. I loved the Cramps but initially I didn't even entertain the thought. I was busy with my own band.

Adult Kicks

"Early in 1986, I read in the *LA Weekly* that the Cramps were supposed to go on tour soon and still didn't have a bass player. I have a bad travel bug and that tour sounded pretty appealing. I had Lux and Ivy's number so I called them up and asked Lux if the job was still open, he said 'yep' and that was that. I started rehearsing, getting gear, wardrobe and passport. It was really a dream and I dug it immensely. It was to be a temporary arrangement: three to four months then back home, keeping in mind that my husband and partner, Gary, would be musically on hold and waiting till I got back to town. I had to learn the songs from the record *A Date With Elvis*. I knew many of the older songs like 'Sunglasses After Dark' and 'Human Fly'. We worked up some Elvis tunes ('Heartbreak Hotel' and 'Do The Clam') and Ricky Nelson's 'Lonesome Town' – those songs were a lot of fun. It wasn't brain surgery, the good stuff usually isn't. Simple repetitive arrangements, fun and easy to learn."

Although it had been almost two years since the Cramps last visited Europe, their popularity remained undiminished. 'Can Your Pussy Do The Dog' had whetted appetites for its subsequent album and the single (which also featured covers of Dave 'Diddle' Day's 1957 single 'Blue Moon Baby' on the seven-inch release, with a version of Jackie Lee Cochran's 1959 B-side 'Georgia Lee Brown' also added to the 12-inch edition) sailed to the top of the UK Independent Chart, as well as selling in healthy quantities on the continental mainland. When *A Date With Elvis* hit the UK shelves in late February, it sold equally well, hitting the number one slot in the Independent listings at around the same time the Cramps touched down in England to begin their European Tour. Their first port of call was Tyne Tees Television studios where the group recorded 'What's Inside A Girl', a powerhouse performance of 'The Hot Pearl Snatch' and 'Can Your Pussy Do The Dog?' for *The Tube*. The band unveiled a new, glamorous look: Lux in gold trousers and little else, Ivy in a similarly coloured burlesque belly dancer outfit, and 'Fur' Dixon in an appropriately furry pink bra with a matching puffball tail. As ever, Nick sat implacably at the back, dressed entirely in black.

The British leg of the tour began in earnest on March 14 with the first of a three night stint at Hammersmith Odeon, with support from Bristol

Journey To The Centre Of The Cramps

rockabillies the Stingrays. Despite some sound problems and sniping from the section of the music press that always seemed to take a dislike to any new member of the group and duly described Fur's bass playing as 'basic', their starving legion of London fans was delighted to have the Cramps back in town. These shows were followed by a further 10 gigs that saw them reunited with their provincial fanbase, as well as an enthusiastically received return to Scotland. As ever, Lux indulged in all manner of PA climbing and general writhing around, while Ivy appeared in a succession of sexy, vintage outfits. "Before we did that *Date With Elvis* tour I couldn't make that connection. Like I'd say, 'Boy, it's too bad that we're not in that era.' I'd be looking at old magazines of burlesque stars and I'd think, 'Wow, I wish I lived in that age.' I'd rather be part of that.' And Lux said, 'You can be whatever you want when you step out on the stage.' And that's when I started wearing like, those belly dance outfits, like forties burlesque outfits," she explained. "And then that was frustrating because we would play concerts like, in England, with punks where they're spitting and I'm wearing a $1,000 outfit. I'm like, 'How can you spit on this?' And they did."

Cleaning bills notwithstanding, Ivy's sartorial adventurism was another manifestation of the Cramps' continuing desire to put on a show. "We've always been interested in flamboyancy," declared Lux. "We've been seeing rock'n'roll bands all our lives, I guess it comes from the Velvet Underground, it comes from the Stooges, it comes from the Dolls, it comes from Screamin' Jay Hawkins. I guess that's a lot of the darker side of rock'n'roll, I guess some people would put it that way, although those people I mentioned are all multi-faceted people that have to do with life."

To coincide with the release of 'What's Inside A Girl' as the second single from the album (issued on purple vinyl with a cover of Andy Starr's lust-crazed 1956 rockabilly single 'Give Me A Woman' on the B-side, and a version of 'Get Off The Road' from Herschell Gordon Lewis' 1968 biker exploitation classic *She Devils On Wheels* on the 12-inch), the Cramps hit France at the start of April. This lengthy run of around 30 gigs was Fur's first exposure to the rigours of life on the road in foreign climes. "The tour was not easy or smooth," she recalls. "Our semi-truck equipment

Adult Kicks

driver was supposed to sleep on arrival at the venue, so he could be up all night later driving to the next gig. He wasn't doing much sleeping, but he *was* doing a lot of drinking and partying. On the way to Nice, France, he fell asleep at the wheel on a bridge and the top of the semi-truck was ripped almost clean off. The jagged metal stuck up gloriously about 15 feet in the air above the truck, until they managed to strap it down so it was 'legal'. Luckily, nothing but the catering food was lost."

After shows in France, Belgium, Holland and across Scandinavia, the tour took the Cramps to Germany, where Lux treated the Munich crowd to a new twist on his ripping-up-the-stage-floor trick, which he'd memorably unveiled at Hammersmith Palais five years earlier. "Lux jumped up in the air and since the stage was so crumbly, he went through it where he landed," explained Ivy. "I had been chopping away at this one spot on the stage with my microphone stand and I landed on the exact same spot I had been hacking at, I just kept going right through the floorboards," added Lux. "All you could see was a gaping hole with this wire going through it, but you could still hear me singing through the PA system."

"Eventually, he tore his way back out through the imploded hole and was ripping and throwing chunks of wood everywhere. I don't know how he managed to get back out of that hole and keep singing the entire time," marvelled Ivy.

As the group headed progressively further east, the group experienced some of the hazards often associated with rock'n'roll groups and customs checkpoints and events became increasingly harrowing. "The tour manager told us to dump any illegal drugs because we were driving through the East German Corridor," Fur recounts. "All Nick and I did was drink and smoke hash. We were pot heads but there's no pot in Europe. What Lux and Ivy were up to I wasn't aware of. Anyhow, we threw out the hash before hitting the road that day. We were stopped at four checkpoints, given the once-over then waved on through. We came to one last check point, guards ordered us to get out of the van. Lux and Nick were put in one holding room, me and Ivy in another. We thought for sure we were going to be strip searched. A lot of talk in German went on between the guards. The female guards were hideous. I looked on a table and there

Journey To The Centre Of The Cramps

were little Petri dishes with little rocky substances that had undergone chemical tests to see if they were drugs. We were let go without a search so we piled back into the pimp van. A mile or so down the road Nick took his boots off for the long drive ahead. Stuck to his sock was a nice size chunk of hash. Could have been a bad show with no drummer at the gig that night. I had nightmares of being arrested in East Germany for years after.

"Then, there were *nasty* anti-American demonstrations going on through Germany and Italy, due to Reagan ordering the bombing of Libya. We seemed to drive right through the middle of pretty horrible demonstrations in every town we arrived in. Talk about feeling tense before a show. Shows were stopped a few times in Italy because the 'Fuck you, Americans' chanting was so loud and the stage being pelting with cans, chair seats – whatever wasn't nailed down. That stopped however, when Chernobyl blew. Things got real quiet and calm and scary. I was 24 and freaked out. I was told, 'The show must go on', which I knew, but not much in the way of comfort though."

After a final burst of British dates in May and June (which included a gig at Brighton's Top Rank that saw Lux remain on the stage for over 10 minutes at the end of the gig, stark naked, creating feedback with the microphone and speakers before he was led away), Fur had had enough and parted company with the group, necessitating the cancellation of a planned Australian tour. However, once back in the States, fate again intervened to drop a permanent replacement directly into Lux and Ivy's laps in the shape of Connie del Mar. "We were at the Liquor Barn in Hollywood, and they have this little tiny parking lot for this very large liquor warehouse, and we were both aiming for the same parking spot with our two cars," Ivy recollects. "We were challenging each other; 'No, that's my spot', and she recognised Lux and myself. We'd heard about her before – a friend of ours said that we should get her in our band, but she was in high school and we weren't interested in pursuing that. It would be trouble."

Sexy and sassy, with a penchant for chewing gum and blowing huge pink bubbles onstage, Connie – who became better known as 'Candy' –

Adult Kicks

certainly looked like trouble. This, along with a lengthy list of shared influences, made her ideal Cramp material and she was briskly inducted into the group ahead of their US tour. "She's the fourth member of the Cramps who's been into the music that the rest of the Cramps are into," Ivy announced. "It's been really hard finding someone. I guess we're really demanding with what we want out of a member. To play the music the Cramps make, you have to like a lot of the music that we collect and listen to, whereas if you were just a fan of the Cramps, that's not important at all. You don't need to know anything at all – just show up, and it's fine. But to make the music, you have to have a pretty profound understanding. You have to really live this music. It can't just be an idea; you've got to have been listening to it."

Strangely, Candy had a habit of bumping into Cramps personnel. In addition to her fateful encounter with Lux and Ivy, while on a trip to Florida she'd also run into her most notorious predecessor, Bryan Gregory. "There was an underlying eeriness and weirdness in the air when he showed up," she recalled. "He truly looked out of this world and like one of the wickedest mofos I've ever seen in person. Dressed to the nines, he also had on a crinkled, fitted cowboy hat with a real stuffed scary looking Cobra snake head protruding from the base of the brim. He also had a dark blue painted-on mask (like Zorro) across his eyes to his ears. Later that evening I was supposed to meet up with him at the lounge of the lodge we were staying at, but I felt like I was sort of kept from going – the way the evening unfolded, let's just say, it was probably a good thing."

Despite having less than a month to prepare, Candy slotted into the Cramps effectively, quickly gaining experience and confidence as the group travelled around North America during July. The following month, she accompanied the band on their rescheduled antipodean debut, which saw the Cramps play 10 shows in Australia and New Zealand, their August 30 set at the Galaxy in Auckland subsequently emerging as the *Rockin'n'Reelin' In Auckland New Zealand* live LP. After the gig the sound engineer had presented the band with an excellent quality tape of the performance that enabled them to arrange a release on Big Beat with Roger Armstrong. The disc sold out its 40,000 pressing almost immediately. "In

Journey To The Centre Of The Cramps

America there's no independents like Big Beat Records," observed Ivy. "Independent labels have successes in England, but we couldn't get a major label to put it out and it's not worth doing an independent in America – they can't do anything. So it just kinda broke our heart that it didn't come out that way."

After reconvening for a trio of shows at the Ritz in New York at the end of 1986, the Cramps took an extended break that saw them make just a handful of public appearances before they hooked up to record their fourth studio album at the Music Grinder facility on Hollywood Boulevard in October 1988. With Lux and Ivy again ensconced within their private world, their profile was so low that during a Los Angeles radio broadcast in late 1987, Joey Ramone announced that Lux had died. While this was fairly representative of Ramonic humour, it came as something of a surprise to Lux, who after checking carefully, realised that he was as undead as ever and announced, "I'm not dead at this time."

As had been the case with *A Date With Elvis*, the absence of any record deal was a significant factor in ensuring that Cramps fans would face another lengthy wait for any new material to become available. "Some people have asked if we're always going to have four years between albums," said Ivy. "That's part of the reason why we needed a record company; it's been very hard for us just to get records out by ourselves." Having failed to secure a US release for their previous album, Ivy was keen to arrange a deal that saw their next disc available everywhere. Although the group played a quartet of Californian gigs that coincided with their return to the studio, including a show in San Francisco on October 31 that would initiate an intermittent practice of appearing there for Halloween, aside from the occasional one-off gig in New York or Los Angeles, the Cramps largely remained on hold throughout 1989 as the search for a viable label dragged on.

In June, they recorded three tracks for inclusion in *Cry-Baby*, maverick director John Waters' forthcoming homage to juvenile delinquent movies, released the following year with Johnny Depp in the lead role. Being fans of Waters movies, which included such kitsch cult classics as *Pink Flamingos* and *Hairspray*, Lux and Ivy agreed and set about laying down a

Adult Kicks

trio of songs on a two-track. The song titles, 'King Of The Drapes', 'Teenage Rage' and 'High School Hellcats', had already been pre-selected for the movie. "We were told that John Waters wanted us to write the songs for the movie *Cry-Baby*, and we told him that we do not write songs on speculation and that's where our songs came from," Ivy explains. "It turned out that they had actually gone to many songwriters including a man named Ben Vaughn who's in Pink Slip Daddy and asked them to write songs too – they just said 'Write songs and give them these titles'. So we wrote ours thinking we were the only people writing the songs." Worse still, having jumped through the hoops that the film production company had set before them, the tracks recorded by the Cramps were rejected. "It turned out to be music business crap," lamented Lux. "[John Waters] never even got to hear the songs. Somebody in LA was choosing the songs. Later we released the songs on the B-side of a record and somebody played it for him and he said, 'I wish I would've heard this, I would've put it in the movie.'"

Shortly after this disappointment, the long-awaited new album was finally given the green light when Ivy agreed a one album deal with Californian independent label Enigma. "They're some of the few people that we know that don't treat us like Hell's Angels from outer space. They have some degree of respect for us, it's great," enthused Lux. "They're kind of achieving major status in America, but they're also in touch with having been an independent originally," explained Ivy. "They just offered us more freedom – not just on paper, but in a vibe. They don't want us to modify anything that we've done. They're willing to put a lot of push behind what we do without us changing anything, they really have a lot of faith, they're really impressed with the Cramps and so we have a lot of faith in them."

With the album requiring only mastering, the band was back in business – although its release was put back to February 1990 to enable Lux and Ivy to move house before embarking on the obligatory promotional touring. This time around there were no cross country trips for the couple, who simply relocated to the Los Angeles suburb of Glendale, close to Forest Lawn Memorial Park Cemetery, the final resting place of many Hollywood notables including Sammy Davis Jr., Errol Flynn and Walt Disney. "I love Forest Lawn. It's like an amusement park. It's very pretty – and with a gift shop," Ivy declared. "Every couple of weeks there's been a smell like a house burning down," added Lux. "One time we went outside and our next-door neighbour said, 'It smells like it's coming from up there.' So we called the fire department. And they said, 'Well, you know Forest Lawn's right up there and they don't like to talk about it, but they cremate bodies every couple of weeks at night.' It's a really strange smell, especially when you know what it is."

The first fruit of the Cramps' deal with Enigma fell to earth in January with the release of a pre-album single, 'Bikini Girls With Machine Guns'. Notable for the effective way in which the rhythm section locks together to drive the track relentlessly forward as Ivy cuts loose with controlled distortion and slashing, reverb-drenched chords, the track was promoted by a video based in part upon *Robot Monster* – a gloriously unhinged Cold War monster movie that was among Lux's favourites. Introduced by Lux in full-blown psychedelic guru mode, who informs us that 'all things now are possible, in the limitless void of counter-actuality', the promo fell afoul of MTV's ever-twitchy censors, who demanded cuts before they would air the footage. "MTV said they wouldn't play our video unless we changed some things and we quite like the idea of having a censored version," Lux explained. "So we did that, and then there's a scene where Ivy's shooting a machine gun and her bikini bottoms fall down around her ankles, and we had to take that out. And they kept saying, 'Take this out, take that out . . .' I think the actual truth of the matter is though, unless you give them $200,000 or something under the table, they don't play your video anyway."

Stay Sick hit stores the following month to demonstrate that the Cramps don't change, they just dip into their bulging grab-bag of influences and pull out different subversive elements on which they perform their customary aural alchemy. "The name of the album is *Stay Sick*, and the reason we called it that [is because] we're sick and tired of rock'n'roll getting such a good name and getting so respectable," announced Lux, reiterating his disgust at the creeping propriety that was infecting rock'n'roll. "They're

Adult Kicks

feeding starving people and the good things happened in rock'n'roll, like happen in the regular world, and we don't like that. We like to keep it unhealthy and sick, like it's supposed to be. It can't be rock'n'roll unless it is, and it's not."

As with *A Date With Elvis, Stay Sick* included just two actual covers (again alongside one adaptation of a traditional song) – the first being a cover of Macy Skipper's 1956 Sun Records cut 'Bop Pills'. "That was originally like a kind of wimpy calypso song – it wasn't even rock'n'roll. But we liked the words and we liked the idea because we knew from talking to those people when we were recording down there in Memphis that you hear all this talk about how Elvis got into the studio because he recorded a demo for his mother and all this sort of thing," recounted Lux. "The solo I play is straight out of [Duane Eddy's] 'Ramrod', but no one picked it up, it's weird," Ivy recalls. "These are like salutes, these are like fireworks, these are like a 21 gun salute to our heroes, but I don't think it's understood that that's what we're doing."

While 'Bop Pills' got *Stay Sick* off to a throbbing part, the album's other cover – a version of country yodeller Jimmy Rodgers' 1930 song 'Mule Skinner Blues' – finds the band back in the barnyard as Lux delivers a genuinely demented vocal performance, projected lunatic laughter and unhinged hollers onto the primal rock'n'roll canvas kicked up by Ivy, Candy and Nick. The group again adapted a page from the great American songbook with a lung-busting version of the traditional number 'Shortnin' Bread', which saw Candy's pulsating bass combine well with Ivy's subtle use of reverb. "'Shortnin' Bread' sounds like a peculiar choice, but actually there's a tradition," said Lux. "In the early sixties a lot of surf bands covered 'Shortnin' Bread'. I don't know why, but you find a lot of versions if you look in surf discographies. We do a stomp and surf version." Although the gaga spankfest of 'Mama-Oo-Pow-Pow' owes its title to the Rivingtons, the song was a largely improvised recording adorned by such mouth-watering lyrics as 'I'll eat your heart out like an Aztec – I don't give a hoot'. "When I did that take, I had no idea what to play on it," revealed Ivy. "I was just kind of stumped as to what to play on that song and that's what I did, that's what's on it. They were saying, 'You

Journey To The Centre Of The Cramps

sure? Don't you think you need to do another take?' I said no. I kind of liked the idea they were horrified enough to think that I should do another take. I thought it was kind of an amusing guitar part. I just winged it from beginning to end. I thought it might have been something horrible at first, but when I heard it that evening I really dug it."

The balance of the original material included on *Stay Sick* includes some stone cold Cramps classics. In particular, 'All Women Are Bad' is a triumphant representation of the group's strengths that incorporates Lux's lyrical wit and slapback vocal, Ivy's guitar subtleties and Nick's non-stop primal pounding into a genuine *gestalt* that is so close to the band's pure essence that the song would not have seemed out of place on *A Date With Elvis*. 'Creature From The Black Leather Lagoon' drops the Cramps' lyrical penchant for horror and science fiction into the midst of a fetish night, while 'God Damn Rock'n'Roll' reiterates the link between rock'n'roll and sex as Lux preaches from the gospel of sin. Ivy unveils different facets of her increasingly agile guitar technique, bringing the tripped-out noise to psychedelic cut 'Journey To The Center Of A Girl', making a sound like Satan's sax on the pulsing, bass-driven 'Everything Goes' and bending notes into new, unnatural shapes across the 'Human Fly' referencing 'Saddle Up A Buzz'.

Additionally, her increasing confidence as a producer is apparent as several of the tracks segue together inventively, linked by bubbling and sizzling sounds, overdubbed to give the album an extra dimension. "Some songs on the new album had to be recorded live," she explained. "'Muleskinner Blues', 'Shortnin' Bread' and [bonus track] 'Her Love Rubbed Off' couldn't be recorded any other way because of the way we have to interact with each other and Lux singing. Other ones though, were tracked with drums and bass first, although we do that together. We try to track the rhythm together; it makes it easier to record songs." This process was enhanced by Candy's precise bass orthodoxy, which enabled her to combine with both Ivy and Nick as the song's structure demanded. "We can play better now than we could before," asserted Lux. "Until Candy, we never had another band member that could play very good. We would always write songs and then we couldn't do them."

Adult Kicks

Whereas *Stay Sick*'s sleeve featured the latest in Lux's sequence of provocative and alluring photographs of Ivy, the reverse depicted the whole band as a sexy girl group – even Nick, who looked quite coquettish in a long black wig and mini-skirt. "It arose out of Halloween," revealed Ivy. "We did this photo spread for a magazine called *Rip* and they wanted us to dress like monsters, a kind of more clichéd thing, for the Halloween issue. We didn't want to do something so obvious, so we decided that since it's also the drag holiday, that would be our Halloween testament. The wig Lux is wearing, the white one, is the *A Date With Elvis* wig. We recycle our clothing!" The album's visuals also served to indicate to the casual browser that what was contained within was dangerous music; nasty, corrupted rock'n'roll – just how it should be. "I think that's what's wrong with rock music today," Lux insists. "It's music for adults, it's respectable and it's good, and it's art, and it's all these kinds of things. That's fine for music, but people don't understand the difference between rock'n'roll – which is a lifestyle, a fashion, a music, it's sexual intercourse – it's a lot of things, and 'rock music' is just merely music. Rock'n'roll is much bigger than that and people confuse rock music with rock'n'roll. Rock'n'roll's much better."

Beginning at the Brixton Academy on February 12, the Cramps duly embarked upon their usual post-album tour, playing concerts in the UK and across Europe, before returning to the States in April for a further tour that took them through until June. While the group were on the road, Enigma issued two further singles – 'All Women Are Bad', which featured all three *Cry-Baby* songs on the 12-inch version's B-side, and 'Creature From The Black Leather Lagoon'. Having experienced issues with MTV over their 'Bikini Girls With Machine Guns' promo, Lux and Ivy decided to give the station something to really get their teeth into this time around. "It kind of had everything that you're not supposed to have on a video. It was just good clean fun," declares Ivy. "It showed Lux getting born at the beginning of it, his head comes out from between this monster's legs. It was like everything you can't show on MTV. I don't think there was any part that could be cut out of that; it's got everything . . . we had other videos that were getting played but that one was just our video."

Journey To The Centre Of The Cramps

"We tried to make it so that you couldn't cut out any parts. That's the mean streak coming out in us," adds Lux.

The single also featured the Cramps' version of 'Jailhouse Rock', originally recorded for the *Last Temptation Of Elvis* double album. Sponsored by *NME*, the two disc set featured everyone from Paul McCartney to Motörhead's Lemmy covering 26 of The King's songs that had featured in films. "It was a tribute to Elvis and it sounded like a good idea for a record," recalled Ivy. "The theme for it was a song from an Elvis movie, we were one of the last bands involved, yet nobody had picked 'Jailhouse Rock', the rock'n'roll song. Everybody went for the weird songs and everybody leaves the most rock'n'roll song from the movies."

After appearing at around half a dozen outdoor festivals during the summer, Candy quit the Cramps to play in a succession of bands with her partner, Andy Gortler, while Nick Knox brought his long association with the band to an end due to his increasingly poor health. "He's really not up to touring. We loved everything he did but he likes to drink and whatever. We always wanted members who could match our energy and it was clear that wasn't happening any more. Candy just changed interest in music and started listening to seventies stuff," explained Ivy. "Nick was so loyal for 13 years. To me it was a technicality that there was Cramps before that and there'd been other members."

"He's kind of a rock'n'roll casualty," concluded Lux.

The Cramps step out in Pasadena, 1998 – [L-R] Slim Chance, Ivy, Lux, Harry Drumdini.
LARRY HIRSHOWITZ/CORBIS

"We go to France and it's incredible – You just wouldn't believe it" – Bryan, Nick, Lux and Ivy on the first French tour, March 1980. CLAUDE GASSIAN/RETNA PICTURES

Losing touch with reality – an outtake from the *Psychedelic Jungle* photoshoot.
DONNA SANTISI

Lux donates some fluids at the Futurama Festival, Leeds, 1981. DAVID CORIO

Queen of the hollowbody – Ivy with her trademark Gretsch 6120. DONNA SANTISI

Midwest Monsters – Nick's cousin Ike Knox [aka Mike Metoff, far right] joins the party, 1983.
CHRIS WALTER/PHOTOSHOT

"It's one of the few things you can do where you don't have to grow up" – Lux in typically uninhibited form at the Eldorado, Paris in June 1984. CLAUDE GASSIAN/RETNA PICTURES

Hollywood Hellbillies Lux and Ivy take stylish shelter from the warm California sun. LINDSAY BRICE

Ivy: "I have an allergy to latex from wearing it too much. I have an amazing collection of latex garments and I wore it to death." LINDSAY BRICE

The Cramps [with bassist Candy del Mar, left] on the set of the 'Bikini Girls With Machine Guns' video shoot, directed by Rocky Schenck (front), 1989. ROCKYSCHENCK.COM

On tour in the UK with bassist Jennifer 'Fur' Dixon [left], March 1986. IMAGO/PHOTOSHOT

'Lemme give you some advice' – The Cramps on Candy and Nick's last European tour, 1990.
JOE DILWORTH/RETNA/PHOTOSHOT

Lux wigs out at the 1990 Reading Festival.
GEOFFREY SWAINE/REX

Ivy's captivating thousand yard stare, which she attributes to short-sightedness.
BRIAN RASIC/REX

Ghouls and boys – The Cramps induct Kid Congo Powers into the madness, 1981.
HAMON/IDOLS/PHOTOSHOT

Featuring the surprising sight of a fair-haired Lux, the Cramps tear up the London Astoria during their final UK show in August 2006. JO HALE/GETTY IMAGES

Lux and Ivy – The recipe for a whole different kind of American love story.
WENDY LYNCH/REDFERNS

CHAPTER TWELVE

The Ones That Got Away

We tried to get old, but it didn't work.
Lux Interior

We're lucky that there's the two of us because I think we keep each other from wiping out.
Poison Ivy

GIVEN that in the past, line-up changes had played no small part in creating the extended gaps that occurred between Cramps albums, anyone aware of the band's history would have been forgiven for assuming that Nick and Candy's departures would likely serve to usher in another lengthy hiatus. However in little over a year, Lux and Ivy recruited a new rhythm section, organised new licensing arrangements, got the Cramps back on the road, and wrote, recorded and released a new studio album called *Look Mom No Head*. "Before, there was a little bit of self-satisfaction creeping into the Cramps, which really flipped us out," revealed Lux. "On *Stay Sick* one of the members wasn't doing so good and the other was having terrible problems and we just couldn't play the songs. On this LP, we had been playing these songs for five hours every day for two months before we went into the studio. We could play them like a blast furnace."

Lux had chosen his words well. *Look Mom No Head* emerged in November 1991 as a superheated mixture of pounding rock'n'roll and transgressive intent. With the exception of the album's reverb-laden closer, 'The Strangeness In Me' (which was based upon the Runabouts' 1961 B-side 'When I Get The Blues'), the relentless nature of the set

Journey To The Centre Of The Cramps

ensured that it was easily the Cramps' most forceful release thus far. In part, this can be attributed to Ivy's increasing mastery of production, which resulted in crispness and clarity being allied to considerable depth and range. Equally, some credit for the pumpin' corpus of songs recorded for the disc should be given to Slim Chance and Jim Sclavunos, the engine room that drove *Look Mom No Head* unstoppably onward. Flaxen haired bassist Slim had previously served time in the Mad Daddys – an association that had placed him directly on Lux and Ivy's radar.

"I really loved his bass playing in that band," said Ivy. "We'd met him before because we knew the singer in that band. We were just trying to get members who were really dedicated. We'd got to the point where we felt like Lux and I were kind of carrying the thing. The rest were acting like a back-up band. We just wanted it to feel more like it did when we started, like a real gang." Beat maestro Jim Sclavunos had been in the Cramps' orbit for some time, having been a member of Teenage Jesus & the Jerks and Tav Falco's Panther Burns, the group that had also included Alex Chilton. "We usually call up all our friends and say, 'Hey, have you seen anybody lately?'" Lux explained. "We're not changing direction in any way, it's just not quite as drunken sounding," added Ivy.

The key to the group's quick recovery from having their membership suddenly reduced by half was the intensive way in which Lux and Ivy drilled Nick and Candy's replacements into shape. "During my tenure I was almost daily in the company of Lux and Ivy, which made for a most unusual time well spent," Jim recalled. "Every day, after our typical six-hour non-stop rehearsal, we would decamp to Lux and Ivy's living room, where the man of the house would deliver lectures in an almost paternal manner. It was like belonging to a weird family – in the Manson sense of family."

The fierce rehearsal regime paid dividends, resulting in an album that is precise and accomplished to the extent that it imparts a degree of irony on the Cramps' origin as a group of non-musicians. From the moment opening track 'Dames, Booze, Chains And Boots' crashes in and Ivy's guitar strafes the bedrock of jackhammer rock'n'roll kicked up by the new rhythm section it becomes clear that the Cramps have been working out –

The Ones That Got Away

it is a muscular album. Despite Slim's employment of blistering low-end distortion on tracks such as 'Two Headed Sex Change' and 'Eyeball In My Martini' and Jim's forceful drumming on those and several other numbers, there is also much subtlety and complexity in evidence. Ivy is again ubiquitous – coaxing sounds from the outer limits on 'Blow Up Your Mind'; providing deceptively simple-sounding layers to the rolling rockabilly of 'Don't Get Funny With Me'; and putting in a triple shift of lead, rhythm and all-purpose manic urgency as 'Eyeball In My Martini' unfolds at breakneck speed.

In addition to sounding as if the Cramps had been at the pep-pills, *Look Mom No Head* was to some extent the band's transgressive album. Lux again appears within the disc's artwork practising his own unique interpretation of cross dressing, while tracks such as 'Two Headed Sex Change', the pumping sex and death declaration of 'Bend Over, I'll Drive', and 'I Wanna Get In Your Pants' (which gives sixties bubblegum a fetish makeover) extend the perversely lascivious theme. "'I Wanna Get In Your Pants' is about me wanting to wear women's clothes," Lux explains. "I like the feel of it." Lyrically, the album finds Lux in his usual dextrous and witty form, splicing pop-cultural references to the kind of wordplay reminiscent of Ghoulardi. He also demonstrates considerable vocal adaptability, adding richness and tone to the slaughterhouse blues cover of Captain Beefheart and Ry Cooder's 'Hardworkin' Man', managing to sound seductive while singing about 'Sunday panties' on 'I Wanna Get In Your Pants' and adding a higher than usual croon to 'The Strangeness In Me'. Once again, the Cramps had rummaged around in their store of influences to emerge with material that combined them in new and exciting ways. "They're just all like postcards from the Cramps," observed Lux. "There isn't a difference except I suppose that we're different people. Right now, we're very interested in flying saucers – we read tons of books on it and spend all our time on that. When our first record came out we were very interested in something else, I don't know what it was at the time – probably staying alive and not getting killed in New York."

Unusually, the Cramps' cover of the Flower Children's 1968 garage cut 'Miniskirt Blues' featured a guest vocalist thanks to a chance encounter

Journey To The Centre Of The Cramps

with Iggy Pop. "I went to get a bottle of wine next door to the studio and he was in there buying Budweisers and I said, 'Come over and say 'hi' to the band,'" Lux recalled. "Then when he came in he said, 'Do you have anything you want me to sing?' and we said, 'Yeah.' It was very strange though because that song that he sung, we'd wanted him to sing for a long time, but we'd never been able to get in touch with him and then right when it came down to the point where we were actually recording it, it was like magic – he was just there buying Budweiser and so it actually happened."

For *Look Mom No Head*'s release, Ivy again turned to Roger Armstrong who issued the disc on Big Beat in the UK, while Enigma subsidiary Restless Records picked up the American end of things and additional deals were negotiated for Germany and Australia. The switch to Restless had been prompted by their parent company's collapse. "Just when we liked the idea of being on one label," lamented Ivy. "We were horrified that there would be another long gap between releases. It's been stop and start all our lives." After recording the album, Jim Sclavunos left the band to devote his considerable energies to a number of projects that included Kid Congo's latest group Congo Norvell, Lydia Lunch and former Birthday Party guitarist Rowland S. Howard's Shotgun Wedding combo, and a return to Tav Falco's Panther Burns. "I quickly learned that despite appearances both Lux and Ivy took themselves and their music very, very seriously and held rockabilly, garage, the blues and the other forms of music that they emulated in the utmost regard," he later observed. "From their point of view, it was art of the most sublime order, no matter how trashy its reputation."

His replacement for the subsequent tour arrived in the shape of Nickey Alexander, who'd previously played with Los Angeles punks the Weirdos and commercial rockers LA Guns, who had originally included Axl Rose among their number. This time around, the group's touring started slightly ahead of the album's release with a show in Newcastle on October 15, which initiated a run of 13 UK dates, culminating with four nights at North London's Town & Country Club. Although the band's London fanbase had the opportunity to see the group as relatively recently as the

The Ones That Got Away

previous summer, when the Cramps had appeared at the Reading Festival, their passion for the group remained undiminished. "A couple of fans brought along a human skull that they'd dug up," Lux recounted. "One of these guys really was a gravedigger. They'd cleaned it up and got all the meat off it, and brought it for us. It was pretty fresh, they knew the guy's name. I guess it's the reason we started the band, to meet those kinds of people. It's better than having a job in a high-rise and meeting people who are so boring that you commit suicide one day."

A lengthy European tour that occupied the whole of November generated equally unusual displays of enthusiasm. "In Greece, there were some fans masturbating in the front row – that's a little different," remarked Lux. "Spain is the weirdest, Barcelona," observed Ivy. "They're very high. We're told that they take mescaline there, which is something you don't hear about anywhere usually. It seems like Lux'll just do some minor gesture with his hand and a wave of people'll fall backwards or something. It's a really strange kind of energy and there's people sitting on each other's shoulders and stuff. Their culture was very cut off for years under this Franco regime, and now they've just gotten the equivalent of London in the sixties, Swinging London. They're just, uh – all flaming youth there right now."

After a turn-of-year break, the Cramps resumed gigging with a bumper sequence of around 40 American shows that also took them into Canada and Mexico as they snaked their way around the continent. "We love playing America," asserted Ivy. "In a way, we're happiest here. There's great crowds here and it feels more like home. In some ways it's similar, but in some ways, Europeans understand our background more, the roots of our music. Oddly enough, most Americans don't seem to know their own history." Whereas Ivy particularly enjoyed the gigs in New Orleans, New Jersey and New York, Lux was literally struck by the reception the band received at the legendary Back Room club in Austin, Texas on February 4. "People were just throwing chewing tobacco onstage, bras, panties; somebody threw a fake eyeball," he marvelled. "Every night, we have no idea what to expect. It's never boring."

For much of the tour, which wrapped up back on home territory at Los

Journey To The Centre Of The Cramps

Angeles' Palladium on March 27, support was provided by the Reverend Horton Heat, perhaps the foremost contemporary group whose sound and style was informed by the Cramps and their influences. "We like anything that's truly dangerous and rockin', which Reverend Horton Heat is very capable of being when they want to," observed Ivy. "There seems to be a lot of bands that treat it too reverently," added Lux. "They sing about boppin' in the soda shop and all this kinda stuff and that ain't what rockabilly is supposed to be about. It's really supposed to be about sex. And I like Reverend Horton Heat, they do something new with it, and there are a few other bands that do."

While the band was on tour a few copies of a new Cramps EP slipped out. Entitled *Blues Fix*, the four track disc featured a collection of covers – the already available 'Hardworkin' Man' was joined by versions of Lightnin' Slim's 1954 blues classic 'It's Mighty Crazy', Walter Brown's innuendo infused 1958 rocker 'Jelly Roll Rock', and, from the same year, Sheriff & the Ravels' slice of doo-wop dementia, 'Shombalor'. While copies of the CD found their way to America, the version of the Big Beat EP that wound up in the hands of eager collectors had not been intended for release. "Our friend Roger Armstrong at Big Beat happened to be out of town at the time they put that out. I don't know who it was – somebody decided they were gonna make it sound real good, but they fucked it up – made it sound horrible," explained Lux. "It sounds like disco," added Ivy. "By re-cueing it, you can almost make it sound like another mix and they recued it to bring out the drums. It was just like this pounding, 'boom boom boom', kinda making it sound more modern, I guess . . . But they're a great label. That's just something that happened."

Around the same time, Lux received an invitation to lend his vocal talents to Francis Ford Coppola's lavish adaptation of *Dracula*, which was released in November 1992. "Francis Ford Coppola's daughter liked the Cramps. She basically told him that she liked the way I screamed and so he called us," he explained. "We did go to his house and record me screaming, sobbing and sighing for three hours. But I don't think all the screams are me. Sofia Coppola is a really big Cramps fan and came up with the idea: 'Daddy, the Cramps would do a beautiful job.'" Although Lux's

The Ones That Got Away

contributions to the finished film are unclear and unaccredited, the invitation was an indication of the way that the legend of the Cramps had spread. "We've been around long enough now that the little monsters who came to see us when we started out are now in positions of power," enthused Lux. "It's a wonderful thing that these people come to us."

Legions more came out to see the Cramps as they undertook a summer of festival appearances at home and abroad before taking another lengthy hiatus, breaking cover only to play the occasional outdoor event, their customary Halloween shows and appear at CBGB's 20th anniversary show in December 1993. The celebration took place across two months and featured groups such as the B-52's and the Damned making returns to the venue, with an album that included the Cramps' performance of 'What's Inside A Girl' emerging in 1994. "That place has changed a lot," Lux observed. "It's much cleaner now. Before you were always looking around you to make sure you didn't get stabbed."

Nickey Alexander had left the group at the beginning of 1993, his place taken by Harry Misenheimer, previously a member of Californian hardcore combos Stalag 13 and False Confession. Once again, it seemed that Lux and Ivy found they were on the familiar path of recruiting new personnel and sourcing a new album deal before the whole record/release/tour cycle could begin once more. "I think that's perhaps why we have all these personnel changes. We will do whatever we have to do to attain this dream. It always seems just out of reach," mused Lux. "You either really love it and really want to do it with everything you got, or else it's too much work. If you're looking to use this to make some money or for something down the road, I think people can't take that. You have to like this life every day."

While Harry adopted the literal surname of 'Drumdini' and made his live debut with the band at Belgium's Graspop Festival in August 1993, Lux was fending off further Hollywood interest in the form of an invitation to appear in the doomed comic book adaptation *The Crow* (during the making of which, the film's leading man, Brandon Lee, was accidently shot and killed). Meanwhile, Ivy struck a deal with Creation Records founder Alan McGee to issue the Cramps' next studio album. "We met up

Journey To The Centre Of The Cramps

with Alan McGee who used to come and see the Cramps all the time and he seemed real cool," Lux recounted. "He was the first one who rang and said, 'I just want you to make a real raw Cramps record. Just do whatever you want to do and I'll put it out. I'll make it into a hit.'"

This arrangement resulted in the recording of *Flamejob* at engineer and former Halfnelson guitarist Earle Mankey's Psychedelic Shack in Thousand Oaks, which was a swift drive west along Route 101 from Lux and Ivy's Glendale pad. Recorded during the first half of 1994, *Flamejob* was a gear-grinding representation of Lux and Ivy's passion for automobiles. The couple had become fascinated by the hot rod and car club subcultures that were prospering in California at the time and Lux had spent plenty of time working on old cars. "Back when I first started buying cars, I'd always buy 'em, they wouldn't be running, and I'd have to put a new engine in 'em or something. I'm about a half-ass mechanic, I'd say. Course, I couldn't work on one of these cars today, but the old cars I can. You open up the hood on these cars today and it looks like a computer," he explained. "Lux knows how to fix cars and all, but he doesn't ever want to," Ivy declares. "He also usually has very long fingernails, but he breaks them on the first gig – so no one ever gets to see them. It's always been funny because he gets under the hood and he knows how to do everything, but he'll be shrieking like a woman because he broke a nail."

Given their taste for the retro-futuristic aspects of fifties design, it was natural that Lux and Ivy also dug classic automobiles. "We had a beautiful car – we had a '72 Riviera, it's called a boat-tail; it looked like the Batmobile. We put a zebra interior in it. Somebody bought it in Japan. We couldn't find out if they bought it because it was a Cramps car," Lux recounted. Cars such as the Riviera and the couple's '56 Dodge added a further layer of aesthetic to their practice of listening to music while driving. "It's easy to maintain a cool car in LA because it doesn't snow. I think it's important to stay in a certain mood when you play music," said Ivy. "I think the one that I play the most, over and over, is 'The Time Funnel' by Jan Davis. There's something about it, I have to play it again as soon as it ends."

Aside from its title, Lux and Ivy's immersion in Californian car culture is

The Ones That Got Away

clearly represented throughout *Flamejob*, as tracks such as album opener 'Mean Machine', 'Sado County Auto Show' (which comes complete with overdubbed engine noise), and bass-heavy growler 'I'm Customised', loudly evoke the gearhead scene. Less pounding than its predecessor, *Flamejob* again provides a showcase for Ivy's prodigious guitar talent. She brews up febrile waves of superheated reverb and creates a one-woman wall of sound across the infectious fetish-a-go-go breadth of 'Ultra Twist', provides a precision note-bending lead to the psychedelic 'Nest Of The Cuckoo Bird', mutates bluegrass into something irresistibly dangerous for a blast through Junior Thompson's 1956 cut 'How Come You Do Me', creates vertiginous drones during a rendition of Keith Courvale's fifties obscurity 'Trapped Love' and applies a crepuscular lead to a mesmeric cover of swamp blues pioneer Slim Harpo's 1958 B-side 'Strange Love'. "We just happened to be listening to it in the studio and just decided to do it," she explained.

In addition to a rolling version of Hillbilly rocker Hayden Thompson's 'Blues Blues Blues', *Flamejob* also includes two truly remarkable covers that clearly demonstrate how the Cramps' knack for the transmogrification of old songs remained as strong as ever. Their version of 'Sinners' (which had made appearances in the group's live set for over a decade) is the album's hidden gem. Freddie & the Hitch-Hikers' original damnation song is mutated into a nightmare descent into the netherworld, as Lux spits unholy fire and brimstone and Ivy kicks up sulphurous six-string winds as a means of demonstrating that the Devil most certainly has the best tunes. The group's cut of the done-to-death standard 'Route 66 (Get Your Kicks On)' is scarcely less remarkable: adorned by Lux's intimate vocal and enlivened by a dynamite instrumental break, the familiar number is uniquely interpreted; at times sparse and atmospheric, it repeatedly shifts up through its gears to add new emphasis and resonance to the song. "Until people heard it, they'd say, 'Why are you doing that?'" Ivy recalled. "But on *Flamejob*, a lot of our songs seem to have an automotive edge to them, so we decided to do a kind of psychedelic version, where 'highway' meant getting high."

Flamejob was trailed by the seven-inch release of 'Ultra Twist' in

Journey To The Centre Of The Cramps

October 1994. Backed by 'Confessions Of A Psycho Cat', a fun-filled psychedelic variant graced by Lux's insidious vocal and Ivy's reverberating boogaloo, the single was promoted with a video that featured a black-PVC-clad Cramps, leading a captive retinue of twisters, while Ivy showed little mercy in her 'Den of Persuasion'. In addition to the cut aired on MTV, an uncensored version was also produced that drew on the titillating end of the exploitation movie spectrum. "Some of those things have great titles: *House On Bare Mountain, Kiss Me Quick, Too Much Sex Quiz, Ultimate Degenerate*," recalled Lux. "But the non-nudie clips came from a reel called *Unidentified Twist Films* – that was the actual title." Directed by long-time Cramps fan and B-movie enthusiast Jimmy Maslon, the video took 12 hours to shoot. "People kept coming up to us, going, 'Are we gonna get a break? Are we gonna get lunch?" And we would go, 'Just shut up and keep dancing,'" recounted Ivy. "They knew they had been through something once they did that video," Lux added. "There was actually lots of sado-masochism going on there – Ivy would be screaming at 'em and they'd be like, 'Oh, OK.' The next day, they had bloody feet!"

Flamejob hit the shelves shortly after, arriving wrapped in a sleeve that depicted Ivy in a PVC cat-suit, impossibly high heels, welding goggles, holding an oxy-acetylene torch and featuring a quote about the nature of criticism from modernist artist Man Ray. "That Man Ray quote was, we thought, useful," Ivy explained. "We've been criticised as being a parody or joke, even by people who are our fans – that we're not a real band but a kitsch shtick. The quote is from the thirties, and shows that certain types of artists have always been seen in that way. It was kind of a retort."

"Marcel Duchamp is quite an inspiration for this new LP, because he kind of single-handedly demolished all that had gone before, and made a brand-new art. Man Ray was great too. When he glued those nails onto the face of that iron, the iron like you'd use to iron clothes, so you couldn't use it for that any more? I like to think the Cramps do that kind of stuff – stop the practical thing from being practical any more," observed Lux. "We're just people who remain ever-curious. We're just attracted to whatever comes in handy. Again, like the Surrealists, anything you run

The Ones That Got Away

across is actually beautiful; within a single city block, you find miraculous things. It's a good planet – and good things can happen."

The album was licensed for US release on Warner subsidiary Medicine Label, and its subsequent promotional American tour ran throughout November and December, took a break for the holiday season then continued through the first two months of 1995. It included several highlights including returns to Cleveland and Sacramento State University (the latter for KWOD Radio's Christmas show on December 7) and an appearance on NBC's *Late Night With Conan O'Brien*, where the Cramps performed 'Ultra Twist' during the November 25 edition. The broadcast was the band's second unexpected appearance on national television that month, as three weeks earlier they'd shown up in an episode of teen drama *Beverly Hills 90210* performing 'Mean Machine' and 'Strange Love' in an episode entitled 'Gypsies, Cramps And Fleas'. "[The series' leading man] Jason Priestley's wife wrote that episode and she also likes the Cramps," explained Lux. "It was real easy. We spent one day there and it was kinda like playing a gig. We just played the songs one time and walked off." Five days after the American tour concluded in Arizona on February 19, the group arrived in Dublin to commence a European leg that would take them through 12 countries before reaching its conclusion in Madrid on March 27.

Even as Lux approached his 50th year, he took the rigours of touring in his stride. Despite the (largely self-inflicted) battering he'd taken during the hundreds of gigs the Cramps had played since they first stepped out at CBGB in 1976, he continued to climb speaker stacks, punch out the occasional party pooper and launch himself into crowds with reckless abandon. Similarly, despite the stresses of managing, producing and writing the bulk of the Cramps' music, Ivy looked considerably younger than her actual age. "It gives us energy," she declared. "There's a myth that rock'n'roll destroys and has to burn up those who use it. But I think it's a myth perpetuated by non-rock'n'roll demon forces. Unfortunately, a lot of people who are rock'n'rollers buy into the myth. The opposite is true. There's life-force energies in the atmosphere you can tap into, and that's what happens when you play rock'n'roll. It's nothing that comes from us, it goes through us – we don't own it."

Journey To The Centre Of The Cramps

While this line-up of the Cramps had developed into a hard working touring band capable of producing devastating new material, and the crowds that turned out to see them contained a mixture of old and new fans, Lux and Ivy were disappointed by the way that their role in the New York punk scene had been largely overlooked in recent books including *Punk* magazine founder Legs McNeil and Gillian McCain's oral history of the period, *Please Kill Me*. "People still continue to write books about that scene without including us like it never happened. I was really disappointed that there wasn't anything written about the band in the book, *Please Kill Me*, which was one that was quite good," observed Lux. "That's true," agreed Ivy. "We knew all those people, we were around them every day. I think that you needed to die to make it in that one. But here we are, not quite dead."

Continuing proof of the couple's enduring vitality was provided throughout a summer tour of Australia and New Zealand and an 11-date US jaunt during October and November. After a New Year's Eve show at San Francisco's recently re-opened Fillmore, Ivy began 1996 again looking for a new album deal as Creation had apparently lost interest in the band, with communication from the label having dried up. "Being ignored was bizarre," recalled Ivy. "I think Alan was the only fan and I don't know why he couldn't have phoned us and said sorry and explained. I think he's not supposed to associate with bad influences." Ivy was equally keen to find another US label, as Medicine's connection to the Warner empire had not proven at all beneficial and the subsidiary had recently gone out of business. "Our last album was distributed through Warner Brothers and they did a horrible job. They didn't sell any records, it's the worst thing," explained Lux. "It seems like in America, the media works in conjunction with the record companies and the record companies invent bands and the whole thing is just product. All the bands that are really doing something cos they love music and they're really good at it and everything – it's the same story as with us when we started: the record companies don't want to know about it, it's too weird, they could never sell it, it doesn't fit. One of the main things that record companies say when they criticise bands is, 'It doesn't sound like what's on the radio now.'"

The Ones That Got Away

The disappointing performance of their labels and distributors was nothing new to Ivy, whose resolve to pursue her and Lux's ongoing rock'n'roll mission remained undimmed. "I think any achievements we've made have been on our own, through word of mouth or through our live shows," she asserts. "Being involved with majors, it just gets confusing and messy." More positively, Ivy eagerly seized an opportunity to contribute a song to the *Shots In The Dark: Del-Fi Does Mancini* compilation, which also included bands such as Alabama surf-rockers Man Or Astroman? and Quentin Tarantino approved Los Angeles combo the Blue Hawaiians. "We were at a friend's house, and he said he was going to be doing something for it," she recounted. "He had a list of what everybody was doing, and I was pretty amazed that no one was doing 'Peter Gunn', so I just said, 'Oooo! Here's my chance!' Del-Fi seemed excited to have my track on there, too. They seemed like nice people, and they're based in LA, too. So it was easy to do."

Founded in 1958, the Del-Fi label was best known for issuing singles by doomed rock'n'roll pioneer Ritchie Valens and had also released a variety of early rock'n'roll and surf records. "I used to collect their records before we were in a band, and I never thought I'd have a song on Del-Fi," enthused Ivy. "That's probably a silly thing to get excited about, but I was even excited about having a record on RCA in Spain. Most people would think, 'Well, that's a major,' but to me, it was the label Elvis was on: 'Wow, I'm on the label *Elvis* was on!' It was great – Del-Fi had a lot of cool stuff on it."

The Cramps celebrated their 20th anniversary as a performing group with a gig at Los Angeles' House of Blues on November 1, part of a run of six Californian dates including a Halloween show at San Francisco's Warfield Theatre, which featured suitably spooky support from the Phantom Surfers and the Groovie Ghoulies. These would prove to be the band's last gigs for almost a year, as after they had taken their usual end-of-year break, Ivy struck a deal with Epitaph Records and the collective focus shifted to recording a new album.

Owned by Bad Religion guitarist Brett Gurewitz, Epitaph had grown from its do-it-yourself hardcore origins to enjoy considerable success by

Journey To The Centre Of The Cramps

releasing records by punk-influenced groups such as Rancid, the Offspring and NOFX, all of whom made varying impacts upon the mainstream. "We called them," Ivy explained "They did our vinyl for *Flamejob*, our previous album. A lot of labels in America don't put out 12-inch vinyl – he did a deal with our record company to do the vinyl and he did a real good job. Also we were touring with an Epitaph band – Gas Huffer were opening for us and we kept seeing all this really great promotion for Gas Huffer and we wished we were getting that sort of promotion, it was more like underground fanzine promotion. So that was what we wanted."

After the disappointment of the Medicine Label arrangement, Lux was pleased to be on a label that understood who the Cramps were and had some appreciation of what the group were all about. "They know what they are doing in regards to a lot of things. I just like the people there. The record company we were with before that was a label distributed by Warner Brothers, and that was a real horrifying experience. Warner Brothers was the only real major label that we dealt with so it's really refreshing to be with Epitaph who are actual real people," he declared. "Everybody sees something different in the Cramps and there's been times in the past where the record label would say, 'Oh, you're a freak show!' "You're weirdos!' 'We really got to push that freaky thing!', and that's a part of it. Yeah, it's a freak show to some guy in a polo shirt but who cares about them. It's much better to have a record company who says we know who you are, we know who your fans are and this should be something sincere to everybody involved and honest and that's the best thing to do."

Although Epitaph was instrumental in popularising a range of contemporary variants of punk rock, by the mid-nineties the term had travelled as far from its 1976 interpretation as the Sex Pistols had been from the Shadows Of Night. As Lux perceived the sixties underground garage movement to be the initial representation of punk, he felt little connection to many of the more pop-orientated bands on Epitaph's roster. "Everybody's got a different idea of what punk rock is. I think of it as what was going on in the Bowery when we started playing, but the fast melodic punk rock that's coming out now: I think it's great, I think it's a good thing, and it's doing its job for a lot of people, but I don't listen to it too

The Ones That Got Away

much. Although they've got quite a lot of good stuff on that label, and they've got another label called Fat Possum that's got an amazing record by T. Model Ford, which I really love."

Commencing in May 1997, the making of *Big Beat From Badsville* was a fairly local affair. In addition to returning to Earle Mankey's Thousand Oaks studio, Epitaph's headquarters was a convenient distance from Lux and Ivy's Glendale home. The 14-track album saw the Cramps reiterate their passion for rock'n'roll, favouring rockin' material over the other sub-generic forms that the band had previously explored. "That really doesn't change," declared Lux. "We still listen to a lot of the same old records that we listened to back then, so it seems perfectly natural to us. We just like rock'n'roll. It's no effort to keep doing this. It would be an effort to do something else cos this just seems like the bullseye of what's fun and what gets us out to an exciting show in a town near you." In addition to the rock'n'roll authenticity of 'Devil Behind That Bush' and 'Hypno Sex Ray', the group also mutate and extend the 'Teenage Werewolf' mythos with 'It Thing Hard On', a consciousness-infecting creature feature that sees the horny monster archetype irradiated beyond the point of sanity.

Additionally, the Cramps reach across into the Ramones' lyrical heritage to develop the series initiated with 'Judy Is A Punk' in 1976 with the finger-clicking rumble-fest of 'Sheena's In A Goth Gang'. "That particular song was from hanging around Johnny Ramone," explained Lux. "We were watching the news on TV and nothing particularly scandalous had happened that week, and some kids had gone into some old deserted graveyard out by where we live in LA and dug up a corpse and put a cigarette in its mouth. Just some goth kids you know, and all of a sudden they started having this big exposé on goth gangs in LA. They started making them sound like the crooks and the blood and the goth, like it was going to be like *Clockwork Orange*, scaring all of these adults into thinking that it was going to be like there were all these bands of roving goths that are out there."

Although further rockin' cuts such as the lusty 'Burn She Devil, Burn' revisit the group's rockabilly fixation, *Big Beat From Badsville* is a wholly

Journey To The Centre Of The Cramps

imaginative album, as the Cramps again demonstrate their ingenuity for mutating and adapting elements of rock'n'roll. This is particularly evident on 'Super Goo', which sees Slim and Harry lay down a conventional rockin' rhythm that enables Ivy's subtle flourishes and imaginative lead to impart a sense of otherness to a track rendered more unorthodox by Lux's twisting lyrical onomatopoeia. "We always experiment," stated Ivy. "Lux has a pretty good range, and he can sing things in different keys, but sometimes a song just sounds more exciting if he sings it higher. Or just the opposite; depending on the nature of the song and the tempo, it might sound more sinister if he sings it low. So we'll rehearse it in like three different keys, and they'll all have different feels to them. Even if he can sing all of them, maybe one of 'em, he's straining his voice, and sometimes straining his voice makes it sound more exciting, so we'll go with it. So we experiment a lot. I think we work harder than some bands in that department. Doesn't sound like it. The way it comes off, they say we have simple boneheaded songs that don't evolve, but there's a lot of work there."

In addition to opener 'Cramp Stomp' and the frug-til-you-drop 'Badass Bug' harking back to the kind of dance craze mania that first infected Lux as a teenager back in Stow, and 'Monkey With Your Tail' referencing both 'Jungle Hop' and doo-wop, *Big Beat From Badsville* also finds time to progress the group's ongoing fascination with fetishism. The pneumatically enhanced bump'n'grind of the dirty blues-infused 'Queen Of Pain' has Lux expressing his heartfelt deviant desire (while observing that 'These marks'll be hard to explain') and the album's sole single 'Like A Bad Girl Should' sees the horny devil expressing his admiration for all manner of feminine nastiness. Issued on red vinyl with a mesmeric cover of 'I Walked All Night' on the flip, the single was promoted with a spectacular video that runs the full gamut of sexual peccadilloes, as Lux crawls around the floor, surrounded by women's shoes, pouring out his devotion to Ivy, her boots, her pantyhose, 'picnic basket' and 'pink jellybean'. "We have our calmer moments," assured Ivy. "We're pretty well-rounded, in our own weird way. Our albums do reflect aspects of our lives – all that's real, the fetish clothes and all – but I've got a homebody side."

The Ones That Got Away

Ivy's contribution to *Big Beat From Badsville* is once again monumental in impact and scope as she provides an impressive clean lead to 'Hypno Sex Ray's break, infuses 'Sheena . . .' with shuddering reverb, switches styles at will to provide additional weirdness to the Theremin infused 'Wet Nightmare' and demonstrates some truly astounding high-speed accuracy during the escape velocity closer, 'Haulass Hyena'. "It's got shifting keys," she explains. "I think I got out like 10 different guitar boogie records and I thought 'Can I cram all this into one song?' Our poor drummer, he's so good on it, but boy, when we first wrote the song we were like 'Okay, when this part comes you do like this, and then you stop, and then you . . .' and he was just staring into space. But then they did it, and they learned it pretty quickly." With Slim becoming the only member of the band besides Nick Knox to record three albums with Lux and Ivy, the six-year understanding between bassist and guitarist is evident throughout the album as they combine to spectacular effect on tracks including 'Like A Bad Girl Should' and the urgent sonic apocalypse of 'God Monster'. "In a way, we're still acting like a two-guitar band," Ivy observed. "He does very un-typical things for a bass. A lot of the fuzz is on bass. The fuzz pedal immediately takes all the low end out anyhow. So it really hasn't been much of a change. The place I notice the difference is on rockabilly songs. It's given them more power. It's nothing slicker. I've heard people say it's slicker. It's just that you have an octave. With Brian Gregory and the Kid, we had them playing bass lines on the guitar. They were playing everything on the fifth and sixth strings, just literally bass lines. Nothing's changed, in that way. To me, it's just more primitive and prehistoric and heavy, and it just evolved naturally."

Released in October 1997, *Big Beat From Badsville* featured another of Lux's spectacular cover snaps, depicting Ivy as a knife-wielding bad girl. "He just loves to take pin-up photos and he's a really good photographer," declared Ivy. "On *Big Beat From Badsville*, I took the photo of him on the back, but he still set it up. It was a high lighting set-up and it was his camera, and I was like, 'I want a picture of you like that.' So, it wasn't that I took the photo – it was like we took the photo. I enjoy doing that. And when he's not shooting me, he's shooting dolls. I'll like buy him dolls for

Journey To The Centre Of The Cramps

Christmas and he makes these really elaborate tableaux." While Lux's passion for photography led to his involvement with a local 3-D camera group, presenting him and Ivy with an opportunity to feature in spreads for several magazines, his interest in dolls attracted an altogether stranger form of attention. "We've got lots of Lux and Ivy voodoo dolls, they're pretty strange – we look dead," Ivy explained. "The guy who sent them to us writes to us a lot; sometimes from a mental hospital, and other times when he's out. All around the margins of his letters he'll have magic symbols and weird things, and he'll talk about how incredible it is that we write the songs just for him. He even set up an appointment to meet us at this Hyatt hotel at a certain time and he said, 'I'll be wearing a red shirt and carrying a coke' – we didn't go."

Instead, the Cramps headed out on the road for a national tour that was preceded by another short run of relatively local gigs around Halloween, which again saw the group make a particular effort to put on more of a show than usual when they played their annual San Francisco celebration. "We like to play there on Halloween because they like to dress up insane and go all-out. That's the one night we dress up; like I'll wear a dress or something. We're not just the 'normal' Cramps that night. Last year our drummer went as Elizabeth Taylor," Lux recalled. "I just like putting on a dress, any old dress. I've got a great one Ivy found in a junk store in Knox-ville, Tennessee and said, 'Here, this is you.' It's like something Liberace would wear at home. It fits me perfectly and it's like photographs of material with buckles and photographs of leather straps all over it, it's really great."

"I love touring. Unfortunately, it seems to require that you have a record out so it's been a while," observed Ivy. "Its self expression to us and I guess it's evolved. We just do what we do. The stage is our playground and it's the ultimate self expression. We're as loud as we're legally allowed to be at every gig. What we wear is our taste in clothes, what we play is our taste in music. If it's crazy it's because we're crazy and we get paid for it."

Starting at the Electric Ballroom in Tempe, Arizona on November 2, the remainder of the Cramps' tour comprised a month's worth of shows

The Ones That Got Away

in smaller venues throughout the US and also included a pair of Canadian appearances. "We play small clubs, it's really fun," said Lux. "We just played in Montreal in a club that holds 650 people. It's like two floors and the floor's just like 10 feet from the stage, the bottom floor is right at the edge of the stage, and it goes all around the stage so I mean nobody was farther away than 20 or 30 feet. And there's like 650 people crammed in there and that was just chaos." The band put in another four weeks of domestic gigging beginning in late February 1998, before travelling to Europe for a spring tour that took them through until May. A month later they played a quartet of concerts in Japan, before wrapping up the *Big Beat From Badsville* world tour with trips to Chile, Argentina and Brazil in October. After completing close to 100 gigs touring behind the album, Lux, Ivy and Harry took a break, while Slim left the band, bringing to an end a period of line-up stability that had lasted more than five-and-a-half years. "We did a lot of albums with Slim but it didn't seem to be quite as much fun there towards the end," explained Ivy.

Former Pressurehead guitarist Doran Shelley and bassist Tim Ferris (who had been introduced to Lux and Ivy by L7's Donita Sparks) handled the bass duties during the small number of shows the Cramps played across the next three years. Given that the band was largely inactive during this period, neither new member had much opportunity to carve out much of an identity within the group, as Lux and Ivy retreated to spend time with each other, their cats and pursue their wealth of hobbies and interests. "I don't think either me or Lux are very goal-oriented or ambitious," observed Ivy. "We think more of the near future, or the immediate present, and maybe by not worrying we can keep carrying on – I mean, whatever comes of this is just fine."

In January 2001, news broke of Bryan Gregory's death from what a spokesman for the Anaheim Memorial Hospital described as a 'multiple systems failure'. Bryan, who had recently formed a new band named Shiver, had been in poor health subsequent to a heart attack and his ashes were buried at Rose Hill Memorial Park, in Whitter, California. During the previous decade, Bryan had written to Lux and Ivy and the two factions had made their peace. "While it's true that Bryan didn't actually

Journey To The Centre Of The Cramps

play on some of the seminal recordings that are attributed to him (he wasn't always present for *Songs The Lord Taught Us*), he could be a truly charismatic live performer when the spirit moved him – particularly in the CBGB/Max's Kansas City days, when spirit was everywhere in the air," remembered Ivy. "He wasn't anything like the myth promoted by his record company and subsequently the press; the real Bryan had a kooky charm the public doesn't even know about – the truth was far stranger than fiction."

After spending time revisiting the Bryan Gregory era during the compiling of *How To Make A Monster*, Ivy subsequently observed that she looked back at the period around the time of *Gravest Hits* as being among her favourite periods in the band's history. "That's one of them, I wouldn't have known it 'til we made this album. Nobody was burned out, nobody was a junkie, everybody was at the peak of their form."

CHAPTER THIRTEEN

Buy The Ticket, Take The Ride

One thing I learned from the Cramps – it's about celebrating life and that life is there to be boiled and nothing should stand in the way of that.

Kid Congo

BY the summer of 2002, many Cramps fans were wondering if they had already seen the group for the final time. They had scarcely gigged during the previous 18 months and the sole evidence of any recent activity came when Lux unexpectedly popped up in animated form, fronting a band called the Birdbrains on an episode of the popular cartoon series *Spongebob Squarepants*. "Our next door neighbour does the background artwork, and he just came by and said, 'I've told my boss that we live next-door and he asked if you would do a song for us' – that simple. It was a lot of fun," explained Lux. "There was a Lux Interior puppet; it was a parrot that had sunglasses, no shirt, black shiny pants and pointy boots with high heels. They made the rest of the band look like Cramps and they gave him his puppet later," recalls Ivy. "It was just me singing," added Lux, "but the band was Peter Strauss from the Dwarves – he recorded this great track that sounded like the Cramps; fuzz guitar, really nasty sound. They sent it to New York for the lawyers to sit around and listen to and decide whether it was appropriate and everything. The lawyers said, 'Fuzztone? That's the Devil's music! When that singer says going "down, down, down" he's talking about going down to Hell, not beneath the sea.' This went on for six months. They hire Lux Interior to be himself and then they said it was too sinister – well what did you expect, y'know?"

245

Journey To The Centre Of The Cramps

Any notion that the Cramps had taken some kind of early retirement were proven to be unfounded, as in August 2002 news emerged that the band had begun recording their eighth studio album and had recruited Scott 'Chopper' Franklin, formerly of LA sleaze rockers the Joneses, as the new permanent bassist. "Chopper asked to be in our band back in 1999 (we already had chosen somebody else who ended up annoying us) and then we kept running into and hanging out with him at concerts and car shows," Ivy recounted. "We became friends. He shares the same passions as we do and every time we ran into him he looked like he was ready to step onstage with the Cramps. He was in Mr. Badwrench and before that he was in the Mau Maus when he was a teenager."

The new album was to be released on the band's own Vengeance Label, which Lux and Ivy had recently reactivated as a means of re-issuing the Cramps' post-IRS albums (with the exception of *Flamejob*). "We wanted to start with reissues just to learn how to be a label because we do everything – if you see an ad in a magazine it's because we called and placed the ad," explained Ivy. "We started with the six issues in the fall of 2001. We wanted the new album to come out last year but we missed the deadline because we're a band and we're not really deadline oriented. We had a personnel change because we had to get the right line-up to get the album done."

Although hardly rich, Lux and Ivy could now afford to fund their own releases, which enabled the Cramps to avoid the kind of hassles they had had with practically every label that they had signed for, with the exception of Big Beat. To a degree, the final motivation to return to self-releasing was provided by the breakdown of their relationship with Epitaph. "We weren't happy there, so we told them we wanted to leave and had to make a deal with them, give up something that they owed us in exchange for leaving," Ivy revealed. "The guy who signed us had left the label, he had some personal problems right after he signed us and the guy who took over really wasn't a fan."

Again mixed and mastered at Earle Mankey's studio, with production duties shared between Lux and Ivy (as they had been for the previous two albums), the resulting *Fiends Of Dope Island* LP was a triumphant return

Buy The Ticket, Take The Ride

that ranks as one of the Cramps' finest recordings. Opening with the heralding single, 'Big Black Witchcraft Rock' – a sorcerous stomper featuring Olympian amounts of distorted bottom end and topped with a gloriously manic vocal – the disc presented 13 sinful selections that roamed freely around Lux and Ivy's broad corpus of influences.

As is often the case with so many of the Cramps' best songs, the processing of much of this source material resulted in music that sounded unlike anything else. In particular 'Fissure Of Rolando', which owes its lyrical provenance to the 1957 sci-fi shocker *The Brain From Planet Arous* (the film starred Shirley Temple's former husband John Agar, to whom the album is dedicated), sees the trio of musicians lock together with assured confidence to deliver a hayride to the centre of the mind while Lux snarls with evil intent and laughs like a crazed axe-man. Lux is also in particularly fine fettle during 'Dr. Fucker MD (Musical Deviant)', which casts him in the role of a mad medic vaguely reminiscent of Elvis Presley's 'Dr. Nick' – 'Take two week's worth of drugs, and call me in the morning.' The number features some spectacular Theremin infusions from Ivy, who also brews up a sumptuous lead break for one of the album's standout tracks. Equally appealing is the cinematic enchanted island mesmerism of 'Taboo'. Loosely based on an easy-listening standard from the forties, the track is a richly lyrical, bongo-driven slither of exotica that has a similar vintage vibe to 'Kizmiaz' and reprises the outsider ideas framed within 'Garbageman' courtesy of lines such as, 'What's for me, ain't for you.' "That was meant to be a B-side, we were in the studio and I told the band we'll be an hour late because I'd told Lux that I'd had this idea about doing a hoodlum version," Ivy recalls. "I'd always wanted to do an entire exotica album, but as the hoodlum band that we are."

In addition to referencing the darker aspects of Elvis' life in 'Dr. Fucker', *Fiends Of Dope Island* also included 'Elvis Fucking Christ', a hunk of classic Cramps voodoo rockabilly that Ivy revealed to be semi-autobiographical: "The song is not about Elvis; it's about Lux – the true King of rock'n'roll." Another tip of the fez to Lux and Ivy's pantheon of heroes can be found within the gloweringly malevolent 'Color Me Black', which finds Ivy paying homage to Link Wray's 'Rumble', generating

Journey To The Centre Of The Cramps

intense, physical layers of reverb that deliquesce into the real bad stuff. Album closer 'Wrong Way Ticket' has the Cramps kicking down the exit door as Ivy slashes and smashes her way through a series of supercharged accelerations for this high-octane, manic panic, rockabilly romp. "It's a very exhilarating song to play," enthused Ivy. "It's very athletic mainly for Drumdini. It's wild, crazy and we never play it the same way twice. In fact after we did the take of that song we liked finally, the engineer told us he ran out of tape; we about killed him. Then we had to do another one and I thought we did it even wilder because we were fuming but I think it was good for that song to be in such a jacked up state. It has to be done live in the studio. It's not a song where people just come in and do their parts."

The Cramps made their long awaited return to live action by commencing a 40-date American tour at Nita's Hideaway in Tempe on March 18, 11 days after *Fiends Of Dope Island*'s release. "We really love playing, we love writing songs, and I love playing guitar," enthused Ivy. "It is hard work doing gigs but we're outside the music business so we don't have all that dispiriting crap to put up with." Despite the fact that the group were approaching the 1,000 gig milestone and that the Cramps had criss-crossed the US innumerable times, Lux and Ivy still took great pleasure in discovering new towns and attractions. "Recently we've just discovered Asheville, North Carolina, it's a really cool city – old beatniks live there. It's beautiful, it's hill country, where some of the best bluegrass came from," says Ivy. "We went to eat in this one restaurant where it was home cooking and they're selling wine in big gallon jugs, with a little ring on the top of it so you could go like that [mimed drinking]," added Lux. "Another city I like is Pittsburgh," Ivy continues. "There's a cool restaurant there called Joe Momma's, with all these fake eight-by-10 photos, and we fell for it at first because we thought that all these celebrities had been there, until we started seeing Albert Einstein. It wasn't until we got to the Elvis one that we realised that it was a joke – they had all these fake autographs and fake dedications to the owner, Joe. There's all these crazy pictures, the food is great and it's just nutty looking."

Less amusing was a gig in Chicago during May that resulted in a

Buy The Ticket, Take The Ride

full-blown onstage brawl. "Security wasn't doing anything," recounted Ivy. "The whole band stopped playing and Harry had to step out from behind the drums because no one was taking care of us. Our stage tech got dragged into the audience and then the house security thought he was part of the crowd and tried to throw him out. Then Chopper pulled him back onto the stage, his face had gotten ripped open. Then I accidentally got clocked with a mike stand and then I was half knocked out so I didn't see the second fight. There was a trail of blood from Chopper's side from the guy they took offstage and on my side there was a trail of blood from the guy who worked for us."

While there was the occasional punch up at Cramps gigs, the enthusiastic nature of the band continued to meet with equal fervour by their fans, many of whom had not been born when Lux and Ivy embarked upon their mission. "I'm more amazed by the truly faithful fans, the people who've stuck with us so long," observed Ivy. "It seems like there's so many variables in life but these are people who still love the band, and there's always a lot of younger ones, too – we played in South Carolina a while ago and met a 15-year-old kid who'd waited all night to meet us because she was too young to get into the show, but she was so into the band. I guess some people look up to us the way I would have looked up to Jerry Lee Lewis when I was a kid."

Such devotion from their hardcore fans and excitement among the younger generation underlines the way in which the Cramps' unique nature has inspired singular and enduring loyalty. "We love our band more than anything," declared Lux. "A lot of people, they get in bands and they think they're rock stars. We've seen it even with our band with some members, all of a sudden they think they're the chosen ones and they're better than everyone else and there's a reason why they should be here because they're such a great wonderful thing. You can really build that out of proportion where you think you deserve all this great stuff. With us it was always a respect for the band, the Cramps is us and our fans – it's one big thing and we're part of it."

Although such mutual respect between band and following was central to the group's long term popularity and subsequent legacy, the partisan

Journey To The Centre Of The Cramps

nature of the Cramps' fans sometimes led to high-spirits boiling over at shows, or – as maverick one-man-band Quintron discovered while supporting the Cramps in Los Angeles during June – made them a hard crowd for anyone else to win over. "They were throwing stuff at him when he first started because he opened with a puppet show, instead of opening with music," Lux explained. "All these Cramps fans were champing at the bit and everything like that and going crazy and they're all fuelled by drugs and he comes out, 'Well, hi Beaky how're you doing', 'I'm doing fine Larry' – we're playing this huge place and he's got these hand puppets and nobody could see what he was doing." Essentially, the Cramps represented the continuance of an irresistible spirit of rock'n'roll rebellion that can be traced directly back to the moment that Little Richard first struck fear into the quivering heart of square America. "We're a true rock'n'roll band, which is more than just a musical group," asserts Lux. "We kind of stand for something; we represent our fans and say the things that we think they'd want us to say. It's a little bit like we're diplomats in a foreign land or something."

After the band took a summer break, during which Lux and Ivy took the golden opportunity to record a new version of Wanda Jackson's classic 'Funnel Of Love' with the rockabilly Queen for her *Heart Trouble* long player, the band set out on a European tour without Harry Drumdini, who'd apparently fallen from grace and off the wagon. "We had plans to put out a new album of all new stuff and our old drummer decided to become a professional alcoholic so we fired him," explained Lux. For the dates, Lux and Ivy roped in 'Jungle' Jim Chandler, who had recently joined Spokane garage punks the Makers after honing his chops with his own band, the Down'N'Outs. After the tour, Jim – a committed Cramps fan who sports 'Big Beat From Badsville' and 'Bikini Girls With Machine Guns' tattoos – hung around long enough to lay down his primal beat for the handful of Californian shows the Cramps' played during the last quarter of 2003.

The new year found Lux and Ivy exhuming the Cramps' archive to compile material for *How To Make A Monster*, a two disc compilation of demos, rehearsals and early live performances that was released on

Buy The Ticket, Take The Ride

Vengeance in late summer. "We had these multi-tracks we'd been storing for years, we'd been paying to have them stored but when we moved to Glendale they were just in the garage, so we have our label now and we thought . . . we ended up mixing 19 songs," says Ivy. "It's all about how to make a rock'n'roll band," explained Lux. "So people are supposed to listen to it, and when they hear how rotten we were when we started it should inspire them to think they're not so horrible. I don't know if that's a good thing to do or not, but that's what we're doing." Although the couple found the project enjoyable, it also turned out to be far more exhaustive and time consuming than they had initially bargained for. "It was a gas and it was a strain, it was hard to do – we thought it would be easy, but we bit off more than we could chew," admits Ivy. "It was about four times as long as it finally ended up," added Lux. "We had to throw out all the illegal stuff, when somebody told us it was illegal, because we don't ever do anything illegal."

Soon after *How To Make A Monster* became available, an important link with the Cramps' past was severed when Johnny Ramone became the third member of the Ramones to die, succumbing to prostate cancer on September 15. In addition to being a key component of the group that helped the Cramps become established during their formative days in New York, Johnny – like his former bandmate Joey – had established an enduring friendship with Lux and Ivy. "Johnny and Joey used to come out when we played, but we had to put them in separate rooms – Johnny was cool about it, he wasn't bothered, but Joey didn't want to be near John," recounted Lux. "They stuck together when they hated each other," confirmed Ivy." "We were very close, and we saw a lot of each other over the past year. Watching his deterioration was just gut-wrenching. It's still hard to process it all, because it seems so mythologically weird – first Joey, then Dee Dee, and now Johnny. They left such a mark, and knowing them personally, it's still really hard. Even talking about it, I'm having trouble. It's just too recent and too much."

A week later the Cramps toured behind the new album, playing over 30 dates around the country with new permanent drummer Bill 'Buster' Bateman in tow. "We have Buster Bateman who was with the Blasters and

Journey To The Centre Of The Cramps

Blue Shadows and now he's all ours," Ivy announced. "We've known him for 20 years, I don't know what took us so long, but now he's with us." Despite the stress and discomfort of life on the road, both Lux and Ivy retained their enthusiasm for playing live.

The same sense of wild adventure that had compelled Ivy to climb into a car with Lux all those years ago in Sacramento and that inspired the couple to embark upon a madcap plan to move to New York and start a band ensured that their commitment to the group never diminished. "It's kind of exhausting, but we do like touring," said Ivy. "We love playing live and we haven't for a while, so it's kind of exciting – we've been having a lot of fun. We also like travelling to different places and touring enables us to do that. It's kind of fun being in the business that we're in because there's a lot of adventure connected to it, if we did something else for a living we wouldn't experience that."

Furthermore, like the Ramones the Cramps were an American band that had developed out of the culture that had given rise to rock'n'roll, one of the USA's most significant and enduring innovations. "It's a wonderful place, or a wonderful ideal of a place," observed Ivy. "I think the original idea of what America should be is a wonderful thing, I hope it stays that way. I think we're very American. I think Americans are unaware – maybe because America is so new they don't know some of the things that are great or unique about America."

After the tour's concluding gig in Long Beach on November 7, the Cramps again dropped off the radar. By now, extended hiatuses had become part of the band's profile, and when a short run of six European dates was announced for August 2006, few of those eagerly snapping up tickets would have seriously entertained the notion that these shows would provide them with their last opportunity to see the band.

With Harry Drumdini restored to the fold, the Cramps kicked off with an appearance at the Lokerse Festival on Belgium on August 9. After three Scandinavian concerts, the group travelled to London for a one-off show at London's Astoria that featured support from London girl-group the Priscillas – one of generations of bands who have drawn inspiration from the Cramps and the influences that Lux and Ivy have

Buy The Ticket, Take The Ride

repeatedly cited. While many present were surprised to see Lux sporting a new fair-haired coiffure, they were delighted to find him in masterful wine guzzling, wise-cracking form. "I haven't figured out how to comb it right yet," he declared. "I've gotta figure out the right process – I wanna make it a bit bigger." Ivy stood implacably to his left, giving the benefit of her 1,000-yard stare to those gathered before her, while looking sultry and untouchable in her slinky black dress. "I bought it in Cincinnati and I nearly got beat up by all the hookers outside the store, it was like this sex shop," she recounts. "They thought she was moving in on the territory," added Lux. "All these girls were saying, 'What are you doin' here?'"

Although the band mixed their early material with choice cuts from *Fiends Of Dope Island*, to Ivy's subsequent relief Lux managed to keep at least some of his clothes on as the floor erupted into wild dancing. "Sometimes I do and sometimes I don't, it's not really part of the act," he explained. "Almost got in trouble in Stockholm. The cops came up afterward to Bob [Woodrum], our tour manager, and they said, 'Incidentally, the exposure of the testicles – this was unintentional, isn't that correct?' And Bob says, 'Oh, absolutely – he's never done that before!'"

"I'd have to pull that whole scam every time he wrecked the joint. I'd be upset and I'd have to say, 'I don't know what got into him – I'm scared to be near him!' And they'd feel so sorry for me they'd say, 'OK now, just go,'" explains Ivy. "I've never dropped my trousers onstage," insisted Lux. "It's never happened before. It's a completely made up lie. I'm a pretty nice guy – everyone says that." The Astoria gig was followed by a final European show in Portugal, after which the band returned home via a Heathrow stopover to play one-off shows in Los Angeles and New York. When they resurfaced for another brief burst of live action in October and November, Chopper had departed to be replaced on a temporary basis by former White Zombie bass titan Sean Yseult.

Sadly, the Cramps' concert at the Marquee Theatre in Tempe, Arizona was to be their last. The band's absence from the public arena during 2007 and 2008 was nothing new, and the announcement of Lux's death from a tear to his aortic wall on February 4, 2009 came as the worst kind of

Journey To The Centre Of The Cramps

surprise. A memorial service was held 17 days later at the Windmill Chapel on Sunset Boulevard. "I just thought he was the greatest, he was so inspiring and so alive," Mike Purkhiser declared. "It's hard to think of him as dead right now because he was so alive. It just seems like he was somewhere else right now. And it's the same with Ivy; I swear I never heard those two down. They were so kind and so down to earth, and you'd expected that when you went to see them it would be some kind of horror show or they would act real creepy. But they were just very, very genuine people."

"Lux Interior, like the artists that inspired him, was a true American eccentric who lived his life solely as he saw fit, demanding integrity and commitment of his self and others to the music he loved to a degree devoid of compromise," declared Jim Sclavunos.

As a simple, heartfelt statement on the band's official website thanked the legions of fans who had expressed their love and sympathy and requested that Ivy's understandable need for privacy and solitude be respected, the sense that someone irreplaceable had been lost was overwhelming. It quickly became apparent that Lux was not merely liked, admired or respected – he was loved. His embodiment of rock'n'roll's wild spirit, glorious sense of fun and genuine, charismatic personality had endeared him to countless fans across the globe. Of course, Lux's death also brought the Cramps to an end. As Ivy told me in 2006, "That's all the Cramps is – a *folie à deux*."

During their 23 year existence, the Cramps included a number of exciting and fascinating personalities within their ranks. However, as captivating as the likes of Nick Knox, Bryan Gregory, Kid Congo Powers or Candy del Mar could be, there was never any doubt that the Cramps *were* Lux and Ivy. This was a group born out of their love for one another and their shared passion for rock'n'roll. "We formed this band because we love this kind of music," asserted Lux. "When you start that way, as opposed to starting out with no love of music cos you want to have a career and be a success, that's fine too – but if you start out because you love music and

Buy The Ticket, Take The Ride

you love to make songs, then you're a success already – all you have to do is keep doing that somehow."

In an age when the mawkish aspects of celebrity culture customarily leads to famous couples declaring themselves to be 'soul mates', then splitting up amid highly public rancour and back-biting, Lux and Ivy's relationship restored the overused term's resonance. "There's not anything that we deny each other," explained Ivy. "We don't feel that either one of us has any right to say anything about the other's needs. We just have to trust that person and what that person is entitled to. Fortunately, we happen to like a lot of the same things, but even if we didn't, that shouldn't matter. We're both real free-thinkers. We're nice to each other. There's all those reasons why we're together, but I think it's also karmic. We're karmically entwined."

"We always do everything together," Lux declared. "In a way it's kind of one thing, me and her, but she's also very much an individual and very strong. She grows like a tree. She's faceted like a diamond. There's a million sides to Ivy and I just love all of them."

Lux and Ivy's *folie* brought the world a remarkable band that produced some of the most exciting and influential rock'n'roll ever committed to vinyl and shone a light on the darker corners of the culture that had inspired them, enabling those influences to be shared and adapted by many others. In addition to unwittingly setting the psychobilly ball rolling, the Cramps influenced generations of bands – from the Gun Club to the White Stripes – and that influence continues to resonate across a vast array of differing acts including popular chanteuse Imelda May, Danish rock'n'roll/metal fusion outfit Volebeat, indie behemoths the Horrors, and all-girl garage/psychobilly titans the Eyelids. We are in many ways fortunate that Lux and Ivy chose to share aspects of their private world with us, and while Ivy's withdrawal from public life has robbed the world of one of the finest guitarists of her generation, it is as logical as it is understandable. "I speak to Ivy a few times a year and if I'm in LA I go and see her," explained Kid Congo. "We keep a nice communication, I feel very close to Ivy especially and since Lux passed away, there's a lot of good people around her and everyone feels like

Journey To The Centre Of The Cramps

that. She's great, she's wonderful, she's doing great, a beautiful, beautiful person."

The story of the Cramps is very much the story of Lux and Ivy. It is a great American love story.

ACKNOWLEDGEMENTS

A number of people have provided invaluable assistance, without which this book would have proven impossible to write. Chief among these are Ivy and Lux for their patience, kindness and consideration. Other kind and noble folk who answered questions, provided valuable material or information or just generally helped include: David Barraclough, Eugene Butcher, Chris Charlesworth, Jayne County, Fur Dixon, Barry 'Scratchy' Meyers, Kris Needs, Carlton Sandercock and Chris Spedding, Thanks to you all and apologies to anyone I left out. Special thanks to Donna Greene for her customary long-suffering endurance.

Sources

The following sources have proven invaluable in producing this book. The author would like to express his thanks to the following authors, journalists and publications:

Books

Adinolfi, Francesco. *Mondo Exotica: Sounds, Visions, Obsessions Of The Cocktail Generation* (Duke University Press, 2008)

Bangs, Lester. *Mainlines, Blood Feasts And Bad Taste: A Lester Bangs Reader* (Serpent's Tail, 2001)

Bangs, Lester. *Psychotic Reactions And Carburetor Dung* (Serpent's Tail, 2001)

Bashe, Philip. *Teenage Idol, Travelin' Man: The Complete Biography Of Rick Nelson* (Hyperion Books, 1993)

Brackenridge, Craig. *Hell's Bent On Rockin': A History Of Psychobilly* (Cherry Red, 2007)

Bright, Kimberly J. *Chris Spedding: Reluctant Guitar Hero* (iUniverse Inc., 2006)

Chusid, Irwin. *Songs In The Key of Z: The Curious Universe Of Outsider Music* (A Cappella Books, 2000)

County, Jayne & Smith, Rupert. *Man Enough To Be A Woman* (Serpent's Tail, 1995)

Crouch, Kevin & Tanja. *Sun King: The Life And Times Of Sam Phillips, The Man Behind Sun Records* (Piatkus, 2009)

Décharné, Max. *A Rocket In My Pocket: The Hipster's Guide To Rockabilly Music* (Serpent's Tail, 2010)

Feran, Tom & Heldenfels, R.D. *Ghoulardi: Inside Cleveland TV's Wildest Ride* (Gray & Company, 1997)

Gacy, John Wayne. *They Call Him Mr. Gacy* (McClelland Associates, 1989)

Gimarc, George. *Punk Diary: The Ultimate Traispotter's Guide To Underground Rock 1970–92* (Backbeat, 2005)

Journey To The Centre Of The Cramps

Gribin, Anthony J & Schiff, Matthew M. *Doo-Wop: The Forgotten Third Of Rock'n'Roll* (KP Books, 1992)

Groia, Philip. *They All Sang On The Corner* (Phillie Dee Enterprises, 2001)

Guralnick, Peter. *Last Train To Memphis: The Rise Of Elvis Presley* (Abacus, 1995)

Heylin, Clinton. *From The Velvets To The Voidoids* (Helter Skelter, 1993)

Hopkins, Jerry. *Elvis: A Biography* (Warner Books, 1977)

Johnston, Ian. *The Wild Wild World Of The Cramps* (Omnibus Press, 1990)

Jovanovic, Rob. *Big Star: The Story Of Rock's Forgotten Band* (Fourth Estate, 2004)

Kasher, Steven. *Max's Kansas City: Art, Glamour, Rock And Roll* (Harry N. Abrams, 2010)

Kristal, Hilly. *CBGB & OMFUG* (Harry N. Abrams, 2005)

Krogh, Daniel. *The Amazing Herschell Gordon Lewis And His World Of Exploitation Films* (Fantaco Enterprises, 1983)

Kunzle, David. *Fashion & Fetishism* (Sutton Publishing, 2004)

Meyers, Ric. *For One Week Only: The World Of Exploitation Films* (New Century, 1983)

Morrison, Craig. *Go Cat Go! Rockabilly Music And Its Makers* (University of Illinois Press, 1998)

Perkins, Carl & McGee, David. *Go, Cat, Go: The Life And Times Of Carl Perkins* (Atlantic Books, 1996)

Pierce, Jeffrey Lee. *Go Tell The Mountain: The Stories And Lyrics Of Jeffrey Lee Pierce*, (2.13.61, 1994)

Poore, Billy. *Rockabilly: A Forty Year Journey* (Hal Leonard, 1998)

Presley, Priscilla Beaulieu. *Elvis And Me* (Berkley, 1986)

Vale, Vivian [editor]. *Search & Destroy: The Authoritative Guide To Punk Culture Vols 1&2* (V/Search Publications, 1997)

Vale, Vivian & Juno, Andrea. *Incredibly Strange Music* (Re/Search Publications, 1993)

Various. *Rockabilly: The Twang Heard 'Round The World* (Voyageur Press, 2011)

White, Charles. *The Life And Times of Little Richard: The Quasar of Rock* (Harmony Books, 1984)

Worth, Liz & Gold, Gary 'Pig'. *Treat Me Like Dirt: An Oral History Of Punk In Toronto And Beyond* (ECW Press, 2011)

Sources

Magazines, Newspapers and Periodicals

Altercation (10/2003), Justin Habersaat

Alternative Press (04/1990), Darren Ressler

Bean-O (06/1981), Jonny

Beyond The Blackout (06/1984), Unaccredited

Boston Rock (04/1983), Sheena

Boulder Weekly (29/05/2003), Amy Stonehouse

Chicago Tribune (20/10/2004), Steve Knopper

City Limits (10/10/1991), Ian Johnston

College Times (16/04/2003), Eddie Shoebang

Cosmik Debris (10/1997), DJ Johnson

Cleveland Scene (060/10/2004), Eric Davidson

CP Fanzine (11/1979), Teri Morris

Creem (08/1980), John Mendelsohn

Creem (10/1980), Robert A Hull

Daily Oakland Press (24/10/2004), Gary Graff

Dayton City Paper (13/10/2004), Tim Death

The Devil's Space Cake (08/1997), Demott Campbell

The Face (07/1980), Alain de la Mata

The Face (07/1984), Fiona Russell-Powell

Fanzeen (07/1977), Robert B Frances

Fuz Brains (10/1986), Unaccredited

The Georgia Straight (01/1996), Ron Yamauchi

Girlyhead (03/1999), Sunny M Anderson and Kevin Chanel

Go-Go (21/12/200), Judy B

Good Times (17/08/1981), Paul Gallotta

The Guardian (17/03/2003), Ian Aitch

Guitar Player (08/1990), Jas Obrecht

Guitar Player (07/1997), Jesse Gress

Guitar Player (09/2003), Unaccredited

Kaleidoscope (04/1998), Unaccredited

Hartford Courant (19/02/1992), Roger Catlin

Hot Press (04/2003), Peter Murphy

Journey To The Centre Of The Cramps

Hot Wacks (09/1979), Unaccredited
The Independent (10/05/1998), Unaccredited
Kerrang! (21/09/1991), Morat
Maryland Daily News (24/09/2004), Steve Wildsmith
Matter (09/1984), Bill McRobb
Maximum Rock'n'Roll (11/1994), Chris Davidson
Melody Maker (09/06/1979), Penny Kiley
Melody Maker (09/11/1991), Steve Gullick
Melody Maker (17/10/1994), Cathi Unsworth
Mojo (11/1995), Susan Compo
Mojo (09/2003), Bill Holdship
Montreal Mirror (13/11/1997), Rupert Bottenberg
New Musical Express (10/06/1978), Paul Rambali
New Musical Express (23/06/1979), Nick Kent
New Musical Express (29/03/1980), Max Bell
New Musical Express (25/07/1981), Paul Rambali
New Musical Express (13/08/1983), Cynthia Rose
New Musical Express (11/01/1986), Mat Snow
New Musical Express (20/01/1990), Edwin Pouncey
New Order (07/1977), James Marshall
New York (03/02/2003), Christopher Bonanos
New York Rocker (07/1978), Howie Klein
New York Rocker (09/1979), Andy Schwartz
New York Rocker (09/1980), Richard Grabel
New York Rocker (10/1980), Michael Corcoran
New York Rocker (09/1981), Roy Trakin
New York Times (05/02/2009), Ben Sisario
Nosebleed (12/1995), Unaccredited
The Offense (08/1981), Don Howland
The Observer (14/12/2009), James Sclavunos
The Poser 04/1980), Unaccredited
Praxis (11/1980), John T Phillips
Propaganda (06/1999), George Petros

Sources

Pulse! (03/1990), Bill Holdship
Ohio Beacon Journal (02/2009), Malcolm X Abram
Option (09/1990), Dana Meyer
Q (04/1980), Mat Snow
Ram (20/06/1986), Mark Demetrius
Record Collector (02/1997), Rob Hughes
Reflex (10/1990), Jenny McGuire
Rip (10/1987), Jonny Whiteside
Rock & Folk (10/1982), Unaccredited
Rock & Folk (11/2003), Isabelle Chelley
Rue Morgue (04/2009), Unaccredited
Select (11/1994), Sian Pattenden
Skin Two (05/1992), Trevor Watson
Slash (08/1978), Unaccredited
Smash Hits (14/05/1981), Mark Ellen
Sooprize Package (08/1994), Unaccredited
Sounds (31/12/1977), Sandy Robertson
Sounds (22/03/1980), Pete Silverton
Sounds (30/05/1981), Mick Wall
Sounds (17/12/1983), Lindsay Hutton
Sounds (24/12/1983), Sylvie Simmons
Sounds (23/06/1984), Sandy Robertson
Sounds (01/02/1986), Edwin Pouncey
Spin (08/1990), Bill Holdship
Star Hits (06/1984), Mark Coleman
The Stool Pigeon (06/02/2013), Gary Mulholland
Suburban Relapse (05/1983), Barry Soltz
Tease (05/1995), Helen Highwater
Trebuchet (19/04/2013), Sarah Corbett-Batson
Trouser Press (02/1984), Don Howland
Uncut (08/2004), Simon Goddard
Vintage Guitar (25/04/2004), Lisa Sharken
Wire (05/2003), Richard Henderson

Journey To The Centre Of The Cramps

XLR8 (09/80), Unaccredited
Zigzag (07/1979), Teri Morris
Zigzag (06/1980), Hugh Jarse
Zigzag (02/1981), Marts
Zigzag (07/1981), Marts
Zigzag (07/1984), John Wilde

Discography

Singles/EPs

All singles and EPs are seven-inch discs unless stated otherwise. Listed in order of release date.

Surfin' Bird / The Way I Walk
Vengeance 666, 1978, US
Two pressings – 1st pressing has a crimson back sleeve; 2nd pressing has a mauve back sleeve

Human Fly / Domino
Vengeance 668, 1978, US
Three pressings – 1st pressing has glow-in-the dark logo; 2nd pressing does not; 3rd pressing has a white border around the front and back of the sleeve.

Gravest Hits EP (12″)
Human Fly / The Way I Walk / Domino / Surfin' Bird / Lonesome Town
Illegal ILS12013, 1979, UK
[Black sleeve]
Two black vinyl editions – One with a standard IRS label, the second with a skull logo label. Also in blue vinyl
IRS SP-501, 1979, US
[Red Sleeve]
IRS SP 70501, 1981, US
[Black Sleeve]

Fever / Garbageman
Illegal ILS0017, 1980, UK
Two pressings – 1st pressing has a group shot on the sleeve and was withdrawn, 2nd pressing features four individual portraits.

Garbageman / Drug Train
IRS IR9014, 1980, US

Journey To The Centre Of The Cramps

Garbageman / TV Set
Illegal CBS8401, 1980, France

Drug Train / Love Me / I Can't Hardly Stand It
IRS ILS0021, 1980, UK

Goo Goo Muck / She Said
IRS PFP1003, 1981, UK
Pressed in black and transparent yellow vinyl editions.

Goo Goo Muck / She Said
IRS IR9021, 1981, US
Pressed in black and transparent yellow vinyl editions.

The Crusher / Save It / New Kind Of Kick (12″ single)
IRS PFSX1008, 1981, UK

You Got Good Taste / Faster Pussycat
New Rose NEW28, 1983, France
Picture disc (NEW28P) also issued

I Ain't Nuthin' But A Gorehound / Weekend On Mars
New Rose NEW33, 1983, France
Several coloured vinyl pressings produced: Brown, White, Blue, Green,
Clear

Can Your Pussy Do The Dog? / Blue Moon Baby
Big Beat NS110, 1985, UK
Pressed in black and orange vinyl editions.

**Can Your Pussy Do The Dog? / Blue Moon Baby / Georgia Lee
Brown** (12″ single)
Big Beat NST110, 1985, UK

**Can Your Pussy Do The Dog? / Blue Moon Baby / Georgia Lee
Brown** (12″ single)
New Rose NEW64, 1985, France

Can Your Pussy Do The Dog? / Georgia Lee Brown
New Rose NEW66, 1985, France

Discography

Can Your Pussy Do The Dog? / Blue Moon Baby / Georgia Lee Brown (10″ single)
New Rose CRAMPS2, 1985, France
Pressed in black, pink and orange vinyl editions

What's Inside A Girl? / Give Me A Woman
Big Beat NS115, 1986, UK
Pressed in black and purple vinyl editions

What's Inside A Girl? / Get Off The Road / Give Me A Woman (12″ single)
Big Beat NST115, 1986, UK
Pressed in black and white vinyl editions

Kizmiaz / Get Off The Road / Give Me A Woman (12″ single)
New Rose NEW70, 1986, France
Pressed in black, blue, red, white, pink and transparent vinyl editions

Kizmiaz / Give Me A Woman
New Rose NEW71, 1986, France

Kizmiaz / Get Off The Road / Give Me A Woman (CD single)
New Rose NEAT 3 CD, 1989, France

Get Off The Road / People Ain't No Good / Give Me A Woman / How Far Can Too Far Go? (12″ single)
Planet Records MOP2002, Sweden

Bikini Girls With Machine Guns / Jackyard Backoff
Enigma 203 696 7, 1990, US

Bikini Girls With Machine Guns / Jackyard Backoff
Enigma, ENV 17, 1990, US
Also issued in a picture disc edition (ENVPD 17)

Bikini Girls With Machine Guns / Jackyard Backoff / Her Love Rubbed Off (12″single)
Enigma, 12ENV 17, 1990, UK
Also issued in a fold-out sleeve

Journey To The Centre Of The Cramps

Bikini Girls With Machine Guns / Jackyard Backoff / Her Love Rubbed Off (12″ single)
Enigma, 060-20 3696 6, 1990, Europe

Bikini Girls With Machine Guns / Jackyard Backoff / Her Love Rubbed Off (CD single)
Enigma ENVCD 17, 1990, UK

All Women Are Bad / Teenage Rage
Enigma 203 818 7, 1990, US

All Women Are Bad / Teenage Rage
Enigma ENV19, 1990, UK

All Women Are Bad / [*Cry-Baby* Suite]: King Of The Drapes / Teenage Rage /High School Hellcats (12″ single)
Enigma 12ENV19, 1990, UK
Also issued in a picture disc edition (ENVPD 19)

All Women Are Bad / [*Cry-Baby* Suite]: King Of The Drapes / Teenage Rage /High School Hellcats (CD single)
Enigma ENVCD19, 1990, UK

Creature From The Black Leather Lagoon / Jailhouse Rock
Enigma ENV22, 1990, UK

Creature From The Black Leather Lagoon / Jailhouse Rock / Jackyard Backoff / Beat Out My Love / Her Love Rubbed Off (live) (12″ single)
Enigma 7 73617-1, 1990, US

Creature From The Black Leather Lagoon / Jailhouse Rock / Beat Out My Love (12″ single)
Enigma 12ENV22, 1990, UK
Some copies were supplied in black shrink-wrapped plastic with two stickers.

Creature From The Black Leather Lagoon / Jailhouse Rock / Jackyard Backoff / Beat Out My Love / Her Love Rubbed Off (live) (CD single)
Enigma 7 73617-2, 1990, US

Discography

The Creature From The Black Leather Lagoon / Jailhouse Rock / Beat Out My Love (CD single)
Enigma ENVCD22, 1990, UK

She Said / What's Inside A Girl? / Mama Oo Pow Pow (12″ single)
RCA 74321205531, Spain

Eyeball In My Martini / Wilder Wilder Faster Faster
Big Beat NS135, 1991, UK

Eyeball In My Martini / I Wanna Get In Your Pants / Wilder Wilder Faster Faster (12″ single)
Big Beat NST135, 1991, UK

Eyeball In My Martini / I Wanna Get In Your Pants / Wilder Wilder Faster Faster (CD single)
Big Beat CDNST135, 1991, UK
Includes insert detailing the Cramps' 1991 tour dates.

Eyeball In My Martini / I Wanna Get In Your Pants / Wilder Wilder Faster Faster (12″ single)
Intercord IRS 910.205, 1991, Germany

Eyeball In My Martini / I Wanna Get In Your Pants / Wilder Wilder Faster Faster (CD single)
Intercord IRS 977.502, 1991, Germany

Dames Booze Chains And Boots / It's Mighty Crazy / Jelly Roll Rock / Shombolar (CD single)
Intercord IRS 977.506, 1992, Germany

Blues Fix EP
Hard Workin' Man / It's Mighty Crazy / Jelly Roll Rock / Shombalor
Big Beat CDNST 136, 1992, UK

How Come You Do Me? / Let's Get F★cked Up
Medicine Label 7-18045, 1994, US

Ultra Twist / No Club Lone Wolf
Medicine Label 7-17976, 1994, US

Journey To The Centre Of The Cramps

Ultra Twist / Confessions Of A Psycho Cat
Creation CRE180, 1994, UK

Ultra Twist / Confessions Of A Psycho Cat / No Club Lone Wolf
(12″ single)
Creation CRE180T, 1994
UK

Ultra Twist / Confessions Of A Psycho Cat / No Club Lone Wolf
(CD single)
Creation CRESCD180, 1994, UK

Ultra Twist / Confessions Of A Psycho Cat / No Club Lone Wolf
(CD single)
Creation SCR 660884 2, 1994, Europe

Naked Girl Falling Down The Stairs / Let's Get F★cked Up
Creation CRE196, 1995, UK
Pressed in transparent red vinyl

Naked Girl Falling Down The Stairs / Confessions Of A Psycho Cat
Medicine Label 7-17932, 1995, US

Naked Girl Falling Down The Stairs / Let's Get F★cked Up / Surfin' Bird (live) (CD single)
Creation CRESCD196, 1995, UK

Naked Girl Falling Down The Stairs / Let's Get F★cked Up / Surfin' Bird (live) (CD single)
Creation 661258 2, 1995, Europe

Like A Bad Girl Should / I Walked All Night
Epitaph 6257-7, 1997, US
Pressed on red vinyl

Like A Bad Girl Should / Wet Nightmare / I Walked All Night (CD single)
Epitaph 6527-2, 1997, US

Discography

Big Bad Witchcraft Rock / Butcher Pete
Vengeance 676, 2004, US
Pressed on red vinyl

The Mad Daddy / Rockin' Bones
Vengeance 669, 2014, US
Limited edition for Record Store Day 2014, pressed in clear and orange vinyl

Studio Albums

Twelve-inch vinyl unless stated otherwise, listed in order of release date.

Songs The Lord Taught Us
TV Set / Rock On The Moon / Garbageman / I Was A Teenage
Werewolf / Sunglasses After Dark / Strychnine / The Mad Daddy /
Mystery Plane / Zombie Dance / I'm Cramped / What's Behind The
Mask? / Tear It Up / Fever
IRS SP007, 1980 US
Illegal ILP 005, 1980 UK [also pressed in dark translucent red vinyl]
Illegal ELPS 4123, 1980 Australia
Vinilissimo MR–SSS 501, 2011 Spain [also pressed in red vinyl]

Songs The Lord Taught Us **(CD)**
TV Set / Garbageman / Rock On The Moon / I Was A Teenage
Werewolf / Sunglasses After Dark / Strychnine / The Mad Daddy /
Mystery Plane / Zombie Dance / I'm Cramped / What's Behind The
Mask? / Tear It Up / Fever
IRS X2-13121, 1989 US
IRS 7131212, 1989 Europe
IRS ILPCD 5, 1990 UK

Songs The Lord Taught Us (CD)
TV Set / Garbageman / Rock On The Moon / I Was A Teenage
Werewolf / Sunglasses After Dark / Strychnine / The Mad Daddy /
Mystery Plane / Zombie Dance / I'm Cramped / What's Behind The
Mask? / Tear It Up / Fever
[Additional Tracks]: I Was A Teenage Werewolf (False Start) / Mystery
Plane (Original Mix) / Twist And Shout / I'm Cramped (Original Mix) /
The Mad Daddy (Original Mix)
Zonophone 7243 4 93836 2 3, 1998 UK/Europe

Journey To The Centre Of The Cramps

Psychedelic Jungle
Green Fuz / Goo Goo Muck / Rockin' Bones / Voodoo Idol / Primitive /
Caveman / The Crusher / Don't Eat Stuff Off The Sidewalk / Can't Find
My Mind / Jungle Hop / The Natives Are Restless / Under The Wires /
Beautiful Gardens / Green Door
IRS SP70016, 1981 US, UK, Canada
IRS ILP 009, 1981 Europe
Illegal ELPS 4235, 1981 New Zealand
Vinilissimo MR-SSS 502, 2011 Spain [also pressed in green vinyl]

Psychedelic Jungle (CD)
Green Fuz / Goo Goo Muck / Rockin' Bones / Voodoo Idol / Primitive /
Caveman / The Crusher / Don't Eat Stuff Off The Sidewalk / Can't Find
My Mind / Jungle Hop / The Natives Are Restless / Under The Wires /
Beautiful Gardens / Green Door
IRS CD 00009, 1989 US
Zonophone 7243 96504 2 8, UK/Europe

A Date With Elvis
How Far Can Too Far Go? / The Hot Pearl Snatch / People Ain't No
Good / What's Inside A Girl? / Can Your Pussy Do The Dog? / Kizmiaz /
Cornfed Dames / Chicken / (Hot Pool Of) Womanneed / Aloha From
Hell / It's Just That Song
Big Beat WIKA46, 1986 UK [reissued in 2013 pressed on orange vinyl]
New Rose ROSE81, 1986 France [also pressed on blue vinyl and issued
with tour poster]
Liberation Records LIB 5076, 1986 Australia
WEA Records CRAMP1, 1986 New Zealand
Planet records MOP 3044, 1986 Sweden
Vengeance 671, 2001 USA

A Date With Elvis
How Far Can Too Far Go? / The Hot Pearl Snatch / People Ain't No
Good / What's Inside A Girl? / Can Your Pussy Do The Dog? / Kizmiaz /
Cornfed Dames / Chicken / (Hot Pool Of) Womanneed / Aloha From
Hell / It's Just That Song
[Additional Tracks]: Blue Moon Baby / Georgia Lee Brown / Give Me A
Woman / Get Off The Road
Enigma DEI2009-1, 1990 USA

Discography

A Date With Elvis (CD)

How Far Can Too Far Go? / The Hot Pearl Snatch / People Ain't No Good / What's Inside A Girl? / Can Your Pussy Do The Dog? / Kizmiaz / Cornfed Dames / Chicken / (Hot Pool Of) Womanneed / Aloha From Hell / It's Just That Song

Big Beat WIK46, 1986 UK

New Rose ROSE81 CD, 1986 France

A Date With Elvis (CD)

How Far Can Too Far Go? / The Hot Pearl Snatch / People Ain't No Good / What's Inside A Girl? / Can Your Pussy Do The Dog? / Kizmiaz / Cornfed Dames / Chicken / (Hot Pool Of) Womanneed / Aloha From Hell / It's Just That Song

[Additional Tracks]: Blue Moon Baby / Georgia Lee Brown / Give Me A Woman / Get Off The Road

Enigma 7 73579-2, 1990 USA

Restless Records 7 72765-2, 1994 USA

Vengeance 671, 2001 USA

Stay Sick!

Bop Pills / God Damn Rock'n'Roll / Bikini Girls With Machine Guns / All Women Are Bad / The Creature From The Black Leather Lagoon / Shortnin' Bread / Daisys Up Your Butterfly / Everything Goes / Journey To The Center Of A Girl / Mama Oo Pow Pow / Saddle Up A Buzz Buzz / Muleskinner Blues

Enigma 773 543 1, 1990 US, Canada, France

Enigma ENVLP 1001, 1990 UK

Enigma ENVLPD 1001, 1990 UK [picture disc]

Enigma 105228-1, 1990 Australia

Enigma 064-7 73543-1, 1990 Germany

Enigma 3543-1, 1990 Sweden

Enigma 64 7735431, 1990 Italy

Hispavox 068 7735431, 1990 Spain

Vengeance 672, 2001 US [pressed on blue vinyl]

Journey To The Centre Of The Cramps

Stay Sick!

Bop Pills / God Damn Rock'n'Roll / Bikini Girls With Machine Guns / All Women Are Bad / The Creature From The Black Leather Lagoon / Shortnin' Bread / Daisys Up Your Butterfly / Everything Goes / Journey To The Center Of A Girl / Mama Oo Pow Pow / Saddle Up A Buzz Buzz / Muleskinner Blues / Her Love Rubbed Off

Enigma DEI2004-1, 1990 US [pressed on red vinyl]

Stay Sick!

Bop Pills / God Damn Rock'n'Roll / Bikini Girls With Machine Guns / All Women Are Bad / The Creature From The Black Leather Lagoon / Shortnin' Bread / Daisys Up Your Butterfly / Everything Goes / Journey To The Center Of A Girl / Mama Oo Pow Pow / Saddle Up A Buzz Buzz / Muleskinner Blues / Her Love Rubbed Off

[Additional Tracks]: Her Love Rubbed Off (live) / Bikini Girls With Machine Guns (live)

Big Beat WIKD126, 1994 UK

Stay Sick! (CD)

Bop Pills / God Damn Rock'n'Roll / Bikini Girls With Machine Guns / All Women Are Bad / The Creature From The Black Leather Lagoon / Shortnin' Bread / Daisys Up Your Butterfly / Everything Goes / Journey To The Center Of A Girl / Mama Oo Pow Pow / Saddle Up A Buzz Buzz / Muleskinner Blues / Her Love Rubbed Off

Enigma 773 543 2, 1990 US
Enigma CDENV 1001, 1990 UK/Europe
Enigma 105228-2, 1990 Australia

Stay Sick! (CD)

Bop Pills / God Damn Rock'n'Roll / Bikini Girls With Machine Guns / All Women Are Bad / The Creature From The Black Leather Lagoon / Shortnin' Bread / Daisys Up Your Butterfly / Everything Goes / Journey To The Center Of A Girl / Mama Oo Pow Pow / Saddle Up A Buzz Buzz / Muleskinner Blues / Her Love Rubbed Off

[Additional Tracks]: Her Love Rubbed Off (live) / Bikini Girls With Machine Guns (live)

Restless Records 7 72753-2, 1994 US
Big Beat CDWIKD126, 1994 UK

Discography

Stay Sick! (CD)

Bop Pills / God Damn Rock'n'Roll / Bikini Girls With Machine Guns / All Women Are Bad / The Creature From The Black Leather Lagoon / Shortnin' Bread / Daisys Up Your Butterfly / Everything Goes / Journey To The Center Of A Girl / Mama Oo Pow Pow / Saddle Up A Buzz Buzz / Muleskinner Blues / Her Love Rubbed Off

[Additional Tracks]: Her Love Rubbed Off (live) / Bikini Girls With Machine Guns (live) / Beat Out My Love / Jailhouse Rock / Jackyard Backoff

Vengeance 672, 2001 US

Look Mom No Head!

Dames, Booze, Chains And Boots / Two Headed Sex Change / Blow Up Your Mind / Hardworkin' Man / Miniskirt Blues / Alligator Stomp / I Wanna Get In Your Pants / Bend Over, I'll Drive / Don't Get Funny With Me / Eyeball In My Martini / Hipsville 29 BC / The Strangeness In Me

Big Beat WIKAD 101, 1991 UK [repressed in 2013 on red vinyl]

Big Beat WIKPD 101, 1991 UK [picture disc]

Intercord IRS 951.945, 1991 Germany [repressed in 2013 on red vinyl, some green vinyl editions also exist]]

Vengeance 673, 2001 US [pressed on green vinyl]

Look Mom No Head! (CD)

Dames, Booze, Chains And Boots / Two Headed Sex Change / Blow Up Your Mind / Hardworkin' Man / Miniskirt Blues / Alligator Stomp / I Wanna Get In Your Pants / Bend Over, I'll Drive / Don't Get Funny With Me / Eyeball In My Martini / Hipsville 29 BC / The Strangeness In Me

Big Beat CDWIKAD 101, 1991 UK

Big Beat PDWIKAD 101, 1991 UK [features limited edition photo on disc]

Liberation Records D30739, 1991 Australia

Intercord IRS 986.945, 1991 Germany

Journey To The Centre Of The Cramps

Look Mom No Head! (CD)

Dames, Booze, Chains And Boots / Two Headed Sex Change / Blow Up Your Mind / Hardworkin' Man / Miniskirt Blues / Alligator Stomp / I Wanna Get In Your Pants / Bend Over, I'll Drive / Don't Get Funny With Me / Eyeball In My Martini / Hipsville 29 BC / The Strangeness In Me / Wilder Wilder Faster Faster

Restless Records 7 72586-2, 1991 US

Look Mom No Head! (CD)

Dames, Booze, Chains And Boots / Two Headed Sex Change / Blow Up Your Mind / Hardworkin' Man / Miniskirt Blues / Alligator Stomp / I Wanna Get In Your Pants / Bend Over, I'll Drive / Don't Get Funny With Me / Eyeball In My Martini / Hipsville 29 BC / The Strangeness In Me / Wilder Wilder Faster Faster

[Additional Track]: Jelly Roll Rock

Vengeance 673, 2001 US

Flamejob

Mean Machine / Ultra Twist / Let's Get F★cked Up / Nest Of The Cuckoo Bird / I'm Customised / Sado County Auto Show / Naked Girl Falling Down The Stairs / How Come You Do Me? / Inside Out And Upside Down (With Me) / Trapped Love / Swing The Big Eyed Rabbit / Strange Love / Blues Blues Blues / Sinners Route 66 (Get Your Kicks On)

Creation CRELP170, 1994 UK

Creation CRELP170L, 1994 UK [picture disc]

Creation SCR 477923-1, 1994 France

Epitaph 86449-1, 1994 US [pressed on red vinyl]

Drastic Plastic DPRLP-39, 2014 US [pressed on 200g vinyl]

Drastic Plastic DPRLP-39, 2014 US [limited pressing of 1500 on red vinyl]

Flamejob (CD)

Mean Machine / Ultra Twist / Let's Get F★cked Up / Nest Of The Cuckoo Bird / I'm Customised / Sado County Auto Show / Naked Girl Falling Down The Stairs / How Come You Do Me? / Inside Out And Upside Down (With Me) / Trapped Love / Swing The Big Eyed Rabbit / Strange Love / Blues Blues Blues / Sinners Route 66 (Get Your Kicks On)

Creation CRECD170, 1994 UK, Europe

Medicine Label 9 24592-2, 1994 US

Medicine Label CD 24592, 1994 Canada

Discography

Flamejob (CD)

Mean Machine / Ultra Twist / Let's Get F★cked Up / Nest Of The Cuckoo Bird / I'm Customised / Sado County Auto Show / Naked Girl Falling Down The Stairs / How Come You Do Me? / Inside Out And Upside Down (With Me) / Trapped Love / Swing The Big Eyed Rabbit / Strange Love / Blues Blues Blues / Sinners Route 66 (Get Your Kicks On)

[Additional Tracks]: Confessions Of A Psycho Cat / No Club Lone Wolf

[Videos]: Ultra Twist / Ultra Twist (X-rated version)

Castle Music CMRCD832, 2003 UK

Big Beat From Badsville

Cramp Stomp / God Monster / It Thing Hard-On / Like a Bad Girl Should / Sheena's In A Goth Gang / Queen Of Pain / Monkey With Your Tail / Devil Behind That Bush / Super Goo / Hypno Sex Ray / Burn She-Devil, Burn / Wet Nightmare / Badass Bug / Haulass Hyena

Epitaph 86516-1, 1997 US

Big Beat WIKAD 210, 1997 Europe [repressed in 2013, orange and white pressings exist]

Vengeance 674, 2001 US [pressed on red vinyl]

Big Beat From Badsville (CD)

Cramp Stomp / God Monster / It Thing Hard-On / Like a Bad Girl Should / Sheena's In A Goth Gang / Queen Of Pain / Monkey With Your Tail / Devil Behind That Bush / Super Goo / Hypno Sex Ray / Burn She-Devil, Burn / Wet Nightmare / Badass Bug / Haulass Hyena

Epitaph 86516-2, 1997 US, Europe, Australia

Paradoxx Music 1309105-1, 1997 Brazil

Big Beat From Badsville (CD)

Cramp Stomp / God Monster / It Thing Hard-On / Like a Bad Girl Should / Sheena's In A Goth Gang / Queen Of Pain / Monkey With Your Tail / Devil Behind That Bush / Super Goo / Hypno Sex Ray / Burn She-Devil, Burn / Wet Nightmare / Badass Bug / Haulass Hyena

[Additional Tracks]: Confessions Of A Psycho Cat / No Club Lone Wolf / I Walked All Night / Peter Gunn

Big Beat CDWIKD 210, 2001 UK

Journey To The Centre Of The Cramps

Fiends Of Dope Island
Big Black Witchcraft Rock / Papa Satan Sang Louie / Hang Up / Fissure
Of Rolando / Dr Fucker MD (Musical Deviant) / Dopefiend Boogie /
Taboo / Elvis Fucking Christ / She's Got Balls / Oowee Baby / Mojo Man
From Mars / Color Me Black / Wrong Way Ticket
Vengeance 675, 2003 US

Fiends Of Dope Island (CD)
Big Black Witchcraft Rock / Papa Satan Sang Louie / Hang Up / Fissure
Of Rolando / Dr Fucker MD (Musical Deviant) / Dopefiend Boogie /
Taboo / Elvis Fucking Christ / She's Got Balls / Oowee Baby / Mojo Man
From Mars / Color Me Black / Wrong Way Ticket
Vengeance 675, 2003 US [alternate sleeve image, pressed on red vinyl]

Live Albums

Twelve-inch vinyl unless stated otherwise, listed in order of release date.

Smell Of Female
Thee Most Exalted Potentate Of Love / You Got Good Taste / Call Of
The Wighat / Faster Pussycat / I Ain't Nuthin' But A Gorehound /
Psychotic Reaction
Big Beat NED6, 1983 UK [also pressed in red vinyl]
Big Beat NEDP6, 1984 UK [picture disc edition]
Enigma ENIGMA 21, 1983 US
New Rose NEW25, 1983 France

Smell Of Female
Thee Most Exalted Potentate Of Love / You Got Good Taste / Call Of
The Wighat / Faster Pussycat / I Ain't Nuthin' But A Gorehound /
Psychotic Reaction
[Additional Tracks]: Beautiful Gardens / She Said / Surfin' Dead
Enigma DEI2005-1, 1990 Canada
Vengeance 670, 2001 US [pressed on yellow vinyl]

Smell Of Female (CD)
Thee Most Exalted Potentate Of Love / You Got Good Taste / Call Of ·
The Wighat / Faster Pussycat / I Ain't Nuthin' But A Gorehound /
Psychotic Reaction
[Additional Track]: Weekend On Mars
New Rose NEW25 CD, 1987 France

Discography

Smell Of Female (CD)
Thee Most Exalted Potentate Of Love / You Got Good Taste / Call Of
The Wighat / Faster Pussycat / I Ain't Nothin' But A Gorehound /
Psychotic Reaction
[Additional Tracks]: Beautiful Gardens / She Said / Surfin' Dead
Enigma 7 73578-2, 1990 US
Big Beat CDWIKM 95, 1990 UK
Restless Records/Vengeance 7 72766-2, 1994 US
Vengeance 670, 2001 US

RockinnReelinInAucklandNewZealandxxx
The Hot Pearl Snatch / People Ain't No Good / What's Inside A Girl? /
Cornfed Dames / Sunglasses After Dark / Heartbreak Hotel / Chicken /
Do The Clam / Aloha From Hell / Can Your Pussy Do The Dog? /
Birdfeed
Vengeance 669, 1987 US, Germany [repressed in 2001 on orange vinyl]
Big Beat WIKAD132, 2013 UK [pressed on red vinyl]

RockinnReelinInAucklandNewZealandxxx (CD)
The Hot Pearl Snatch / People Ain't No Good / What's Inside A Girl? /
Cornfed Dames / Sunglasses After Dark / Heartbreak Hotel / Chicken /
Do The Clam / Aloha From Hell / Can Your Pussy Do The Dog? /
Birdfeed
[Additional Tracks]: Blue Moon Baby / Georgia Lee Brown / Lonesome
Town
Big Beat CDWIKD132, 1994 UK
Restless Records 7 72767-2, 1994 US
Vengeance 669, 2001 US

**Frank Furter and the Hot Dogs Recorded Live at CBGB's – Friday,
January 13th 1978**
The Way I Walk / Love Me / Domino / Human Fly / I Was A Teenage
Werewolf / Sunglasses After Dark / Can't Hardly Stand It / Uranium
Rock / What's Behind The Mask? / Baby Blue Rock / Subwire Desire /
I'm Cramped / TV Set
Medicine Label PRO-A-6736, 1993 US [limited pressing of 500 copies
given away as part of CBGB's 20th Anniversary Show]

Journey To The Centre Of The Cramps

Compilation Albums

Twelve-inch vinyl unless stated otherwise, listed in order of release date.

...Off The Bone
Human Fly / The Way I Walk / Domino / Surfin' Bird / Lonesome Town / Garbageman / Fever / Drug Train / Love Me / I Can't Hardly Stand It / Goo Goo Muck / She Said / The Crusher / Save It / New Kind Of Kick
Illegal Records ILP012, 1983 UK, France [issued with 3-D sleeve and glasses]
Illegal Records ILP25847, 1983 Europe
Illegal Records ILP 466723 1, 1983 Netherlands

...Off The Bone
Human Fly / The Way I Walk / Domino / Surfin' Bird / Lonesome Town / Garbageman / Fever / Drug Train / Love Me / I Can't Hardly Stand It / Goo Goo Muck / She Said / The Crusher / Save It / New Kind Of Kick
[Additional Track]: Uranium Rock
Illegal Records ILPIC012, 1985 UK [picture disc]

...Off The Bone
Human Fly / The Way I Walk / Domino / Surfin' Bird / Lonesome Town / Garbageman / Fever / Drug Train / Love Me / I Can't Hardly Stand It / Goo Goo Muck / She Said / The Crusher / Save It
Simply Vinyl SVLP 327, 2001 Europe

...Off The Bone (CD)
Human Fly / The Way I Walk / Domino / Surfin' Bird / Lonesome Town / Garbageman / Fever / Drug Train / Love Me / I Can't Hardly Stand It / Goo Goo Muck / She Said / The Crusher / Save It / New Kind Of Kick
[Additional Tracks]: Uranium Rock / Good Taste (live)
Illegal Records ILPCD012, 1987 UK
Beaky Records CCSCD 348, 1992 UK
Zonophone 7243 4 93837 2 2, 1998 UK

...Off The Bone (CD)
Garbageman / Human Fly / The Way I Walk / Domino / Surfin' Bird / Lonesome Town / Goo Goo Muck / Save It / New Kind Of Kick / Drug Train / Love Me / I Can't Hardly Stand It / She Said
IRS Records 466723 2, 1990 Europe

Bad Music For Bad People
Garbageman / New Kind Of Kick / Love Me / I Can't Hardly Stand It /

Discography

She Said / Goo Goo Muck / Save It / Human Fly / Drug Train / TV Set /
Uranium Rock
IRS Records SP 70042, 1984 US, Canada

Bad Music For Bad People (CD)
Garbageman / New Kind Of Kick / Love Me / I Can't Hardly Stand It /
She Said / Goo Goo Muck / Save It / Human Fly / Drug Train / TV Set /
Uranium Rock
IRS Records 7131192, 1984 Europe
IRS Records CD70042, 1987 US
IRS Records 4479742-2, 1987 Canada

How To Make A Monster
Disc One
Quick Joey Small / Lux's Blues / Love Me / Domino / Sunglasses After
Dark / Subwire Desire / TV Set / Sunglasses After Dark / I Was A
Teenage Werewolf / Can't Hardly Stand It / Sweet Woman Blues /
Rumble Blues (false start) / Rumble Blues / Rumble Blues / Rumble
Blues / Lonesome Town / Five Years Ahead Of My Time / Call Of The
Wighat / Hanky Panky / Journey To The Center Of A Girl / Jackyard
Backoff / Everything Goes / All Women Are Bad
Disc Two
Live at Max's Kansas City 14/01/1977: Don't Eat Stuff Off The Sidewalk /
I Was A Teenage Werewolf / Sunglasses After Dark / Jungle Hop /
Domino / Love Me / Strychnine / TV Set / I'm Cramped; *Live at CBGB
13/01/1978*: The Way I Walk / Love Me / Domino / Human Fly / I Was
A Teenage Werewolf / Sunglasses After Dark / Can't Hardly Stand It /
Uranium Rock / What's Behind The Mask? / Baby Blue Rock / Subwire
Desire / I'm Cramped / TV Set
Vengeance 677, 2004 US

File Under Sacred Music – Early Singles 1978–81 (CD)
Surfin' Bird / The Way I Walk / Human Fly / Domino / Lonesome Town
/ Mystery Plane / Fever / Garbageman / TV Set / The Mad Daddy / Drug
Train / Love Me / I Can't Hardly Stand It / Twist And Shout / Uranium
Rock / Goo Goo Muck / She Said / The Crusher / Save It / New Kind
Of Kick / Rockin' Bones / Voodoo Idol
Munster Records MR CD 315, 2011 Spain
★also issued as a ten single boxed set

Journey To The Centre Of The Cramps

Boxed Sets

Listed in order of release date.

Smell Of Female
A set of four singles containing the six tracks from the original album, plus 'Weekend On Mars':
Call Of The Wighat / Thee Most Exalted Potentate Of Love (LUX 1, black vinyl)
Faster Pussycat / You Got Good Taste (IVY 1, white vinyl)
I Ain't Nuthin' But A Gorehound / Weekend On Mars (NICK 1, blue vinyl)
Psychotic Reaction (CONGO 1, orange vinyl)
New Rose CRAMPS 1, 1983, France

New Rose Singles
Includes the four Cramps seven-inch singles previously issued by New Rose:
You Got Good Taste / Faster Pussycat (NEW28)
I Ain't Nuthin' But A Gorehound / Weekend On Mars (NEW33)
Can Your Pussy Do The Dog? / Georgia Lee Brown (NEW66)
Kizmiaz / Give Me A Woman (NEW71)
Numbered, limited edition.
New Rose CRAMPS 4, 1991, France

De Lux
Includes *Gravest Hits*, the *Smell Of Female* picture disc, plus three 12-inch singles:
Drug Train / Love Me / I Can't Hardly Stand It (ILS 2001)
Fever/ Garbageman / Goo Goo Muck / She Said (ILS 0017)
The Crusher / Save It / New Kind Of Kick (PFSX 1008)
The set also contains a T-shirt, poster and a copy of *The Wild Wild World Of The Cramps* by Ian Johnstone. Numbered, limited edition of 2000.
Big Beat/IRS/Radical Records NED P 6 / WINDSONG 4, 1991, Spain

De Lux (CD)
Disc One:
Human Fly / The Way I Walk / Domino / Surfin' Bird / Lonesome Town / Drug Train / Love Me / I Can't Hardly Stand It

Discography

Disc Two:
Fever / Garbageman / Goo Goo Muck / She Said / The Crusher / Save It / New Kind Of Kick

Disc Three:
Thee Most Exalted Potentate Of Love / You Got Good Taste / Call Of The Wighat / Faster Pussycat / I Ain't Nuthin' But A Gorehound / Psychotic Reaction
The set also contains a t-shirt, poster and a copy of *The Wild Wild World Of The Cramps* by Ian Johnstone. Numbered, limited edition of 3000.
Big Beat/IRS/Radical Records NED P 6 / WINDSONG 4CD, 1991, Spain

File Under Sacred Music – Early Singles 1978–81
Limited edition boxed set of 10 singles, liner notes and memorabilia:
Surfin' Bird / The Way I Walk (7239-1)
Human Fly / Domino (7239-2)
Lonesome Town / Mystery Plane (7239-3)
Fever / Garbageman (7239-4)
TV Set / The Mad Daddy (7239-5)
Drug Train / Love Me / I Can't Hardly Stand It (7239-6)
Twist And Shout / Uranium Rock (7239-7)
Goo Goo Muck / She Said (7239-8)
The Crusher / Save It / New Kind Of Kick (7239-9)
Rockin' Bones / Voodoo Idol (7239-10)
Munster records MR 7239, 2011, Spain

Unofficial Releases
Singles/EPs

Seven-inch vinyl unless stated otherwise, listed in order of release date. Those singles where the release date is unknown, or uncertain are listed alphabetically.

The Cramps Live EP
Human Fly / Caveman / Sunglasses After Dark
Unknown label, 1980, Italy
A limited pressing of 500 singles in a plain card sleeve with a photocopied insert taken from the back cover of *Gravest Hits*, which states that the tracks were 'recorded during the 1980 world tour'. The seven-inch record has an unmarked grey label. Black, white and clear vinyl pressings exist.

Journey To The Centre Of The Cramps

1976 Demo Sessions with Girl Drummer Miriam
Disc One
Don't Eat Stuff Off The Sidewalk / I Was A Teenage Werewolf /
Sunglasses After Dark / Love Me
Disc Two
Domino / What's Behind The Mask? / I Can't Hardly Stand It / TV Set
Fan Club USA, CR-OX2, 1984, US
Limited pressing of 700 in a card sleeve featuring an early publicity shot of
the group. The record label somewhat inexplicably credits 'The Sloths'.

A Vicious Cycle
Heartbreak Hotel / Do The Clam
Scatterbrainchild Records, SR 001, 1986, US
Limited pressing of 500 in a paper sleeve featuring Elvis Presley. Recorded
at Hammersmith Odeon on March 16, 1986. Red and blue vinyl editions
exist.

Lonesome Town / Womanneed
Scatterbrainchild Records, SR 006, 1987, US
Limited pressing of 500 orange vinyl seven-inch singles in a paper sleeve
featuring Lux.

Amsterdam 1990
Tear It Up / What's Inside A Girl? / Psychotic Reaction
Label and release date unknown, Greece
Limited edition of 500, black and clear vinyl pressings exist. Recorded at
the Jaap Edenhal, Amsterdam, March 9, 1990. Picture sleeve features live
photographs of the band.

Blind Vision
Thee Most Exalted Potentate Of Love / Five Years Ahead Of My Time /
Jesus Was A Sinner / Call Of The Wighat
IRStibile Records, AH23817 / BLIND1, Date unknown, US
Issued in a picture sleeve featuring photographs of the band.

Blow Job
Do The Clam / Love Me / Blue Moon Baby / Cornfed Dames
Non-Profit Productions NPP012, Date and country unknown
Recorded in Stockholm, Sweden, April 10, 1986. Issued in black and white
picture sleeve.

Discography

Dance Of The Cannibals Of Sex
Hurricane Fighter Plane / I'm Cramped
Famous Lux, LUX 102, Date unknown, US
Recorded at Max's Kansas City in January 1977. Printed sleeve features illustrations of Lux, Ivy, Bryan and Miriam alongside drawings of cannibals and skeletons. The label credits 'I'm Cramped' to 'M Jackson' and states 'If we see any copies out there that we didn't print, we're comin' for the blood.' A variety of editions exist with different colour printing and cardstock.

From Los Angeles With Love
Her Love Rubbed Off / Is Elvis Dead?
Date, label and country of manufacture unknown
Paper wrap-around sleeve features images of the band in blue and white. Tracks believed to have been pirated from KROQ Radio.

Houston 1997
Garbageman / Cramp Stomp
Date and label unknown, Greece
B-side is incorrectly listed as 'Camp Stomb'. Paper wraparound sleeve featuring a concert poster illustration on the front, and drawings of Lux, Ivy, Nick and Bryan on the reverse.

Human Fly / Domino
Date and label unknown, US
Features a black and white sleeve and a reproduction Vengeance label.

Rock This Dump
Muleskinner Blues / Journey To The Centre Of A Girl / All Women Are Bad / Drug Train
ZAP! Records EHOY 7, release date unknown, UK
Limited pressing of 500. Recorded at Brixton Academy on February 28, 1990. Picture sleeve features live photographs of the Cramps.

Sometimes Good Guys Don't Wear White / Five Years Ahead Of My Time
Date, label and country of manufacture unknown
Green and black vinyl pressings were produced. Record comes in an illustrated paper sleeve. A subsequent pressing of 200 entitled *Heaven Can Wait* was issued by Wardance Records and a different sleeve (with a New Rose Records logo displayed).

Journey To The Centre Of The Cramps

Sunglasses After Dark
Sunglasses After Dark / Human Fly / Caveman
Date, label and country of manufacture unknown
Live EP, paper wrap-around sleeve features images of the band.

Teenage Werewolf
I Was A Teenage Werewolf / Sunglasses After Dark / What's Behind The
Mask? / I'm Cramped
Label unknown EP5. Date and country unknown
Limited numbered edition in a reproduction Sub Pop picture sleeve.

The Band That Time Forgot
The Band That Time Forgot / Twist And Shout / The Way I Walk /
Domino / Human Fly
Unknown label and release date, US
33rpm live EP, recorded at CBGB in August 1979. Comes in black and
white illustrated sleeve featuring Lux, Ivy and Nick. Pressed on red vinyl.

The Most Exaltet Potentates Of Trash (12″ single)
Devil With The Blue Dress / You'll Never Change Me / Sinner / Big &
Fat / Zombie Dance / What's Inside A Girl? / A Walk On Broadway /
Tear It Up
Taylordisco Records TD 45-001, Date unknown, Country unknown

The Smell Of San Diego Live!
Domino / Nuthin' But A Gorehound / Faster Pussycat / Garbageman
Unknown label TC-01 L24265, Date unknown, US
Limited editon of 475 red vinyl and 475 black pressings. Recorded at the
Adams Avenue Theatre, San Diego June 2, 1984. Comes in a picture sleeve
featuring horror movie imagery on the front and photographs of Lux and
Ivy on the reverse.

Venue 1980 Live
Drug Train / Under The Wires / Garbageman / Louie Louie
Unknown label and release date, US
Four track EP in paper wraparound sleeve featuring a photocopied image of
the band on the front and the Creature from the Black Lagoon on its
reverse.

Discography

Voodoo Idols
Human Fly / Love Me / Voodoo Idol
Hot Spot Records NR 16974, Date unknown, Country unknown
Limited initial pressing of 500, comes in fold-out EC Comics style poster
sleeve. Originally pressed in red vinyl; subsequent turquoise and black vinyl
pressings were produced.

What Colour Panties Are You Wearing? And How Long Have You Been Wearing Them?
I Wanna Get In Your Pants / Muleskinner Blues / Aloha From Hell
Label unknown CRA001, Date unknown, Country unknown
Recorded live in Stockholm, Sweden in 1991. EP issued in illustrated
picture sleeve.

You'll Never Change Me / Bacon Fat
PMS 511050, Date unknown, Country unknown
Limited first edition of 300, in an illustrated sleeve. Recorded May 19,
1984 at the Peppermint Lounge, New York. A subsequent Swedish
repressing also exists.

Albums

*Twelve-inch vinyl unless stated otherwise, listed in order of release date. Those
albums where the release date is unknown, or uncertain are listed alphabetically.*

Live Venue April 19, 1980
Intro / Drug Train / Love Me / Voodoo Idol / Rockin' Bones / Weekend
On Mars / Uranium Rock / The Natives Are Restless / Under The Wires
/ Strychnine / Garbageman / Human Fly / I Was A Teenage Werewolf /
Sunglasses After Dark / I'm Cramped / The Mad Daddy / Interlude /
Louie Louie / Hurricane Fighter Plane / Surfin' Bird
Unknown label, 1980, US
Recorded at the Venue, London. Plain sleeve, pressed on red vinyl. Two
repressings have been issued.

Stay Sick Turn Blue
Human Fly / Garbageman / I Was A Teenage Werewolf / Sunglasses After
Dark / Strychnine / Tear It Up / Drug Train / The Way I Walk /
Caveman / Goo Goo Muck / Zombie Dance / The Natives Are Restless /
Surfin' Bird

Journey To The Centre Of The Cramps

Outernational Record Syndicate Inc IRLP9014, 1980, US

Recorded at The Edge, Toronto, July 18, 1980. Editions with green and yellow sleeves exist. Also issued as *Rock'n'Roll Monster Bash* (Turn Blue Records TB-100).

Human Fly

Don't Eat Stuff Off The Sidewalk / New Kind Of Kick / Strychnine / Green Fuz / Human Fly / Goo Goo Muck / Natives Are Restless / Primitive / I Was A Teenage Werewolf / Sunglasses After Dark / I Was A Teenage Werewolf / Sunglasses After Dark / Beautiful Gardens / Green Door / Drug Train / TV Set / The Crusher / Surfin' Bird / The Way I Walk

Unknown label CPS1981, 1982, Belgium

Recorded at De Gigant, Apeldoorn, Netherlands, 12 June 1981. The final two tracks on Side A ('I Was A Teenage Werewolf' and 'Sunglasses After Dark') are repeated at the start of Side B.

Psychedelic Safari

Domino / Human Fly / Sometimes Good Guys Don't Wear White / Five Years Ahead Of My Time / Primitive / Goo Goo Muck / Beautiful Gardens / TV Set / Sunglasses After Dark / Garbageman / Psychotic Reaction

Creepy Records 013, 1984, UK

Hey You! Records WHAT?1, Unknown year and country

Recorded at Astor Park, Seattle, Washington, May 20, 1982. Several subsequent pressings have been produced, including some on green and maroon vinyl. Later issued by Prairie Dog Records on purple vinyl as *The Cramps Totally Destroy Seattle*.

Faster Pussycat

Devil With A Blue Dress / You Got Good Taste / Call Of The Wighat / Thee Most Exalted Potentate Of Love / You'll Never Change Me / Sinner / Bacon Fat / Domino / I Ain't Nuthin' But A Gorehound / Zombie Dance / What's Inside A Girl? / Faster Pussycat / Psychotic Reaction / Garbageman / TV Set / The Mad Daddy / Human Fly

Unknown label CRA001, 1984, US

Recorded at the Hammersmith Palais, London, May 28, 1984.

Discography

Hot Club Philadelphia Nov. '77
The Mad Daddy / The Way I Walk / Rocket In My Pocket / Domino / Voodoo Idol / Rock On The Moon / Jungle Hop / Human Fly / I Was A Teenage Werewolf / Sunglasses After Dark / TV Set / I'm Cramped
Basil Records CRA001, 1985, UK
Two identical pressings were produced.

Demons Of The Swamp Vol. 1
Domino / Human Fly / Primitive / Garbageman / Psychotic Reaction / Tear It Up / Drug Train / Caveman / Goo Goo Muck / Surfin' Bird

Demons Of The Swamp Vol. 2
Everybody's Movin' / Problem Child / Rockin' Bones / Voodoo Idol / Rock on The Moon / I Was A Teenage Werewolf / The Way I Walk / Human Fly/ Twist And Shout / Weekend On Mars / Mystery Plane / Human Fly / I Was A Teenage Werewolf / Beautiful Gardens
Unknown label, 1985. US
Recorded live at Max's Kansas City, 1978. Sleeve features posters and images taken from B-movies.

Kizmiaz (Double album)
Intro / Heartbreak Hotel / Chicken / How Far Can Too Far Go / (Hot Pool Of) Womanneed / People Ain't No Good / Cornfed Dames / What's Inside A Girl? / Blue Moon Baby / Trouble Away / Lonesome Town / Do The Clam / Aloha From Hell / (Hot Pool Of) Womanneed / Love Me / Thee Most Exalted Potentate Of Love / You Got Good Taste / TV Set / Can Your Pussy Do The Dog? / Surfin' Bird / Call Me Wild / It's Just That Song
Skeleton Songs, 1986, Country unknown
Recorded at the Volksbildungsheim, Frankfurt, Germany, 17 April 1986. Comes in a sleeve featuring a topless model.

These Pussies Can Do The Dog (Double album)
Intro / Chicken / How Far Can Too Far Go? / The Hot Pearl Snatch / People Ain't No Good / Cornfed Dames / What's Inside A Girl? / Blue Moon Baby / The Way I Walk / Lonesome Town / Do The Clam / Aloha From Hell / Jungle Hop / Love Me / Thee Most Exalted Potentate Of Love / You Got Good Taste / Can Your Pussy Do The Dog? / Surfin' Bird / Human Fly / Stay Cool / It's Just That Song
Good Taste Records CR3486, 1986, Spain
Recorded at the Paradiso, Amsterdam, Netherlands, 3 April 1986. Features a gatefold sleeve with a large performance photograph of the band.

Journey To The Centre Of The Cramps

Don't Pummel And You Won't Pogo. They Ooze And You'll Throb
(Double album)

Heartbreak Hotel / Chicken / How Far Can Too Far Go? / The Hot Pearl Snatch / People Ain't No Good / Cornfed Dames / Blue Moon Baby / The Way I Walk / Lonesome Town / Do The Clam / Aloha From Hell / (Hot Pool Of) Womanneed / Love Me / Thee Most Exalted Potentate Of Love / You Got Good Taste / TV Set / Can Your Pussy Do The Dog? / Surfin' Bird / Human Fly / Sunglasses After dark / It's Just That Song

Unknown label 1804, 1986, Country unknown

Recorded at the Markthalle, Hamburg, Germany, April 18, 1986. Limited pressing of 500 copies.

Unleashed and Unreleased

Domino / I Ain't Nuthin' But A Gorehound / Faster Pussycat / Garbageman / Hurricane Fighter Plane / I'm Cramped / Her Love Rubbed Off / Lonesome Town / (Hot Pool Of) Womanneed / Human Fly / Love Me / Voodoo Idol / Is Elvis Dead?

Cramped Records CRAMPED1, 1989, UK

Compilation of live and demo material, the album labels misleadingly state 'made in Australia'. Also pressed on blue vinyl.

Same As The Cavemen

The Way I Walk / Everybody's Moving / Domino / Rocket In My Pocket / Human Fly / Rockin' Bones / I Was A Teenage Werewolf / Sunglasses After Dark / I Was A Teenage Werewolf / Uranium Rock / Weekend On Mars / Rockin' Bones / The Mad Daddy

What's The Beef Records SO WHAT2, 1989, Australia

Compilation of live and studio material. Several pressings with alternate coloured sleeves were produced.

Booze Party (Double album)
Disc One

Muleskinner / Chicken / Shortnin' Bread / Hot Pearl Snatch / People Ain't No Good / God Damn Rock'n'Roll / Strychnine / Drug Train / Bikini Girls With Machine Guns / All Women Are Bad / What's Inside A Girl? / Booze Party / Creature From The Black Leather Lagoon / Aloha From Hell / Goo Goo Muck

Discography

Disc Two

Primitive / Sunglasses After Dark / Cornfed Dames / Can Your Pussy Do
The Dog? / You Got Good Taste / Psychotic Reaction / The Mad Daddy
/ The Crusher / She Said
Lux Records LUX1989, 1990, US
Recorded at The Ritz, New York, January 3, 1989. Also pressed on orange
vinyl. Subsequently issued on CD (minus 'She Said') by Exile Records (CD
4017, 1991 Germany) as *The Wild Wild World Of The Cramps*.

Sex & Cramps & Rock'n'Roll
Disc One

Heartbreak Hotel / Chicken / How Far Can Too Far Go? / The Hot Pearl
Snatch / People Ain't No Good / Cornfed Dames / What's Inside A Girl?
/ Blue Moon Baby / Georgia Lee Brown/ Lonesome Town / Do The
Clam / Aloha From Hell / (Hot Pool Of) Womanneed

Disc Two

Love Me / Thee Most Exalted Potentate Of Love / You Got Good Taste /
TV Set / Can Your Pussy Do The Dog? / Surfin' Bird /Human Fly /
Sunglasses After Dark / It's Just That Song
The Swingin' Pig TSP 083-2, 1991, Luxembourg
Recorded at the Volkhaus, Zurich, Switzerland, April 21, 1986 Pressed on
pink vinyl. A subsequent purple and blue pressings and a CD edition were
also produced (TSP-CD-083-2).

Ohio Demos 1979

Twist And Shout / All Tore Up / Mystery Plane / TV Set / Rockin'
Bones / What's Behind The Mask? / Uranium Rock / Under The Wires /
I Was A Teenage Werewolf / Sunglasses After Dark / Jungle Hop / The
Mad Daddy
Alpha Tune CZ144, 1992, Country unknown
A number of different pressings and sleeves are available, including several
with additional tracks.

Trash-O-Rama (Double CD)
Disc One

Dames Booze Chains And Boots / Muleskinner Blues / Aloha From Hell /
Bop Pills / Everything Goes / Jelly Roll Rock / The Creature From The
Black Leather Lagoon / Hipsville 29BC / I Wanna Get In Your Pants /
Hardworking Man / Goo Goo Muck / Human Fly

Journey To The Centre Of The Cramps

Disc Two

Cornfed Dames / Miniskirt Blues / Sunglasses After Dark / Bend Over, I'll Drive / Two Headed Sex Change / Blow Up Your Mind / Eyeball In My Martini / Alligator Stomp / Shortnin' Bread / The Mad Daddy / Surfin' Bird

Rocks Records 92037-8, 1993, Luxembourg

Recorded at the Paradiso, Amsterdam, Netherlands, November 18–20, 1991.

A Date With The Cramps

Muleskinner Blues / Bop Pills / Ultra Twist / Naked Girl Falling Down The Stairs / Mean Machine / I'm Customized / Nest Of The Cuckoo Bird / New Kind Of Kick / Human Fly / Route 66 (Get Your Kicks On) / Let's Get F★cked Up / TV Set

Doctor Doom Records MZE3961-2, France, 1995

Recorded at the Free Wheels Festival, Cunlhat, France, August 19, 1995. Limited red vinyl pressing of 500 copies.

Songs The Cramps Might Have Taught Us

Drug Train / Garbage Man / Rock on The Moon / I Was A Teenage Werewolf / Sunglasses After Dark / Strychnine / The Mad Daddy / Mystery Plane / Zombie Dance / I'm Cramped / What's Behind The Mask? / Tear It Up / Fever

Alien Records WEIRD1, 1998, UK

An alternate version of *Songs The Lord Taught Us* compiled from rejected mixes and including 'Drug Train', which was omitted from the original album by Alex Chilton. Several subsequent pressings have been issued in a variety of different coloured vinyl.

Electric Cheese

Muleskinner Blues / What's Inside A Girl? / Her Love Rubbed Off / Journey To The Centre Of A Girl / All Women Are Bad / You Got Good Taste / Drug Train / Can Your Pussy Do The Dog? / Blues Blues Blues / Ultra Twist / Naked Girl Falling Down The Stairs / You'll Never Change Me

Alien Records WEIRD1, 1998, UK

Recorded at Brixton Academy London, February 25, 1995. Pressed on red vinyl.

Discography

Persecuted Prophets With B–Movie Souls

The Mad Daddy / The Natives Are Restless / Five Years Ahead Of My Time / Lowdown / Zombie Dance / Mystery Plane / Call Of The Wighat [Three versions] / Jesus Was A Sinner / Thee Most Exalted Potentate Of Love / Five Years Ahead Of My Time / Jesus Was A Sinner / Call Of The Wighat

Alien Records WEIRD5, 1998, UK

Compiled from demo recordings and studio out-takes. Pink and yellow vinyl editions were pressed.

Cheer Hell (CD)

Heartbreak Hotel / Chicken / How Far Can Too Far Go? / The Hot Pearl Snatch / People Ain't No Good / Cornfed Dames / What's Inside A Girl? / Blue Moon Baby / Georgia Lee Brown / Lonesome Town / Do The Clam / Aloha From Hell / (Hot Pool Of) Womanneed / Love Me / Thee Exalted Potentate Of Love / You Got Good Taste / TV Set / Can Your Pussy Do The Dog? / Surfin' Bird / Bis / Human Fly / Sunglasses After Dark / It's Just That Song

Sling Blade Records SLING 11, 2000, UK

Recorded live at Brielpoort, Deinze, Belgium, April 6, 1986.

You Betta Duck

Devil With The Blue Dress / You Got Good Taste / Call Of The Wighat / Thee Most Exalted Potentate Of Love / Jesus Was A Sinner / Domino / What's Inside A Girl? / Faster Pussycat / Psychotic Reaction / Garbageman / TV Set / The Mad Daddy

Alien Records WEIRD10, 2001, UK

Recorded at Club Soda, Montreal, Canada, May 16, 1984. A wide variety of different coloured vinyl pressings exist.

Memphis Poseurs – The 1977 Demos

TV Set / Domino / I Can't Hardly Stand It / Lonesome Town / I Was A Teenage Werewolf / Sunglasses After Dark / Human Fly / Love Me / The Way I Walk / Strychnine / Surfin' Bird / I'm Cramped

Embassador Records, 2010, Country unknown

Multiple 'limited' pressings have been produced, many with different coloured cover typefaces, including editions on purple and marbled vinyl.

Journey To The Centre Of The Cramps

Irving Plaza 1979 (CD)

Mystery Plane / Domino / Twist And Shout / Untitled / Voodoo Idol / Zombie Dance / Rockin' Bones / Human Fly / Garbageman / I Was A Teenage Werewolf / Sunglasses After Dark / TV Set / The Way I Walk

Cellar Dwellar Records CD110901604, 2010, US

Recorded at Irving Plaza, New York, August 18, 1979

Rare Tracks (Demos, Rehearsals, B-sides, Soundtracks) (Double album)

Disc One

Blue Moon Baby / Georgia Lee Brown / Give Me A Woman / Get Off The Road / Confessions Of A Psycho Cat / No Club Lone Wolf / I Walked All Night / Peter Gunn / Wilder Wilder Faster Faster / Twist And Shout / Her Love Rubbed Off / Beat Out My Love / Jelly Roll Rock

Disc Two

Jailhouse Rock / Jackyard Backoff / Beautiful Gardens / She Said / Surfin' Dead / Rumble Blues / Lonesome Town / Journey To The Center of A Girl / Sweet Woman Blues / Call Of The Wighat / Jackyard Backoff

Unknown label, 2012, UK

Comes in a large fold-out poster sleeve, pressed on grey vinyl.

A-Sides 1978–2003 (Double album with additional 10″ single**)**

Disc One

Surfin' Bird / Human Fly / Lonesome Town / Garbageman / Fever / TV Set / Drug Train / Goo Goo Muck / The Crusher / Rockin' Bones / You Got Good Taste / I Ain't Nuthin' But A Gorehound

Disc Two

Can Your Pussy Do The Dog? / What's Inside A Girl? / Kizmiaz / Get Off The Road / Bikini Girls With Machine Guns / All Women Are Bad / The Creature From The Black Leather Lagoon / Eyeball In My Martini / Miniskirt Blues / Hard Working Man / Twist And Shout / Let's Get F★cked Up

10″ Disc

Ultra Twist / Naked Girl Falling Down The Stairs / Like A Bad Girl Should / Big Black Witchcraft Rock

Unknown label C-78-03, 2013, unknown country of origin

Comes in a large fold-out poster sleeve

Discography

After Dark (Double album)
Disc One
Heartbreak Hotel / Chicken / How Far Can Too Far Go? / People Ain't
No Good / Cornfed Dames / What's Inside A Girl? / Blue Moon Baby /
Georgia Lee Brown / Lonesome Town / Do The Clam / Aloha From Hell /
Love Me / Thee Most Exalted Potentate Of Love / You Got Good Taste /
TV Set / Can Your Pussy Do The Dog? / Surfin' Bird / Human Fly /
Sunglasses After Dark / It's Just That Song
Trade Mark Of Quality TMQ72127, Date unknown, US
Recorded at the Hammersmith Odeon, London, March 14, 1986. Limited
pressing of 500.

All Aboard The Drug Train
Human Fly / Domino / Caveman / Goo Goo Muck / The Way I Walk /
Zombie Dance / What's Behind The Mask? / Strychnine / Garbageman / I
Was A Teenage Werewolf / Sunglasses After Dark / I'm Cramped /
Mystery Plane / TV Set / Tear It Up
Unknown label CR001, Release date and country of origin unknown.
Recorded at The Stone, San Francisco, May 13, 1980.

All Tore Up
I Was A Teenage Werewolf / Jungle Hop / The Mad Daddy / Rockin'
Bones / What's Behind The Mask? / Sunglasses After Dark / All Tore Up /
Twist And Shout / Uranium Rock / Under The Wires / Mystery Plane /
TV Set
Revisited Records SAFE001, Date of issue unknown, US
Pressed on green vinyl. A second pressing (REVREC0012) was
subsequently issued in an alternate sleeve. Issued as a CD by Hand Made
Records in France (HAM 008).

Beyond The Valley Of The Cramps
Thee Most Exalted Potentate Of Love / Psychotic reaction / Five Years
Ahead Of My Time / Blue Moon Baby / Can't Find My Mind /
Garbageman / The Mad Daddy / Fever / The Crusher / Drug Train /
Green Fuz / Weekend On Mars
Unknown label LUX001, Release date unknown, France
Recorded at The Ritz, New York (date uncertain) and the Lyceum,
London, December 14, 1980.

Journey To The Centre Of The Cramps

CBGB's
The Way I Walk / Love Me / Domino / What's Behind The Mask? / Don't Eat Stuff Off The Sidewalk / I Was A Teenage Werewolf / Sunglasses After Dark / TV Set / The Way I Walk / Domino / Love Me / Jungle Hop / Strychnine / I Was A Teenage Werewolf / Sunglasses After Dark / I'm Cramped / Surfin' Bird
Trademark Of Quality TMQ 721127, Release date unknown, US
Recorded at CBGB, New York, June 10, 1977

Demons Of The Swamp Vol. 1
Domino / Human Fly / Primitive / Garbageman / Psychotic Reaction / Tear It Up / Drug Train / Caveman / Goo Goo Muck / Surfin' Bird
Unknown label (SA-100) and release date, US

Exorcism Night
Mystery Plane / TV Set / Twist And Shout / Weekend On Mars / Voodoo Idol / Zombie Dance / Rockin' Bones / Human Fly / Garbageman / I Was A Teenage Werewolf / Sunglasses After Dark
Unknown label, date of release or country of origin
Recorded at Club 57, New York, August 19, 1979. Also pressed on orange vinyl.

Fetischism
Drug Train / Goo Goo Muck / Green Fuz / Five Years Ahead Of My Time / Blue Moon Baby / New Kind Of Kick / Sometimes Good Guys Don't Wear White / Thee Most Exalted Potentate Of Love / Garbageman / Green Door / The Crusher / Psychotic Reaction / Sunglasses After Dark / Tear It Up
Ghoul-Ash Records, Date and country of origin unknown
Recorded at Larry's Hideaway, Toronto, Canada, June 14, 1982. Also issued as *New Kind Of Kick* (Unknown label) and in Sweden as *Live At Harry's* [sic].

Fetischism Vol. 2
Goo Goo Muck / Voodoo Idol / Primitive / I Was A Teenage Werewolf / Beautiful Garden / Green Door / Garbageman / I'm Cramped / TV Set / The Crusher
Ghoul-Ash Records, Date and country of origin unknown
Recorded at Le Flipper, Marseille, France, June 3, 1981

Discography

Last Time For Nick In Paris (CD)
Muleskinner Blues / The Creature From The Black Leather Lagoon / Chicken / Bop Pils / What's Inside A Girl? / Everything Goes / Mama Oo Pow Pow / God Damn Rock'n'Roll / Primitive / Goo Goo Muck / Her Love Rubbed Off / Daisy Up Your Butterfly / Journey To The Centre Of A Girl / Mystery Plane / Hot Pearl Snatch / Saddle Up A Buzz Buzz / Thee Most Exalted Potentate Of Love / All Women Are Bad / You Got Good Taste / Bikini Girls With Machine Guns / Psychotic Reaction / Shortnin' Bread / Drug Train / Can Your Pussy Do The Dog? / Tear It Up
Recorded at Elysee Montmartre, March 6, 1990 .

Let's Get Ugly
Hungry / Domino / What's Behind The Mask? / Zombie Dance / Save It / Primitive / Green Door / New Kind Of Kick / Strychnine / The Crusher / Beautiful Gardens / Hanky Panky / Drug Train / Fever
Trademark Of Quality TMQ-CLGU001, Release date unknown, US
Recorded at the On Broadway Club, San Francisco, November 6, 1981

Nazibilly Werwoelfen N'Ont Pas De Bausparvertrag (10″ album)
The Gas I Like / Everybody Dying Tonight / Gestapo / Stuka In My Pocket / Human Cry / Rockin' Bones – Heil! / I Was A Nazi Werewolf / Endsieg After Dark
Democrazy Records DR010, Year and country of origin unknown
Recorded live at Palo Alto, California in 1979, this set was put together by someone with an unhealthy Nazi fixation, as is reflected by the change of song titles and the fascist imagery of its packaging and insert. Orange and blue vinyl pressings exist. Also issued as a CD and in 2002 as a Spanish edition on white and transparent red vinyl (Spanish Fly Records 1944), without the Nazi imagery and amended song titles.

No More Cramped For Space
Human Fly / Love Me / Domino / What's Behind The Mask? / TV Set / I Was A Teenage Werewolf / Sunglasses After Dark / Strychnine / Zombie Dance / Voodoo Idol / I'm Cramped / Tear It Up / The Way I Walk / Garbageman
Unknown label, date of release or country of origin
Limited pressing of 150 copies. Recorded at Ole Man River's, New Orleans, December 4, 1979

Journey To The Centre Of The Cramps

Surfin' The Dark
Rumble / Goo Goo Muck / What's Inside A Girl? / Faster Pussycat /
Psychotic Reaction / TV Set / The Mad Daddy / Human Fly / She Said /
Zombie Dance
Unknown label, date of release or country of origin
Recorded at Hammersmith Palais, May 29, 1984. Picture disc. Several
pressings were produced, including a plain black vinyl edition.

Take Me Alive
Intro / How Far Can Too Far Go? / The Hot Pearl Snatch / People Ain't
No Good / Cornfed Dames / What's Inside A Girl? / Love Me / Human
Fly / Can Your Pussy Do The Dog? / Surfin' Bird / Sunglasses After dark /
It's Just That Song
Thrash Records THR001, Release date unknown, US
Recorded at Teatro Tenda, Florence, Italy, April 25, 1986

Tales From The Cramps Vol. 1
What's Behind The Mask? / Love Me / I Was A Teenage Werewolf /
Sunglasses After Dark / TV Set / Don't Eat Stuff Off The Sidewalk /
Strychnine / I'm Cramped / Twist And Shout / I Was A Teenage
Werewolf / Rockin' Bones / The Mad Daddy
Cave Records CAVE001, Date unknown, US
Compilation of early studio recordings with Richard Robinson, Alex
Chilton and Chris Spedding. Subsequently reissued with an alternate sleeve.

Tales Of Terror!!
The Way I Walk / Everybody's Movin / Domino / Rocket In My Pocket
/ Human Fly / Rockin' Bones / I Was A Teenage Werewolf / Twist And
Shout / Weekend On Mars / Rockin' Bones / The Mad Daddy
Unknown label WOLF101, Unknown date and country of release
Compilation of live tracks recorded at the Keystone Club, Palo Alto,
California, February 1979 and demo tracks recorded by Chris Spedding.
Also issued as *This Is Pop* with the same catalogue number.

Teenage Drug Idol
Strychnine / I'm Cramped / What's Behind The Mask? / Love Me / I Was
A Teenage Werewolf / Sunglasses After Dark / TV Set / Call Of The
Wighat / Thee Most Exalted Potentate Of Love / Five Years Ahead Of My
Time / Jesus Was A Sinner / Uranium Rock / Twist And Shout / Rockin'
Bones / I Can't Hardly Stand It

Discography

Tel. International TEL INT 101, Unknown date and country of origin
Compilation of studio out-takes.

The Last Record
Weekend On Mars / Rockin' Bones / I Can't Hardly Stand It / Lonesome
Town / Love Me / Uranium Rock / Twist And Shout / Jungle Hop /
Everybody's Moving / Problem Child / Voodoo Idol / TV Set / Mystery
Plane
Unknown Label LR 2022, Date unknown, France
Combines demos produced by Chris Spedding with live material from
Max's Kansas City, November 10, 1978. Two pressings were produced
with alternate sleeve art.

Voodoo Idols
Goo Goo Muck / The Natives Are Restless / Voodoo Idol / Primitive /
Human Fly / Garbageman / Sunglasses After Dark / She Said / Surfin' Bird
/ Fever / The Mad Daddy
Unknown Label Q-9013, Release date and country of origin unknown.
Recorded at Crazy Al's, Indianapolis, Indiana, July 7, 1981. Limited
Pressing of 500. Also issued as *Psychedelic Jingles*

Voodoo Rhythm
Thee Most Exalted Potentate Of Love / Five Years Ahead Of My Time /
Call Of The Wighat / Jesus Was A Sinner / Call Of The Wighat / Jesus
Was A Sinner / Weekend On Mars / The Mad Daddy / The Natives Are
Restless / Five Years Ahead Of My Time / Lowdown / Zombie Dance
O. KR, Unknown date and country of origin
Compilation of demo, rehearsal and live material.

Werewolf In My Pocket
The Mad Daddy / The Way I Walk / Rocket In My Pocket / Domino /
Voodoo Idol / Rock On The Moon / Jungle Hop / Human Fly / I Was A
Teenage Werewolf / Drug Train / Goo Goo Muck / Green Fuz / Five
Years Ahead Of My Time / Blue Moon Baby / New Kind Of Kick /
Sometimes Good Guys Don't Wear White / Garbageman / Louie Louie
Tel. International TEL INT 101, Unknown date and country of origin
Compilation of live tracks, the first nine at the Hot Club, Philadelphia,
November 10, 1977 and issued as *Hot Club Philadelphia Nov. '77* by Basil
Records in 1985.

Journey To The Centre Of The Cramps

What's Inside A Girl?

What's Inside A Girl? / Blue Moon Baby / Georgia Lee Brown / Lonesome Town / Cornfed Dames / Aloha From Hell / Surfin' Bird / How Far Can Too Far Go? / The Hot Pearl Snatch / People Ain't No Good

Pig Beat & Old Rose Records ROSE 86, Date and country of issue unkown

Live recordings from spring 1986, pressed as a picture disc.

Boxed Sets

Ohio Demos 1979

Three seven-inch singles pressed on red, yellow and green vinyl – blue vinyl copies also exist:

Disc One

Twist And Shout / All Tore Up / Mystery Plane / TV Set (NR16734)

Disc Two

Rockin' Bones / What's Behind The Mask? / Uranium Rock / Under The Wires (NR16735)

Disc Three

I Was A Teenage Werewolf / Sunglasses After Dark / Jungle Hop / The Mad Daddy (NR16736)

Unknown label, 1986 US

Confessions Of A Psychocat

Limited pressing of 350. Three seven inch singles (Disc Three plays at 33rpm). An alternate pressing with a different cover image was also produced.

Disc One

Fever / Heartbreak Hotel / Do The Clam / She Said (NICK954)

Disc Two

Rockin' Bones / Love Me / The Sinner / Human Fly (IVY666)

Disc Three

What's Inside A Girl? / The Hot Pearl Snatch / Can Your Pussy Do The Dog? (LUX706)

C Class, Date unknown, US